A VAGABOND LIFE

*Stories From a
Minnesota Hockey Coach*

TOM PEART

 FriesenPress

One Printers Way
Altona, MB R0G 0B0
Canada

www.friesenpress.com

Copyright © 2023 by Tom Peart
First Edition — 2023

Edited by Chris Middlebrook

ISBN
978-1-03-916469-7 (Hardcover)
978-1-03-916468-0 (Paperback)
978-1-03-916470-3 (eBook)

1. *BIOGRAPHY & AUTOBIOGRAPHY, PERSONAL MEMOIRS*

Distributed to the trade by The Ingram Book Company

TABLE OF CONTENTS

DEDICATION

To My Father, Thomas Leander Peart –
my hero and the inspiration in my life.

To My Mother, Adeline Orayne Peart –
my biggest fan.

To all my teammates…it was an honor to share the ice with all of you.

To Dick Gustafson, Tom Savegeau, Pat Finnegan, Jim Matchefts, Charlie Basch, Bruce Johnson, Don Moore, Bill Taleen, Jim McGlynn, Mike Mulvey, Mark Bergum, Max San Roman, Jeff Whisler, Mike O'Connor, Alex Dampier, Mike MacMacmillan, Dave Prokop, Tom Brophy, Amy Cardarelle, Mark Bahr, Jerrid Reinholz, Carl Davis, Dave Snuggerud, Larry Hendrickson, Pat Westrum, Fred Bandel, Dan Ogdahl, Ken Pauly, Steve Carroll, Jon Bittner, Dennis Fermoyle, Jeff Lindquist, Bill Kelly, Ben Shanahan, Ian Anderson, Ed Saugestad, Steve Houge, Jill Pohtilla, Bill and Barb Halbrehnder, Keith Radloff, Claire Goldsmith, Bob Sherry, Tom Brophy, Ed Roethke, Donnie Williams, Mike Mortelaro, Bill Moore, Bob Brinkman, Jim Windsperger, Denny Malarkey, Maria Swanson, Andy Richardson, Margaret Doer, Chuck Otremba, Mike Jerich, Brendan Bennett, Lindsay Merritt, Marc Lane, Britany Fussy, Joe Lunders, Mark Johnson, Sierra Vadner, Tim Morris, Steve Guider, Pete McKenzie, Jeremy Gunderson, Jeff Bolin, Tim Hunst, Joel Tornell, Denny Johnson, Jim McConnell, and countless other coaches that I worked with or played for in over 50 years in the great games of hockey, soccer, football and softball.

You were the best.

To Wally Odell, Ralph Goldhirsch, Barry Ford, John Perry, Ted Brill, Dick Emahiser, Paul Moen, Doug Woog, Mike Sertich, Kyran Kennedy, Kevin Sullivan, Larry Piedrie, Randy McKay, Steve Steege, Don Olson, Bruce Horsch, Dave Witting, Darcy Way, Bill Corbo, Al Bloomer, Tom Lampl, Scott Koberinski, Tom Carroll, Andy Slaggert, Jim Slaggert, Dave Gilbert, Arnie Caplan, Jim Christensen, Mike O'Connor, Tad Tuomie, Kip Noble, Gerry Sullivan, Mike Sullivan, Dave Gilbert, JJ Bamberger, Tom Rudrud, Matt & Mark Osiecki, Kip Noble, Laura Halldorson, Scott Oliver, Ben Simon, Joe Dusbabek, John Wroblewski, Adara Bonnell Durgin, Kelsey Brovick, Shawna Davidson, Joni Bonnell, Chris Bonnell, Gary Stefano, Sherman Liimatainen, Bill, Tim & Mike Cortes, Shjon Podein, John Bazzachini, Mike Donahue, Jon Westby, Christian Koelling, Mark Palmer, John Peterson, Rick Sainty, Rick Lowe, Bob Driver, Eric Johnson, Tracy Cassano, Chris Erickson, Bob Sherry, Claire Goldsmith, Brian Bergstrom, Jon Bittner, Brad Buetow, Claire Taylor, Fred Perlini, Kent Lane, Alyson Blood, Bill Switja, Craig Barnett, Brianne Brinker, Mike Castle, Amanda Koep, Bill Manuel, Eva-Maria Verworner and countless others for great spring, summer and fall hockey experiences…thank you from the bottom of my heart.

To Tom & Bonnie Richards, Larry & Nancy Ford, Sharon & Jim Sawyer, Steve & Colleen Reiter, Scott & Barb Godin, Laura & Denny Lynch, Kris Bennett, Terry Burton, Danny & Vickie Anderson, Dick & Helen Kruppa, Max & Ginny San Roman, Tom & Jane Palmer, Stan & Lori Volkman, Warren & Susan Myhre, Jim & Lil Wawra, Keith & Ellie Hall, Margaret Hancock, Bert & Bonnie Notermann, Lisa & Mark Richardson, Marcia Blake, Dan & Jane Savage, Noc & Lol Vogt, Jim & Kris Rollwagen, Bill & Sandy Wegwerth, Katie Dykoff, Katherine & Chuck Sawyer, Betty & Steve Beach, Joe & Beth Budaji, Tori & Van Miller, Tim & Nancy Huber, Craig & Linda Cullen, Jay & Jodi Knip, Tom & Cathy Delich, Janet & Derek Bertolas, Lisa Archer & John King, Diane & Matt Clysdale, Cory & Susan Parnell, Carl & Susan Adam, Jim & Kristie Minkoff, Russ & Lisa Ponessa, Rich & Kirsten Vosen, Bruce & Elizabeth Hegedus, Kevin & Nancy Hill, Joe & Lora Oberle, John & Mary Cheasick, Pete & Terry Javorina, Don

& Tami Zurbay, Mike & Nu Zosel, Scott & Colleen Haley, Kent & Sheryl Lane, and countless other parents who truly made hockey and softball the best sports to coach in the world.

To Eric Magdanz, Ed Prohofsky, Ron Charboneau, John Malloy, Mike Smith, Carol Howe-Veenstra, Margie Hughes, and Dave Larson, Dave Turbitt, and Joy Gauster, some of my many bosses that were great to work with and taught me a great deal about how to handle different situations. Thank you for making me a better coach.

To Denny Roach, Matt Roach, Mark Whipple, Jerry Pieper, Jim Larson, Bruce Tilton, Mark Lodge, Bill Kronschnabel, Greg Sheppard, Paul Moen, Jerry Bergstrom, Bill Newhouse, Terry Abram, Scott Parker, Greg Hughes, Rob Shattuck, Bill Rhody, Jeff Shie, C.J. Beaurline, Mark Lodge, and Brian Monahan, Dan Krutzig, Brent Richter, Bill Volbrecht and many more. Thank you for your selfless dedication to the game of hockey and making our sport even better through your efforts as officials.

To Mark Brock: the best pebble in the shoe that one guy deserves. Thanks, big guy for pushing me to finish this project. Love you buddy!

To my Editor: Chris Middlebrook for all the tips on how to publish this book. And for your excellent editorial skills. You are the best. Your help with this was immeasurable. And you are an excellent writer yourself!

And to Kevin McMullen for getting me in touch with Chris Middlebrook, you were always good as a connector, and an even better friend!

To Bill Blanchard, one of the best friends a guy could have. Thanks for convincing me that I would love hockey. You were right. As usual.

To Bob Olson for fostering my love of hockey over the years and always having my back in good times and in bad times.

Last, but certainly not least, to my players…You were one of the greatest gifts in my life. There are far too many to name here, but I will cherish the memories of all of you, today, tomorrow, and always.

INTRODUCTION

It is said that if you love what you do, you will never work a day in your life. I believe this statement completely and I was lucky enough to love what I was destined to do with my life. I truly believe that I was meant to be a hockey coach and to work with young people. The fact that I could do this for thirty-seven years and then continue working in other aspects of the game I love was a cherry on the top. I consider myself one of the luckiest people alive. I have met some incredible people over my coaching years. People who have enriched me and made my life a joy to live. Many of them were the coaches that I worked with and the parents that I met as I coached their young boys and girls. Most of them were the players who loved playing the game of hockey as much as I loved coaching it. I was lucky enough to coach other sports as well, including softball, football, and soccer, but hockey, first playing and then coaching, has always been my true joy. These are some stories of my life playing the game, some from my time growing up and some from my time in the United States Marine Corps and college. Most are about the incredible experiences of coaching in high school, college, and European Pro Hockey. I hope you enjoy them. All these stories are true. Some of the names have been changed so that the people involved will not be hurt or embarrassed. I apologize for some of the salty language. I needed to include it for the full impact of the story to come through. I have made every attempt to attribute the proper credit in the pictures and quotes. Any mistakes are mine entirely.

Why does anyone love hockey?
For many reasons, but one main reason is that hockey tells stories.

THE BEGINNING

Almost every experience that we have, every story that we tell, is shaped by our beginnings, the place that we come from, and the people, parents, grandparents, siblings, and friends, who helped shape who and what we have become.

GROWING UP IN MY HOMETOWN

Growing up in Alexandria, Minnesota was special. I suppose most people who have grown up in a small town feel the same way about their hometown. We never locked our house, or our car. We hung our clothes up on the outside line and we left our unlocked bikes on the front porch, though I did get my bike stolen once from the front yard. My dad said I deserved it because I forgot to put it on the porch. I had to go to the police station myself and report it. The police found it in a creek and there was a great deal of rust right around the handlebars where they connected to the stem. One day I was watching a little league baseball game and a teammate said "Where's your uniform? We play next." I lived close to eight blocks away from the baseball park and needed to get home to get my uniform. I was peddling as hard as I could and as I crossed Broadway (Main Street) I saw some cars coming. I stood up to peddle harder and snap, the handlebars broke off the bike. Down I went. I scraped the heck out my right knee and right elbow. Both were bleeding like crazy. I dragged my bike off the street and started hobbling home. With every step, I was getting madder and madder. By the time I got home I hated that bike! I picked it up by the stem and the seat post and I threw it for all my 11-year-old body was worth. The darn thing didn't fly onto the yard as I had envisioned...no, no, no, both tires hit the curb and it bounced back and cut my left leg open. Not only that, but I sliced my thumb open when I threw it! (Still have both scars to prove it.) Okay, I wasn't the brightest child. Needless to say, I never made it to baseball that day.

It was tough growing up in my neighborhood. The Osterberg boys, Steve and Chuck ran the neighborhood, or should I say, terrorized the neighborhood! They used to make us play football with them in their yard and then throw us the ball so they could kill us with a full-on tackle. One time Bill Theiss had on his brand-new hockey school jersey and one of the brothers ripped it when Bill was carrying the ball. Bill started swearing at both of them, so the two brothers grabbed his bike and threw it into Noonan's Pond. Bill was so mad; he couldn't stop cussing at them. When he finally dragged his bike out of the muck, they then grabbed it and threw it up on Billy Anderson's roof. Like I said, terrorists.

My run-ins with the brothers usually ended up with me going headfirst into a snowbank! Thankfully they didn't skate so Noonan's Pond in winter was a safe haven.

All in all, Alexandria was a great place to grow up. And of course, Alexandria is the Birthplace of America. Or so the legend goes. Some folks believe that the Vikings discovered America. A farmer, named Olof Ohman, found a Runestone with Swedish writing on his farm in Kensington, near Alexandria. No one really has been able to explain how or why the Vikings came to end up in north-central Minnesota, but hey, we have a statue of Big Ole and the Kensington Runestone to prove it.

"Home is where the heart is."
—Pliny the Elder (24 AD–79 AD)

SONS CAN CHALLENGE YOU.
WELL, SO CAN DAUGHTERS

I was watching "This Is Us" on TV and in the show, a three-year-old blind boy made his way on his own to the park. He fell and got hurt. It brought back a memory, well not a memory really, because I was about three years old at the time when I somehow got out of the house and walked down the six blocks from 11th Avenue to Broadway in my hometown of Alexandria. My mom and dad scoured the neighborhood and my Aunt Dutch, and my Grandma Peart were driving the streets trying to find me. My dad finally found me just as I reached Broadway, the busiest street in Alexandria at the time. According to family lore, my dad marched me the six blocks back home swatting me on the butt every couple of steps. Grandma and Aunt Dutch were driving slowly in the car, crying as =much, or more than I was. Or so I was told.

It strikes me that it must be scary at times being a parent. What exacerbated my parent's situation is that I had a brother who died at birth a year and a half before I was born. I am sure that my parents were extremely nervous about my well-being, as I was their only living son. True, I have six older sisters, but having lost one son already, they were probably more cautious with me.

And before anyone goes off on the spanking. I spent the rest of my next fifteen years trying not to do anything that would make my dad ever need to spank me again. Didn't always work of course, but I loved him and respected both of my parents. And they loved every one of us.

Now my sisters? Well, I think that they challenged my parents' way more than I ever did. Or maybe, my mom and dad were worn out by the time I got older...I am not sure.

So, I grew up with six older sisters and I was both the youngest and the only boy. My dad also had six sisters and was also the only boy. The only difference was that he had one sister that was younger. When I was seven, my dad would say "Thomas, let's go for a ride." My father was my hero, so it was easy to run out to the car and go anywhere with him. We would go watch a baseball game or feed the ducks or just go for a long ride in the country. When I got older, 12 or 13...I realized that we went for a "ride" roughly the same time every month. We didn't have a man cave to escape to, so this was my dad's way of escaping. What I did learn growing up was that women are a treasure and that they should be treated with respect. That upbringing helped me greatly throughout my life and especially in my coaching of girls and women in the last half of my career.

> *"A happy family is but an earlier heaven."*
> —George Bernard Shaw (1898–1943)

When you are a young child, the concept of death and dying doesn't enter into your head. I was seven when my Grandma Peart died, and my life was army soldiers and matchbox cars and wearing holes in the knees of my jeans. Seeing Grandma in that strange box, and the fact that she was dead, didn't really register with me, except she wasn't moving, and she felt all cold and waxy. Yes, I had to touch her and see. I've been that way all my life.

"Don't touch that Tommy, it's hot!"

"OUCH!"

At that time of my life, I cried when I was physically hurt or when someone else in my family cried. The rest was just a big mystery to me. Ten months later, and having been through it once already, when Grandpa Peart died it was a much more solemn occasion. I could now understand that he wasn't just going away for a while, like my dad did on his hunting trips. This time, Grandpa Peart wasn't coming back.

When I was eleven, happily riding my bike all over Alexandria, having a fun summer, death struck again. This time, it was my best friend Jimmy Flaig who died. It was a hot summer day in late August. Jimmy and I had planned to meet up for another adventure of some sort. We might go see Jimmy's dad Jerry at the gas station he worked at, or we might have races down Oak Street, which was in front of Jimmy's house. At that time, it was just a long dirt road. We would get going as fast as we could and then slam on the brakes and turn sideways to see how far we could slide. Or we might pool our money and head downtown to the bakery and buy some maple fried cinnamon rolls. We were always doing something together.

Instead, I woke up that morning in August to my sister Patty shaking me.

"Get up Tommy. Jimmy Flaig died."

What did she mean, Jimmy died? How could that be? I just saw him the other day and he was fine; we were going to hang out today. This must be a mistake. I don't recall much the rest of that summer. I remember the funeral and how much different it felt than the funerals of my grandparents. It felt so much sadder, and of course, since I was four years older than when my grandparents passed, I was more aware of the realities of life and the finality of death. What I was also acutely aware of was that my best friend was gone. Never to return.

Jimmy had died from a malformed heart valve on August 22nd, 1968. Apparently, he had the defect since his birth. Starting in June of 1968, he spent six weeks at Children's Hospital in the Cities which was a big strain on his parents, Ardelle and Jerry and his older sister Renee. Both emotionally and financially. After Jimmy died his doctor at Children's Hospital paid for Jimmy's autopsy so he could figure out what happened. That autopsy and my friend Jimmy Flaig's heart helped lead to the development of artificial heart values for children which probably has saved thousands of lives in the last 50 years. Even though Jimmy left us at way to young of an age, his life definitely had great meaning and purpose.

Jimmy's death changed my life in many ways. It especially led me to hang around Bill Blanchard more, which introduced me to the greatest game – Hockey! In essence, Jimmy's tragic death altered the trajectory of my life. I have to say though, Jimmy was the bravest, toughest kid around. He stood up for anyone that was an underdog and never backed down from anything or anyone. If he felt he was in the right or you were a bully picking on one of his friends, he waded right in and stood up to the bullies, even when the bullies were bigger. He was strong, even though he wasn't the biggest kid, and he was talented in so many ways. His biggest asset was that he was a true friend, always and forever. I always admired his courage. To the end Jimmy was there for all the underdogs in the world. Rest In Peace my friend.

"Friends show their love in times of trouble, not in times of happiness."
—Euripides (484 BC–406 BC)

DEATH AMONG US

Even though death is a part of life, learning that at a young age was confusing. I mentioned my grandparents dying and then my friend Jimmy Flaig dying. There were also two other deaths that affected me at a young age. I had a classmate, Greg Merten who died when I was 10 years old. The story was that he was either playing with his dad's shotgun or was cleaning it and accidentally shot himself. A sad day in Alexandria, that is for sure. An even sadder event happened when I was in 9th grade. I had spent that summer hanging out with Ray Devine. We would camp out and throw apples at cars and just generally be little hooligans. Ray was a hockey player. He was a good skater and was a tough defenseman. He loved his family, and he loved the Nebraska Cornhuskers, or maybe it was the Oklahoma Sooners, I can't remember which and I am not sure why he loved one or the other, but he did. I remember when camping out in his yard and he would ramble on about the Sooners and Nebraska Cornhuskers football game. How he wanted to go to a live game someday and how much he also loved duck hunting. That fall Ray told us that he and his brothers had a great duck hunting spot. When we pressed him on which slough or lake it was, he wouldn't tell us.

"It's a secret spot." he told us.

That October, Ray, his brother, and a friend of theirs from the Twin Cities were duck hunting on Lake Reno. It was a notoriously shallow lake in spots that is prone to big waves if the wind is strong. Their boat capsized and Ray, his brother and their friend all died that day. Ray, when they found his body, had one wader on and one off. His brother was found near him with both of his waders on and I am not sure where they discovered the friend. The current had carried him away from the brothers. It appears that Ray's brother tried to get Ray's waders off and that may have doomed them both. Of course, the cold water would have affected them as well. Hypothermia most likely set in. This combined with heavy clothes and hip waders (long boots that allow you to walk in cold water and stay dry) most likely were the cause of all of them drowning. I remember that it took them a while to find all three bodies. They had to drag the lake, and this was always a hit and miss proposition at best. We kept hoping, making up scenarios where Ray had made it to shore and was in some farmer's house, in bed, recovering. This was all just a fantasy of course. Ray and the others were found and the rest of us were left to deal with another friend's death. Another death that was hard for us to understand. We feared death because of the unknown of what happens to us afterward. Where do we go? Will we see our family and friends again when it is our time? All things that religion, our parents and older siblings try to teach us and guide us through when we face these difficult times.

"Like a bird singing in the rain, let grateful memories survive in times of sorrow."
—Robert Louis Stevenson (1850–1894)

THE CONTINUING ADVENTURES OF
A SLIGHTLY MISSPENT YOUTH

Where I lived on Kenwood Street, our house was right across the street from Walter Robel's Evergreen Grocery. Alexandria used to have quite a few small neighborhood grocery stores. I remember my dad telling me about my sister Diane borrowing the car to drive across the street to Evergreen Grocery. Probably cost more to start the car twice, then to drive that short distance. Of course, it was raining out, so that was her explanation.

Poor Walter, we were always pulling childish pranks on him, like calling him up and asking, in a deep voice. "Do you have Prince Albert in a can?" "Yes," he would reply. "Well, you better let him out." Or "This is the power company, is your refrigerator running?" He would respond with a yes. "Well, you better go catch it!"

I once told Walter that my parents said I could charge for goods. You know, important stuff, like Hershey's Chocolate Bars, Ice Cream and Cherry or Apple Pies. All that yummy stuff. Yeah, that went over like a lead balloon when my mom got the bills. The joke ended up being on me, that is for sure.

A group of us kids also used to play ding-dong ditch. In the winter after a big snowstorm, the snowplows would plow the streets and pile up the snow fairly high. We would sneak up to a house and ring the doorbell and then run and jump over the snowbarnk, as we tried to keep from laughing. This was good fun until one guy saw our footsteps in the snow and ran out to the street behind us, scaring us half to death!

Another fun and dumb thing we kids used to do, again after a snowstorm, when the streets were good and snowy, was to wait for a car to pull up to a stop sign. One or two of us would crouch down and grab on to the bumper and hitch a ride. Great fun until we hit a bare patch in the road and went flying!

We also really enjoyed giving friends a ride on our bikes. The best place was up on the handlebars. I once was giving sister Patty a "buck' as we called it and she started to slip, while I picked just that moment to veer and since I couldn't see... bam-we hit a parked car. Patty flew up onto the car's trunk. And what happened to me? Well, I slipped forward off the seat right onto the bar running up to the handlebars. I was rolling around on the grass holding my crotch. Patty was dragging her bruised body off the car when the owner of the car, Bill Melaas came out and pummeled me for hitting his car as if I hadn't been punished enough already. It was definitely not a fun day. I don't think I walked right for a whole week.

There was also a small neighborhood grocery store over by Washington Elementary school where a friend stole seven cartons of cigarettes. We found a really cool hiding place to smoke these ill begotten goods. We were in this little hiding place, puffing away when Billy Blanchard and Linda Lundstrom found us. Linda said she was going to tell our parents and since she was older, we were a little scared of her. They grabbed the cigarettes and laid each of them one after another on the street, all the way home. My sister Mary found out that Linda and Billy had done this, and she then went and picked them all up so she could smoke the cigarettes that didn't get run over by cars. As for the really cool hiding place? We were under the pumps where the fuel trucks would fill up. If there had been a leak, they probably wouldn't have found a speck of us. We definitely hadn't thought about that possibility.

"We do dumb things when we are young,
so we have something to smile about when we are old!"
—Unknown (From Someecards.com)

BUCKSALARSE

I was five years old, the only boy with six older sisters. I was pretty lucky in many ways. However, at five, I didn't always feel that way. One day I decided my sisters were being mean to me, so I made a couple of peanut butter and jelly sandwiches and filled my dad's thermos up with really sugary Kool aide. I then ran away. To the corner of our yard. I sat down right on the curb and waited all day for my parents to get home. My mom and dad finally came home, and they walked over to me.

"What are you doing?" My dad asked.

"The girls were mean to me, so I ran away." I replied.

"You didn't get too far. How long have you been here?"

"All day, but I didn't go any further because you said I couldn't leave the yard." I told him.

My mom and dad exchanged smirks and my dad said, "Let's go have dinner."

Another crisis solved at the Peart household! My dad did get a little ticked off at me the next time he used his thermos. I guess I didn't get all the sugar out when I washed it.

Speaking of sugar, in my house, the coffee pot always seemed to be on and in the winter, I would come home from skating at Noonan's Pond for dinner, cold as the dickens, and pour a cup of coffee. I dumped so much sugar into the coffee that the spoon would stick in the bottom of the cup. My mom would get so mad about that.

My sisters always tortured me, their baby brother. When I was old enough to understand that I had a brother who died at birth, they would tease me and tell me I was adopted. I was about seven years old, and they told me, once again, that I was adopted. I ran to my dad, crying.

He wrapped me up in his arms and said, "What's the matter bucksalarse?" This was his pet nickname for me.

"Am I adopted!" I ask.

He smiles and says, "Who said that?"

I replied, "All the girls!"

My dad laughed, hugged me harder and said, "You go tell them that you were the only one wanted!"

My dad also had six sisters. He knew what I was going through.

I got my sister Patty back later in life. When we were the only two remaining in the house, I used to hide in her closet and grab her when she walked in to get something. She got smart and started to take her pajamas out of the closet early and leave them on her bed. So then, I started hiding under her bed waiting until she turned the lights out and had gotten under the covers. I would then reach up and grab her. She would go through the roof! After a couple of times doing that, she would then close the closet door and check under the bed. So, I had to resort to sneaking out on the roof, which was very easy to get out on, and then come in through the window to startle her Ah, Patty and I had such good times! Of course, I don't think she remembers it quite so fondly.

My sister Mary created my fear of enclosed spaces. Like any little brother, I followed her around...everywhere she went in the neighborhood. A neighbor had a small shed in their backyard. Mary got annoyed that I was following her and her friends, She grabbed me and shut me in the shed and latched it closed. Unbeknownst to her there was a beehive in the shed. I started screaming while I was getting stung about 10 times. Mary got me out, but the damage was done! I have been claustrophobic ever since.

By the way...my dad's nickname for me? "Bucksalarse." I asked him when I was older what it meant.

He smiled and said, "It's Norwegian slang for 'Farts a lot!'

And here I thought it was going to be something cool!

"You are the bows from which your children as living arrows are sent forth."
—Khalil Gibran (1881–1931)

DESTINY IS LEARNED EARLY

I loved playing baseball as a kid. I really wasn't very good, but I could do the basics: hit some of the time, throw the ball, which went where I wanted it to go most of the time and catch, which I could do fairly well. Players that can do the basics and not much more usually are platooned in right field. In the '50s, '60s and '70s, the prevailing thought was that all but a few players were naturally right-handed, so we hit and threw right-handed. Never mind that if you are naturally right-handed, your dominant eye is your right eye and thus you should hit left-handed, but I will leave that up to the sports physiologists and exercise science folks. My point being that if you were good at just the basics they put you in right field, as not many balls got hit out there. Not true today or even as we got older and played a better form of baseball.

In Alexandria Little League Baseball, there was one coach, who doubled as an umpire. Usually, a high school baseball player or maybe a college baseball player who was working a summer job, thus all the players took turns being first and third base coaches and helping direct base runners. One game I hit a single and my teammate batted me around to third base with a double to the fence. This was when my destiny as a coach became evident to me. I saw that the pitcher, Gary Serum wasn't paying attention to me on third base, and I got a great jump and tried to steal home, but I was thrown out. The problem was that I wasn't the fastest runner. I failed to mention that fact when I listed the basics. You see, it was the right time, the right idea, I was just the wrong baserunner to try it. My teammates were not happy with me, but again, had I been faster, I think I would have made it. I came to learn that coaching was a lot easier than playing somedays.

That pitcher I mentioned, Gary Serum, who I grew up, became a professional pitcher for the Minnesota Twins and the New York Yankees. He turned out to be the only professional athlete from my Alexandria graduating class of 1975.

"Timing is Everything."
—Buck Brannaman (By Permission)

A DOG NAMED KING

I was sixteen years old, living with my sister Margaret and her husband Noel in Tonka Bay, Minnesota, a suburb of Minneapolis. I had a summer job working as a night watchman at North Star Marina on Lake Minnetonka. Working nights is solitary and to state that the summer was lonely doesn't quite do it justice. Margaret and my sister Mary discussed the situation and since Mary had a dog, the sisters thought it would be good for me to have a companion for my nights at the marina.

King was a big dog, so his name was very fitting. He was not only big, but he was also friendly. He was definitely the ruler of his kingdom and soon came to be the ruler of my heart. A German Shepard mix, thick golden coat and strong as a bull. I loved that dog. Now anyone that has worked nights knows that you have a limited amount of time to make friends. You are either sleeping or getting ready to go to work. Your world gets a bit turned upside down, and you spend an inordinate amount of time alone. King became my best friend. I took him to work with me every night. I am not sure that I would have made it through that summer without him.

At 16, I wasn't quite worldly. I had my driver's license and a car, but I had never driven a stick shift. The marina had a company pickup that the daytime crew used to make deliveries and pick up parts or what not. One night I saw that the keys were left in the truck and being a little bored, I thought it would be fun to drive it around a bit. King and I jumped in the truck, and I noticed that there was an extra pedal on the floor, but I really didn't think much more about it. I mean, I was a goaltender in hockey and yeah, maybe I had taken a few knocks to the melon, so the extra pedal didn't register in my mind. I turn the ignition on and WHAM, the truck lurches forward and hits a parking post in the parking lot. Thankfully, the truck hadn't built up much speed so there was just a small dent in the front fender. There were other dents in that front fender, so I figured no one would probably notice another one.

King was on the front seat next to me and looked at me like I was a complete bonehead. My sister Mary's husband drove stock cars, so King was used to being around cars and more importantly, stick shifts. He probably could have driven that truck better than I could. Needless to say, after having survived this little adventure, I grabbed the keys and put them inside where they belonged. And, yes, I figured out what that extra pedal was for!

King was such a good dog. I remember one night, he and I were making our rounds in the marina lot, checking the boats that were parked on shore, when we came across a racoon. The raccoon ran towards the lake as King went nuts, barking and snarling, I believe wanting to protect me. King almost broke loose of the leash I used when we patrolled the premises. He leaped and jumped towards the racoon, but I instinctively kept him away as it made threatening hissing noises that I had never heard before. I found out later that a racoon will sit on a dog's head in the water, dig its claws in and use its body weight to drown it. Sometimes my instincts turn out to be correct.

King developed severe hip dysplasia a few years later. He was in so much pain that my sister told me that they needed to take him to the veterinarian and put him to sleep. I was attending school in Virginia, Minnesota when my sister Mary called me with the news that King was gone. I ended up walking around the town of Virginia until about 2 AM thinking about that dog and how much he got into my heart and soul.

"You think dogs will not be in heaven?
I tell you; they will be there long before any of us."
—Robert Louis Stevenson (1850–1894)

THE FURTHER ADVENTURES OF
CHUCKIE AND STEVE OSTERBERG

My friend, Billy Blanchard reminded me of a couple more Osterberg Brothers stories. They were the resident bullies of our neighborhood in Alexandria. Anyway, one of the ways they used to torture us was to hold us down with their knees holding our arms down and let spit fall slowly out of their mouths, almost, until the spit would fall into our mouth. They then would suck it back up to into their own mouth. Of course, sometimes they would fail. Or they would both hold us down and use the knuckle of their middle finger to beat on our chests. They called this the ninety-nines. Oh man that hurt. Sometimes they would do it until we peed our pants! Of course, we would run home, change clothes and come back, only to have them do it again.

The brothers also used to sell us firecrackers out of their bedroom window for the Fourth of July. At a markup of course. They would build model airplanes, cars and boats all year long so they could blow them up over the Fourth using firecrackers and cherry bombs or M-80s. Thank goodness they couldn't get their hands on dynamite, there is no telling what kind of damage those two could have done. Billy thinks we egged them on. US? No, never!

Now, most of the time we didn't torture any of the younger kids in the neighborhood. Mostly because there were not a lot of younger kids to torture. There was Mike Montbrian, but he had Hodgkin's Lymphoma and we all liked him. His dad was a baseball umpire and a nice guy. We never bothered Mike. Now Scott Bentley? He was a different story. Scott used to lip off at us and he was a fast little bugger. Dane Vickstrom, Gordy Vipond, Bill Theiss, Billy Blanchard, and I would chase him. Eventually we would surround him and catch him, Scott would then promise to not lip off anymore, but sure enough, he would get two or three steps away and he would say something smart and start running again. I can't tell you how many hours we spent chasing him around. Of course, the smart and mature thing would have been to ignore him and his comments, but that wasn't us.

There were also the Lehman brothers, Jim and his way more famous brother Tom. They moved into the neighborhood when we entered high school and by then the guys in my neighborhood had discovered cars and those oh so mysterious and interesting creatures, girls. Between chasing girls, trying to pry the car keys out of our parents' hands and playing sports, we didn't bother with the new kids on the block. Besides, we hardly ever saw Jim. And Tom? He was always hitting golf balls in the field next to his house. Lots and lots of practice and look at him now. Famous and rich! All in all, Alexandria was a great place to grow up.

"Youth is wasted on the young."
—George Bernard Shaw (1856–1950)

THE KENWOOD STREET PARTIES

My dad joined the Fraternal Order of the Elks in Alexandria. He worked his way up to be Exalted Ruler of the Club. He then joined the Fraternal Order of Eagles Club, went through the ranks and became President of that Club. He and my mom often went to Conventions out of town, and this forced us hooligans into having a party at my house on Kenwood Street. Usually, one on Friday night and then again on Saturday night. On Saturday afternoon, my sister Patty, Bob Olson and I were lounging about on the couch and easy chair drinking a Schlitz Malt Liquor or two and enjoying a fine Swisher Sweet cigar. We were discussing that evening's soirée and who to invite when we heard car doors slam.

I looked out and said "Oh sh$& it's mom and dad."

They had come home a day early! The three of us bolted for the backdoor. When I arrived there, I suddenly remembered the cigar smoke. I ran back into the house, reached under the kitchen sink, and grabbed a can of air freshener. I then ran to the living room to get rid of the smell. Patty and Bob were probably halfway to Noonan's Pond by then. I sprayed the air freshener all over the living room and suddenly I smelled this gosh awful smell. I looked at the can and realized I had grabbed a can of Raid Bug Spray and not air freshener. Oh my, the smell was horrible.

By now mom and dad are in the kitchen and sitting down after their long drive home. At this point I noticed the garbage bag full of empty Schlitz Malt Liquor cans sitting in the living room. I picked it up, but in my panic, I tried to walk right by my parents with the bag of empty cans. I could have gone out the front door and avoided this ugly scene. But no, that would have required me to use my brain. Ugh.

My father had a booming voice and I heard one word," Thomas!"

I stopped dead in my tracks, put the bag down, and sat down at the table. My dad raised his right eyelid at me in that famous Tom Peart way and says, "What's in the bag?"

"Pop cans." I answered.

My mom is glaring at me, shaking her head and my dad said,

"Wanna try again?"

"Yes sir, we had a party last night. I'm sorry." I replied sheepishly.

I mean, I was caught red handed. My best bet was to throw myself at the mercy of the court.

Just then Bob and Patty came back in, and Bob said the party was his idea and there weren't a lot of people there. Somewhat of a lie.

About that time my mom says "Oh my Lord! What is that smell?"

The Raid/cigar smoke had found its way to the kitchen.

After I explained the Raid mistake, I swear they looked at each other and thought "We actually had this child?"

Patty and I were grounded for a month along with a lot of chores because of that party.

My dad later told me he asked the police to watch the house and gave the police the number to their hotel. The police called them about the party and that is why they came home early. He was always sneaky that way.

Another time, we had a bunch of friends over for a party. A police car pulled to a stop in front of the house. Someone heard the car door slam and yelled,

"Run, it's the cops!"

Everyone took off out the backdoor and the policeman ran around the house and through our back yard. I was just coming out the back door when I heard the policeman swear. He had run chest first into the clothesline and stumbled backwards. I got caught because I laughed when I saw his flashlight fly into the air. I also felt sorry for him, so I just stood there while he retrieved his flashlight.

He brought me to the patrol car and his exact words were,

"So, your parents are out of town, and you decided to have a she-bang, huh?!"

I knew we were busted again. I didn't seem to learn these lessons very easily. However, I did learn a great many important and positive lessons growing up.

Alexandria is my hometown. Always will be, even though I have lived away from it longer than I lived there. Alexandria, while not a perfect place, was a great town to grow up in.

No matter where I go or how long I am gone, Alexandria, for good and bad, is still my hometown.

"Raising Children is an uncertain thing;
success is reached after a life of battle and worry."
—Democritus (460 BC–370 BC)

IRON MIKE'S FIRST TIME DRINKING

I had a high school hockey teammate that loved to tan and loved baby oil so much that he would spray it all over his body and suntan at the beach. The baby oil made him all shiny. Thus, the nickname; "Iron Mike." Mike was not much of a drinker. As a matter of fact, one night when my parents were out of town and the Peart house once again was *party central*, Mike decided to have his first beer. Actually, it turned into his first few beers.

While Mike was losing his beer virginity, some younger kids decided to sneak into the party and steal some of our beer. My house had a big front porch and my mom had peony bushes right in front of the porch. She loved her peonies. We weren't even allowed to touch her flowers. She was the only one allowed to work on them. So, here were the younger kids sitting right behind my mom's peony bushes, backs up against the house drinking our beer.

Mike was three or four beers in by now and he staggered outside to get some air. He proceeded to get sick over the edge of the porch, right on the kids that crashed our party and stole our beer. Mike staggered back in and told me what had happened. I went out to see where the kids were. They were running down the street yelling, covered in Iron Mikes vomit.

Silly, silly boys, you shouldn't have been crashing our party. I don't think Mike did much drinking after that night, but he still loved his baby oil. My mother was confused by the vomit in her peonies. I told her it was my vomit from something I ate. I don't think that she bought that excuse. She was an extremely smart woman who had raised six girls before me. I think that she had pretty much seen everything by the time I was a teenager.

"I live in that solitude, which is painful in youth,
but delicious in the years of maturity."
— Albert Einstein (1879–1945)

FRANKIE AND GORDY

It was the spring of 1975, a group of us hockey players from Alexandria, were at the boys' state hockey tournament. Most of my friends and I were done with high school sports after the hockey season. At that time, both the drinking age and we were 18. So, we decided to make good use of our newfound freedom to drink legally.

Frankie Verdugt, Gordy Vipond, Bob Olson, and I drove down to the Twin Cities together in Bob's car, which Bob named *White Lightning*. Okay, the car was white, but it was far from lighting fast. White Lightning was, however, reliable and got us from point A to point B. Most of our hockey team were also making the three-hour drive down to the Cities. We left on a Wednesday, and it took us about five hours to make the three-hour trip. We made a few stops along the way. Going to the state tourney and the big cities of Minneapolis and St. Paul was a trip we all looked forward to every year. Even some of our girlfriends were staying together in a hotel by the Met Center. It was a big party waiting to happen.

We were staying at Bobby's brother's house in Minneapolis, and we started partying. After an hour or so, we then headed to downtown Minneapolis to check out a few bars. We had connected with our friends Brian Lynch and Pat Maloney, so they were with us, as well. Bob was driving, I was in the front, in the middle and Brian was next to me by the passenger seat. Pat, Gordy, and Frankie were all in the back seat. Bob had gotten turned around and we were lost in an unfamiliar Minneapolis neighborhood. We were driving around aimlessly, trying to find Hennepin Avenue when Bob said that there was a police car behind us. We then saw its red lights go on. The police pulled us over. Before the policemen got out of their car, Brian set a beer on the dash of the car. He started to shove a six pack under the seat when Bob grabbed the beer from the dash and stuck it under my coat. The police came up on both sides of our car and told Bob that he had a taillight out. They asked where we were heading, and Bob told the officers that we were down for the state hockey tournament, and we were trying to find some place to eat and then would be headed back to where we were staying. Unfortunately, we had gotten turned around and weren't sure where to go. They checked out the front and back seats with their flashlights and told Bob to get the taillight fixed. The police gave us directions and they told us to get a bite to eat and get back to wherever we were staying. Of course, we didn't listen, as the night was young!

We finally made it to the Hennepin Avenue strip where we wandered into Moby Dick's, a famous bar in downtown Minneapolis. We walked in and saddled up to the bar. We ordered a couple of drinks and Frankie asked me to play pool, so he and I went over to the pool tables and started playing. Unfortunately, there was a couple playing at the table next to us. Frankie was kicking my butt and I was absently twirling my pool stick. It was a habit of mine when I played pool. The guy at the next table stepped in front of me. He accused me of swinging my pool stick at his girlfriend. I am sure I came back with a clever retort. The guy swore and took a swing at me. I ducked the punch, spun around and threw him on the pool table. I punched him once and the next thing I knew, I was about five feet up in the air, kicking my feet and trying to get loose. One of the largest bouncers I had ever encountered had seen the altercation as it was happening and moved in to calm things down. The bouncer told me to relax and stop resisting. When I did, he put me down. A second large bouncer handled the punk I was tussling with. I had a few Bacardi and Cokes under my belt, and I was a little intoxicated. I am kind of a smart ass most days and even worse when drinking, so I peeked over the bouncer's shoulder and winked at the guy I hit and blew him a kiss. The guy went nuts again, so the first bouncer led Frankie and I out the back entrance, and then escorted the other guy and his girlfriend out the front entrance.

Frankie and I found ourselves in the alley behind Moby Dick's, so we walked down the alley and around the side street back to the front of the bar. Meanwhile, Gordy had gotten into another altercation with a patron. The bouncers grabbed Gordy and pushed him out the front door. Because it was now closing time, they locked the front door so people could get out, but not back in. Gordy was drunk, so he decided to try and get back in. In his attempt he broke the lock on the door. By the time Frankie and I got around the block, Gordy was being taken away in a police car, arrested for destruction of private property. Bob and the rest of the guys stumbled out of the bar, and we found our way to White

Lighting. We figured out where the police station was, and we dropped Bob off there to bail Gordy out.

Frankie and I took the rest of our friends to Bob's brother's house and came back to get Bob and Gordy. Frankie was driving and we parked in front of the station which was on a slight hill. Frankie forgot to put the car in gear, and we rolled back into a police car. Thankfully there were no policeman around who saw this. Bob was waiting for Gordy to be processed and he was talking to one of the policemen. The bail was set at $125. We pooled all the money we had together.

Bob counts it and says, "Sir, all we have is $98.50."

The policeman shook his head, rolled his eyes, and said "Fine, $98.50."

I think Bob was working him a bit before we got there. We collected our wayward friend Gordy and his chief negotiator Bob and got out of downtown Minneapolis before any more trouble came our way.

"Friends are like the walls of a house. Sometimes they hold you up. Sometimes you lean on them. But sometimes it's enough to just know that they are standing by."
—Anonymous (From Search Quotes)

GORDY GOES TO COURT

After the wild Wednesday night on the town, we went to the state hockey tournament games at the Met Center all day on Thursday. All the boys had some beers hidden in their jackets. I hid a pint of rum hidden in my pants. I do remember thinking after that weekend that it would be good to get home and get some blood back into our alcohol streams. Our tickets were way up in the nosebleed section, and we tried our hardest to avoid our head coach Dick Gustafson and assistant coach Tim Cullen, so that they wouldn't smell alcohol on us. I did run into Tim once, but wait, thankfully it turned out to be his identical twin brother Terry instead. Whew. I could never tell them apart. I remember The Met Sports Center fondly. The mezzanine would be jammed with people in-between periods and in-between games. And the lines to the urinals felt like they were a mile long. The games were truly incredible as well.

On Friday we went with Gordy down to the Hennepin County Courthouse for his day in front of the judge. Gordy was nervous and we all wanted to be there for him since we kind of were the four amigos or the four musketeers that whole weekend. We checked in at the information desk and we were directed to the sixth floor. There were police and lots of people everywhere. Some decent looking folks and some really scary looking characters. Gordy checked in with the Court Clerk and was directed to wait for the Public Defender who would be representing him. We waited outside the court room while Gordy was meeting with the Public Defender. I looked over the railing, down some six floors thinking, I wonder if anyone has been tossed off one of these floors before? I know, pretty morbid. After about 45 minutes, Gordy came out and we all filed in to the courtroom to wait for his case to be called. It was a fascinating example of life that paraded before us. Frankie, Bob, and I kept looking at each other with shocked expressions. Person after person would have their case called, their crime described and asked how they would plea. Guilty, Guilty, Guilty. An occasional Not Guilty which took a little time to sort out, but all guilty people would get fined and/or probation. Some would get escorted away, but most were there for misdemeanors and a lot of fines were levied. The Judge asked each person if they had anything to say. Almost to a person they would say something close to "Your Honor, I am working/broke/on welfare/or something similar and I don't get paid until next week/I won't get paid until the end of the month. Etc. The Judge would rap his gavel and tell the miscreant to make arrangements with the clerk. "Case dismissed." Now it was Gordy's turn. The crime was read, the judge asks for a plea and Gordy states "Guilty, your Honor." The Judge levies a fine and a month's probation, which would be cleared if Gordy didn't get into any more trouble.

"You going to cause any more trouble in my city?" The judge asked.

Gordy replied, "No sir!"

The judge said "Anything further to add? "

Gordy started out, " Yes, your Honor, I am still in school and need a couple of weeks..."

BAM! The gavel came down. "Pay the clerk!" The judge yells. "Case dismissed."

I guess the judge wanted to impress upon Gordy and the other three of us, very out of place teens, that we better clean up our act. Especially in his city. I think the guy watched *The Life and Times of Judge Roy Bean* one too many times. We left court that day and though I don't remember if we discussed it or not, I think all four of us made a vow to ourselves not to get so crazy in downtown Minneapolis ever again.

"That might be the subject of a new story. But our present story is ended."
—Fyodor Dostoevsky (1821–1881)

A LESSON FROM BIG TOM

My dad graduated from Jefferson High School in Alexandria in 1933. It was during the Great Depression. Jobs were few and far between. There was a program that was part of FDR's New Deal called the Civilian Conservation Corps (CCC.) It gave manual labor jobs to men eighteen to twenty-five years old. It was later expanded to include seventeen to twenty-eight-year-olds. It paid each man thirty dollars per month, but more importantly gave them food, shelter, and clothing. It also helped with morale and physical conditioning. One project my dad worked on was the building of State Highway 1 in Northern Minnesota. My dad was 5'2 and 120 pounds when he graduated from high school. After his stint in CCC camp, he came home, and my grandmother barely recognized him. He had filled out and grown to 5'11 and 175 pounds. My dad then joined the U.S. Army in 1938. After boot camp in the Army, my dad put on another couple inches and twenty more pounds. Everyone started to call him Big Tom. He had a big, booming voice, a barrel chest and was very, very strong. It was how he carried himself that made him seem bigger though. He wasn't afraid of much and had a very determined way of thinking. Everyone who knew him knew that when his one eyebrow went up, you better just be quiet. Which brings me to my story.

Big Tom worked at Alexandria Light and Power, where he worked his way up from shoveling coal to being a Chief Engineer. When he retired after 36 years, he needed a couple more years for his Social Security to kick in. My sister, Margaret, lined up my dad and mom to work at The Coverleaf Motel on 494 and 35W in Richfield, Minnesota. One night my dad is at the front desk and my mom is in the shower. Two nefarious young men come in and one pulled a gun on Big Tom. They wanted the money in the cash register. My dad thought about it and determined that since it wasn't his money, no problem. He started to get the money out of the register when one of the two robbers says,

"Hurry up old man!"

Now my dad had a Billy club underneath the desk, he grabbed it and hit the guy with the gun in the arm. The man he hit, pulled the trigger, and accidently shot his partner in the leg. My Dad hit the guy again, and then both crooks ran out. I remember later shaking my head at him and asking him what he was thinking. He could have been shot!

He says, "He called me an old man; he made me mad!"

Now fast forward thirty plus years. I was working with a friend of mine, Pete Waggoner, in the scorer's box at a Junior Gold Hockey Tournament at Braemar Arena in Edina, Minnesota. Minnetonka was playing that day and their fans, a large group of young men, were quite boisterous. The arena guys asked us to help keep the kids off the glass around the rink. They kept jumping up on it when Minnetonka would score. I went down to the area where they were jumping up on the case and nicely said,

"Hey guys, do us a favor and stay off the glass. Someone might get hurt."

All of them got down, except one little punk, who yelled,

"F&%$' the old man! Hit the glass!"

I saw red! I grabbed him by the legs, he is hanging on by his fingertips and screaming at me with this abject look of fear on his face. With good cause, as he was maybe 8 to 10 feet off the ground and there was only cement to land on. A dad ran down from the bleachers and said he would handle it, so I let go of the kid and went back to the scorer's box. It hit me that I could have really hurt the kid. He could have landed on his head on the cement or the bleachers. What was I thinking? And then when I calmed down, I looked up and remembered what Big Tom had said,

"He called me an old man; he made me mad!"

Like father, like son.

I love you, Papa! You were always, and still are, my hero!

"A hero is no braver than an ordinary man, but he is braver five minutes longer."
—Ralph Waldo Emerson (1803–1882)

FATHER'S AND GRANDFATHER'S

We all learn things from our fathers and grandfathers. Now this is not to diminish what we learn from our mothers and grandmothers, but today, as I am writing this, is Father's Day so this is about two men who had an incredible impact on my life.

We Peart's have a lack of imagination in naming our sons, or you could say that we loved our fathers and grandfathers so much that we kept naming the Peart boys the same. My great-grandfather was Thomas Peart, a miner turned farmer and politician, who was born in County Durham, England. He immigrated to Ohio as a young man of nineteen. At some point, he moved to Morris, Illinois and he got into politics and farming. There is a Peart Road in Morris named after him.

My grandfather was Thomas Garfield Peart. He was born in Morris, IL and moved to Flandreau, SD. where he married a little French-Canadian woman named Marie "Mae" Bebeaux. Together they had six girls and one boy, my father Thomas Leander Peart. They lived on a farm with crops and some cows and pigs.

My father, Thomas Leander Peart, lived his life with a certain panache. He had a strong sense of morals, and from him, I learned what I like to call a "little Kentucky Windage," meaning that there were usually more ways than one to handle situations. For example, my grandmother was stubborn and due to her poor eyesight, had these thick coke bottle glasses. As she aged, her depth perception got very bad and one day she sideswiped a couple of parked cars when she was driving home. The police came and told her that they needed to confiscate her driver's license. She said no, emphatically. They argued with her, and they finally called my dad. Alexandria was more like a Mayberry type small town at that time in the late '50s, early '60s. My dad knew all the policemen by first name and when he arrived, he listened to the officers and then spoke to my grandma. My dad then brought the officers into the other room where he gave them $5 and said to give it to her in return for her driver's license. The police weren't sure that was going to work, but trusted my dad, so they went back in the other room and gave my grandma the money. She looked at them and grunted and gave them her driver's license. You see, she paid for it, and it was hers unless someone wanted to buy it from her. She was quite the lady.

My dad also told stories of times that he did something wrong, and my grandma would start swearing in French. He would climb up on the roof and hide from her until my grandpa came home. Grandma was deathly afraid of heights and would not go up on the roof or even up on ladders. She would just yell at him and start in again with the French swear words. This is a prime example of the term she and my own mother would use "Wait until your father gets home!" This term was used quite often in my family.

My grandma died in January when I was nine years old. After she died, I would go over to grandpa's house after school to hang out with him and wait for my dad to pick me up after work. I remember sitting on his lap. He would give me a quarter and tell me to save it. He would also tell me that it should have been him to die first. She was his life. He died of a broken heart the next November. Their funerals were two of the three times I ever saw my dad cry in my entire life. The third time was when John F. Kennedy was assassinated. He loved his parents, and he thought JFK was the best President we have ever had in our country.

My dad also was a sneaky SOB! I would use the car and the next day, he knew how far I had driven, as he always checked the odometer before and after. He also knew if I had taken a turn too sharply. He even knew which way you turned too sharply. He used to put boxes on each side of the trunk. If the right-side box was askew, he knew you took a right turn a little too fast. If the left side was messed up...he knew you went that way too fast. I didn't get away with anything.

I learned those tricks from my dad and when I started coaching at Roosevelt, I put them to good use. Every season, early in the year, I would plan an overnight trip to help the team bond and prepare for the bulk of the season. I figured out how to know which rooms, if any, broke curfew without staying up sitting in the hall. I took pennies and put one on the door handle of each room. We had a couple of all team runs before breakfast when I found some pennies on the floor. My girls' teams were a little sharper. They figured out the penny trick, as the pennies would make noise when they fell after the door was opened. They would then put the penny back on the handle and gently close the door. It worked sometimes, probably more often than not. With my girls' teams, I switched to small pieces of paper that I would put in the door jam. This worked even better. I really don't know how my grandfather, or my dad survived raising seven kids each, but some of those two generations of lessons sure benefited me when I started coaching.

"By the time a man realizes that his father was right,
he usually has a son who thinks he is wrong!"
—Charles Wadsworth (1814–1882)

MOM

I would be remiss if I didn't tell a story of what my mother, Adeline Orayne Max Peart, truly meant to me, and how she affected my life and development as a person, a teacher and as a coach.

"Life began with waking up and loving my mother's face."
—George Eliot (1819–1880)

CHICKEN LEGS

I was born a year and a half after my brother, who was still born and never had a chance at life. On the other side of the coin, had he been a live birth, he probably would have been Thomas Henry Peart and I. most likely wouldn't be here. It's amazing how life plays out and how fortunate we all are to be here.

My sisters told me that my mother was bleeding internally. The bleeding started one afternoon, and my mom passed out on the floor. My dad was at work when he suddenly felt that he had to get home quickly. When he arrived at home, he found my mother on the floor. He rushed her to the emergency room. He didn't feel that he could wait for the ambulance, so he took her in his car. My brother was still born, and my mom's doctor told her that it would be best if she stopped having children.

My dad had six sisters and no brothers, he and my mom had six daughters and had just lost a son…there was a snowball's chance in hell that my mom and dad were going to listen to the doctor. They were going to try once again to have a boy and Wala! The Golden Child appeared. Me!

I was a skinny little dude at birth and my uncle Rod, upon seeing me for the first time, made the mistake of saying that I had chicken legs. Not something that my mother was going to take laying down and she verbally bit Rod's head off. She now had a boy and for the rest of my life, no one could say anything bad about her son; even though I had chicken legs when I was born. I pretty much made up for those chicken legs later in life. My thighs now are bigger than some people's waists…lots of biking, skating, and running with goalie pads on did the trick.

"God could not be everywhere, and therefore He made mothers."
—Rudyard Kipling (1865–1936)

Thomas H Peart

YOU NEED TO LEARN TO LISTEN TO YOUR FATHER

When I was nine years old, my sister Patty and I were out Trick or Treating on Halloween. My Dad told us we could go anywhere we wanted, but we were to stay away from the Tech School apartments. Did we listen? Wouldn't be much of a story if we did. So, we are on 14th Avenue and Jefferson Street in Alexandria scoping out the uncharted territory that we just knew was ripe for candy. Little did we realize that most of the homes around the Tech School were student housing and the students would be partying and not handing out candy. We saw two guys walking towards us and I could feel tension in the air. Something was wrong, but I was too young to know what to do. One of the guys said,

"You dropped some candy."

Patty turned around, but again something didn't feel right so I turned sideways, not quite believing him. The first guy grabbed Patty's bag of candy and the guy in front of me shoved me and grabbed my bag. I remember both of us crying long and hard that night. We, of course, had to fess up to my dad and mom. This was harder than losing the candy. I absolutely hated disappointing them. My mom looked at us, shook her head and said,

"You need to learn to listen to your father."

She then took pity on us and shut off the porch light and what candy she had left was divided up between us. We became better listeners from then on.

"Example isn't another way to teach, it is the only way to teach."
—Albert Einstein (1879–1945)

STORIES I'M GLAD MY MOM DIDN'T KNOW ABOUT

Growing up, I adored my mom. I had a special relationship with my dad, but there was something unique about my mom. I guess when you are a mother, have six girls and always want a boy, then you lose a boy at birth, when you finally have that son, you develop a special bond. There was a great deal I couldn't tell her while I was growing up, though, because she would worry too much, and I didn't want to upset her. For instance, when I got busted in the head with a beer glass at a bar called The Barn one Saturday night, I remember begging the nurses not to call her and my dad until the next morning. They acquiesced, but I had to turn on the big soulful eyes for a bit to get them to wait.

The times when I would start feeling guilty about one thing or another, which often happened if I drank a little too much, I would conclude that as a good Catholic boy, I needed to go to confession. The problem was, I was three sheets to the wind when I would come to the realization that I couldn't remember what I said to that poor priest during my confession. Whatever it was would not have made my mom very proud.

My mom was a very proper woman and kind of shy, so I know that she would have been upset if she heard about the time Steve H. walked into a house while drunk thinking that it was my house, looked around and said,

"Damn, this isn't the Peart's!"

He had the right house number, just the wrong street. He walked into the corner house on Hawthorne instead of Kenwood. Not sure what those poor residents thought. To my mom, this would be akin to one of her kids running down the street naked. She would be more upset than we probably would have been.

Of course, there was the time I finally convinced my girlfriend to come over to my house. It was a very romantic moment. I had Barry White (I know, I know, but it was the '70s) on the stereo, a fire in the fireplace, as we laid on a blanket in front of the fire. Just as I am about to make my big move, the hall light comes on and my dad comes banging down the stairs. Me, Mr. Romantic forgot to open

Thomas H Peart

the flue in the fireplace and the whole house was filled with smoke. We hadn't noticed because we were lying on the floor. The smoke had scared my poor mom and dad half to death. I had a hard time explaining to them how or what had happened. I told them that we had fallen asleep. The lesson? When you start a romantic interlude with someone, always check the flue in the fireplace to make sure it is open. Especially with your mom and dad upstairs.

"Only mothers can think of the future –
because they give birth to it in their children."
—Maxim Gorky (1868–1936)

A MOM AND HER SON

It struck me today how much cell phones have changed our lives. When I was in college and would call home, inevitably, my mom or dad would always ask,
"What's wrong?"
And then," Do you need money?"
A phone to them was a tool and it wasn't for idle chatter.

When I was younger, we had one phone and we were even part of a party line for a while. I guess when your neighbors could listen in on your conversations, you didn't want to talk long or too in-depth. Today, with cell phones, my sisters speak with their kids nearly every day.

My dad passed away in February of 1991 and my mom in January of 1996. There isn't a day that goes by that I don't miss them both. My mom was not into athletics at all. My dad played basketball, football and baseball in high school and football in the Army. When I was in high school, my mother didn't like coming to my hockey games. I think it was all the fans yelling "sieve" at me! (A sieve is defined as a bad, leaky goaltender, who lets too many goals into his own net, causing his team to lose) My mom would have none of that chant. Well, not after I told her what it meant.

After my brother died at birth, the doctors told my mom not to have any more children. A year and a half later the "Golden Child" came along, and her life changed greatly.

I was quite the hellion growing up. I was rambunctious and would wear out the knees of my pants playing on the floor. Mom would patch them up. Little did I know, I could have left the holes in there and been an early trend setter. One of my favorite memories was playing on the kitchen floor while my mom ironed as the smell of baking bread and fresh homemade caramel rolls wafted through the house while she listened to one of her favorite songs, *Puff the Magic Dragon* playing on the radio. She loved that song.

My mom was also a very good piano player and had the voice of an angel. I would beg her to play "The Beer Barrel Polka" on the piano. I could listen to her for hours.

Growing up, I was a bit of an imp at times. One night I saw that the water was running in the bathtub, along with lots of bubbles. I thought my sister Patty was going to take a bath, so I took a handful or two of those army men, you know the ones with the really sharp edges, and threw them in the bath. I was holding my breath in excitement, waiting for my sister to go into the tub. This was going to be the best prank ever! Then, much to my horror, it was my mom going into the bathroom. I was halfway to hiding in my closet when I heard a horrific scream. My dad came running upstairs and threw open the bathroom door. My poor mom was struggling to get out of the bath. I thought better of hiding in the closet and I started to run downstairs. I was going to head for the hills. As I got to the open bathroom door, I looked in and there is an infantryman stuck to my mom's butt. I knew I was in deep doo-doo! Especially when my mom yelled,

"Thomas! Do something with YOUR son!"

My dad was trying so hard not to laugh when he swatted my bottom. To be honest, it wasn't too hard of a swat, he was laughing too much.

After my dad died, my mom came to visit every late January into early February, right around the anniversary of my dad's passing. She would make all my favorite food, but even better, she loved to come to my hockey games. Somehow, this woman, who hated coming to my games when I played, loved watching my team play and her son coach. She would sit behind the glass in the lobby of Parade Ice Gardens, where it was nice and warm, and we would go out for a bite to eat after the game. If we lost, she would cheer me up and if we won, she usually was happier than I was.

I also remember the time that my girlfriend Kris, my mom and I went to a movie during one of her visits. My mom, like the proper woman she was, sat in between Kris and me. I think she was afraid of being left out, but I also believe she still thought of me as her little boy.

To all of you who still have your parents, call them up, tell them how much you love them and thank them for always being there for you...even when you were a little s$&t!!

Mom...I love you and miss you!

*"There is no occupancy limit on a mother's heart. It expands with each child...
and you just add another room."*
—Heather Lende (By Permission)

DEER HUNTING AND NEAR DEATH

My Dad had a rule regarding hunting and the use of guns when I was growing up. Duck, pheasant, grouse and geese hunting were allowed once I passed my gun safety training. No deer hunting until I was eighteen. Those were his rules, and I abided by those rules. I loved going hunting with my dad. I saw a side of him that you didn't see around my mother and my sisters.

My first deer hunting trip was during the fall of my senior year. We were driving up to the deer camp just outside Littlefork-Big Falls in Northern Minnesota. We would meet my mom's brothers, Rod and Stan at the camp on a Wednesday. As we were driving, my dad started to talk about the rules of deer camp,

"One, double check what you are aiming at. Two, be calm, don't jerk when you squeeze the trigger. And three, for goodness sakes, don't shoot at the orange deer."

Then he looks at me and says, "The most important rule is, what happens at deer camp, what you hear at deer camp, stays at deer camp!"

I'm pretty sure that the advertising executive that came up with *What happens in Vegas, stays in Vegas!* was a deer hunter.

I had spent the entire eighteen years of my life around these three men, and at times, all three would get on me about my language. My dad's last rule hit home as soon as we arrived at the camp. I didn't know that the three of them could cuss like they did, until I heard them at deer camp. They also told some naughty jokes. It definitely was an eye-opener for me. I had used cuss words and my friends, and I often told dirty jokes, but this was the first time I had heard adult men this open about it and this free with the cuss words. And yes, I never told my mom or sisters about what happened at deer camp.

On Thursday morning, after breakfast, we took my Uncle Rod's boat over Black Bay to a peninsula and one of their favorite hunting spots. At first, we saw only a couple deer, but they were too young. We were walking along a road to another hunting spot when nature called out to me. I headed into the woods to answer the call, thinking it would be easy to find my way back to the path. I finished up the paperwork and suddenly realized that I had no idea how to get back to the road. I was lost in the woods. Totally turned around. I couldn't find my way out. I forgot the "stay calm" rule and started to panic. I fired off one shot into the air and then another, as I heard my dad's voice calling out to me. He told me to walk towards his voice. Thankfully I was not far from the road. This experience freaked me out a lot!

Then it started to storm and got extremely windy so Rod, Stan, my dad and I jumped into Rod's boat and began making our way back across the bay. The waves were huge, and we were taking on a great deal of water. My dad gave me a coffee cup and told me to start bailing water. He and Stan were busy with coffee cans shoveling out water up in the front of the boat. I was in the middle, shoveling water with a coffee cup. Uncle Rod was trying his best to guide us across the bay and keep us off the bottom of the lake.

Suddenly we went almost straight up a huge wave, crested it and started straight down to the bottom of the wave. My Dad and Stan dove at me and knocked me down and our combined weight and excellent boating skills by Rod brought the nose of the boat up and saved us from a certain, freezing demise.

Later, when we told my mom, she shook her head and often told people about how she could have lost the love of her life, her son and two brothers all in one fell swoop.

There, but for the Grace of God, go I. Or in this case, the four of us.

"Having a great uncle in your life is like having a great coach, a favorite teacher, a big brother and a best friend all rolled into one."
—Anonymous (From Quote Ambition)

MIGHTY MOE AND GRANDPA'S CHILI

My niece Shelly died in 2021. She had suffered from a rare blood disease since her high school years called Dermatomyositis. The disease causes muscle weakness and painful skin rashes. She had over 30 surgeries in her lifetime from complications of the disease and even lost her leg when she got a staph infection in her knee in 2015. Her life was hard. Much harder than most people, but then life isn't always fair. The thing is, she never complained about her life or her condition. Was she perfect? No. She had her moments, but she had a heart of gold, and loved her family deeply. At the end, she contracted Covid and was on a ventilator. She fought off the Covid. Her oxygen levels got back to near normal, and she came off the ventilator. But then she got an infection that raged through her body. She became septic, and her organs started failing. After a lifetime of fighting physical adversity, the end finally came. She had lived a fighter's life. I believe that she is in a better place now and hopefully romping around with her dog Titan who she lost ten years before she passed away.

Here are a couple of my favorite memories of Shelly when she and her siblings, Lynn and Chad were young. My sister Lynda, Shelly's mom, lived across the street from my parents and me in Alexandria. Lynda worked overnights at an elderly nursing home, and I would sleep at her house to watch over her three kids. When my mom would go to Phoenix periodically to stay with my sister Diane, my dad would oversee the evening meals. Normally this was one of my mom's duties. My dad was a good cook, but he didn't cook very often. During one of my mom's trips, my dad decided to make chili and he loved it spicy and hot. He made a big pot, and Shelly and her siblings ate and ate. To this day, I am not sure where they put it all. Sweat was pouring down their faces and Shelly looks up and says,

"Can we have more chili grandpa? Mom's chili never tastes this good!"

She loved grandpa's cooking.

I think grandpa might be making his chili in Heaven for her. At least I hope he is.

Then of course, because their favorite uncle was, and still is, a bit of a nut job, we watched professional wrestling on television. This would lead to major wrestling matches between the four of us. One day, I came up with nicknames for all of us. Chad was "Mr. Quick" because he was very quick and fast. Lynn was "Mighty Mite" because she was tiny and tough as nails. Shelly was "Mighty Moe" because she was a mini-Lynn. Tough in her own way. I was "Dr. Paralyzer" with *101 ways to cause you pain*. I would pick each of them up over my head and body slam them on the bed, get them in leg locks and pinch nerves in their necks and arms and legs. We had a fabulous time. Lynn even gave me a hand painted mug with Dr Paralyzer embossed on one side and Mighty Mite on the other for Christmas one year. Shelly would always be the last one to "tap out." She could withstand the most discomfort. Maybe it was preparation for the life ahead of her. I am not sure.

I have not had the joy of being a parent during my life. But with six older, "prolific" sisters, I have a plethora of wonderful nephews and nieces who mean the world to me. My life has been richer because of all of them.

RIP Mighty Moe! I love you!

Michelle Rae Logan "Mighty Moe" 4/9/1970–6/22/2021
If nieces and nephews were jewels, I would have the most beautiful gems ever."
—Author Unknown (From Wow4U.com)

ALEXANDRIA CARDINALS

I came to hockey later in my life. Well, later than most kids do today, that is for sure. I started in my teens. One of my best friends and my neighbor, Bill Blanchard talked me into playing when I was thirteen. I have told him that it was because he didn't want to be a goaltender. He laughs and agrees, saying it was partly that, but he also knew that hockey would be good for me. Little did either of us know that hockey would become my career, my livelihood, my lifelong passion, and my reason for being.

Once I started playing hockey, I spent countless hours skating on Noonan's Pond and on the outdoor rink behind our high school. Skating was a way for me to free myself and focus. An ability I certainly lacked in class throughout elementary, junior high and high school. Today, I probably would have been tested for attention deficit disorder, but we didn't know about that in the early '70s. Goaltending turned out to be a perfect position for me. I didn't have to focus constantly, and I could take little mental breaks when the puck was in the opponent's end. Then when the puck was in our end, I was focused completely on the play. This was a pattern I followed throughout my life. Complete focus when it was necessary and important.

Here are some of the incredible stories from my early life as a hockey player.

"Life isn't about finding yourself. Life is about creating yourself."
—George Bernard Shaw (1898–1943)

DICK GUSTAFSON - "THERE WAS A RUSSIAN POLE-VAULTER WITH FIRE IN HIS EYES!"

As I noted earlier, Bill Blanchard was instrumental in my lifelong passion for hockey. He started out playing hockey as a goaltender. He didn't want to continue playing that position. I played in the goal in our playground soccer games in elementary school. Bill saw a way to get out of the goalie net and knew that I was crazy enough to be a goaltender even though I had never played hockey before. He was right. Flip Namur also wanted to play goal and initially, he and I were supposed to trade off wearing the pads, but once I was in the net, I didn't want to share, and Flip ended up playing defense throughout our high school days.

We hockey players were the crazy athletes of the school. I mean we had to be right? We didn't have an indoor arena, so we practiced outside in bone chilling temps. We drove to Detroit Lakes for practices early in the season when we didn't have outdoor ice yet. Often, we would get home at 1:00 am and have to be in school by about 7:30 or so that morning. I'm pretty sure that wouldn't fly with parents today. We also had to play many of our home games at the opposing team's rink because they wouldn't play outside.

Dick Gustafson, our coach who we called Gus, did some amazing things just to keep us playing. How he figured out the travel budget, I will never know. Gus was a marvel in many ways. Gus was a young man when he was coaching us bunch of hooligans. Mid-twenties if my calculations are correct.

One of our biggest rivals was Fergus Falls and they were the closest team to us, being only 45 minutes away. We used to have to change into everything but our skates at the junior high and then go to the fairgrounds, where the rink was, to finish up. Before one game in Fergus, Gus had a big speech ready to pump us up. He came into the locker room, flipped the lights off and said,

"There was a Russian pole vaulter with fire in his eyes!"

Before he could say another word, Bobby Olson. bellows "Turn on the F'ing lights, I can't see to tie my skates."

Gus flipped on the lights and screamed, "Who said that?"

All the while glaring right at me.

"It wasn't me" I said. Thank the good Lord I already had my skates on and was working on my pads, or I would have been in big trouble.

Gus and I had a tumultuous relationship in high school. He was trying to get the best out of a relatively inexperienced goaltender. I had some anger issues, trying to navigate the world, that I thought was tilted against me. Fairly typical of teenagers. I didn't always appreciate or even understand what he was trying to do. Many years later, when my coaching career was winding down, I finally understood Gus and I wrote him a letter to that effect. I will say this now, publicly, I respect Dick Gustafson for all that he did for me and the challenges he overcame in doing so. I learned many things from Gus, both good and maybe, also, how to try different things. He is a part of my life as a fellow coach and as a friend. He has had a lasting impact on my life throughout the years. I consider him a friend and a mentor.

"A good coach can change a game. A great coach can change a life."
—Unknown (Brainyquotes)

COACH TOM SAVAGEAU

During my high school years, we had a new coach move to Alexandria from Fargo, North Dakota. He was a counselor by trade and was a great inspiration to many of us hockey players who were somewhat lost at times due to life's challenges. I happened to be one of those people.

Tom Savageau and his wife Rachel moved into the house right next to mine during my senior year. They were excellent neighbors and Tom was a great help to me in my sorting through some options, as I contemplated going into the service or heading off to college. My original plan was college, but other circumstances, such as a lack of money, factored into my decision to join the United States Marine Corps.

Tom possessed a very calm demeanor and he understood, as well as accepted, his role as an assistant coach. He may have disagreed with our head coach at times, but he always kept his opinions to himself until the coaches were alone and could discuss things away from the players. I attempted to pattern myself after Tom when I became an assistant coach, and it was always a trait that I searched for when I was hiring assistant coaches. With a team, you need a unified voice coming from the coaches to the players.

Tom was someone who was always there for me. He had the innate ability to speak when words were necessary and to be quiet and listen when silence was required. His words of encouragement, his belief in me, helped me become the man and coach that I became. I may have never told him outright, but he was one of the men I aspired to become as I grew to adulthood and wished to be like in my coaching career.

"Whatever you are, be a good one."
—Abraham Lincoln (1809–1865)

WHEN TOMMY LEARNS THE MEANING OF THE WORD IRONY, AND WHAT IT MEANS TO BE A TEAM PLAYER.

Growing up, I was a spoiled boy with six older sisters and by the time I got to high school, all my sisters were out of the house. I won't get into all the details, but my sisters always commented negatively about my teenage years, partially because Dad made a set of car keys for me. They never had a set of their own, so they thought I was a spoiled brat!

I had some anger issues due to some conflicts at home with my mother and got into my fair share of battles on the ice and off. One of those battles happened in Baudette, Minnesota. We would play Indus and Baudette twice every year. Often, instead of spending money on hotel rooms, we would pair up and stay at one of their players' houses. When they came down to play us, they would do the same. We usually could put away our differences for the night. Thankfully we weren't staying with the Baudette players on this trip, due to a fight that broke out in the junior varsity game. During my sophomore year, I was the starting goaltender for junior varsity games and was the backup goaltender for the varsity games. We got beat in the JV game 3-2. It was a hard-fought game and since I was ultra-competitive, it didn't matter if I played well, it just mattered if we won or lost. So, I was not a happy camper and as we were shaking hands, one of their players said, "Ha! Ha! We beat you f'ers!"

I responded by punching him with my blocker. A small fight broke out, but the refs shut it down quickly.

Back then both teams had to climb this long set of stairs that extended out over the concession stand to get to the locker rooms upstairs. The locker rooms were down a long, narrow hall. As we were leaving the ice and walking towards our locker room, some of the Baudette players were behind us. This included my new friend, who decided to mouth off again as we walked down the hall. Of course, I felt duty bound to defend the honor of the Alexandria Cardinals. We exchanged a few punches and our respective JV coaches broke it up.

Gus got wind of the fight and oh boy was he mad. This is when I learned the meaning of the word irony. Gus grabbed me and threw me up against the wall repeatedly, yelling, "You have to learn how to how to control your temper!"

I suppose one could have said it was the pot calling the kettle black at that moment. Afterwards, I was really embarrassed and angry and I'm in the shower because I had decided that I was quitting the team. I would show Gus. Our Assistant Coach, Tom Savageau, stood at the edge of the shower and helped calm me down. At least for a day.

When my dad found out I was thinking of quitting hockey, he was very angry with me and told me that I wouldn't have hurt Gus in the least, if I had quit the team. But I would have been letting my teammates down by quitting and that wasn't acceptable. He then told me that being a team player meant you are there for your teammates first and yourself second. I had to learn a lot of lessons the hard way on that trip. It seemed that a lot of my life was learning a lot of lessons the "hard way."

"We should not look back unless it is to derive useful lessons from past errors, and for the purpose of profiting by dearly bought experience."
—George Washington (1732–1799)

Thomas H Peart

THE NOONAN'S POND ICE BATH

It took a certain type of person to play hockey outdoors in Alexandria in the sixties and seventies. I remember that one year during the early part of the season, practice was scheduled for Noonan's Pond as the ice was not ready at our rink behind school. Gus had us warm up with some resistance drills. One player would be skating backwards and snow plowing as another player skating forwards would be pushing. We would switch on the way back. On this day, we did a couple of sets when Gus called for one more time down and back. I was paired up with Dave Kluver and one of my leg straps came loose, so we stopped so I could fix it. Just then we heard this loud, echoing sound and looked up to see the ice as it tilted downwards and almost the entire team went straight into the water. Pat Rouillard thought he was drowning, but Gus told him to stand up. The water in that area was only about to your waist, with probably a foot of muck and goose poop on the bottom. Needless to say, practice was over for the day, but if I recall, Gus had a look on his face as if he was thinking that the ice on the other end of the pond, seeing ice that was still good. We could skate there. Fortunately, all the players that fell in were already making their way to their cars before Gus could finish that thought and order us back onto the pond to finish practice.

Outdoor ice is always a hit and miss situation early in the season, depending on how cold the weather gets in November. Gus would take us outside and we would do dry land training drills. We would do different speed and agility drills, and then run a mile or two. And Gus, that old son of a gun, would make the goalies run with our leg pads on. Wanna talk about a workout? No wonder Bill Blanchard wanted me to play goal. At that time, goalie pads were vintage leather and stuffed with horse or deer hair. They weighed a total of thirty pounds. That's a lot of weight to run with.

We also held practices out on Lake Latoka, or other ponds and lakes that froze over. If you missed a pass, that puck would go a long way. You would be skating after it listening to the ice cracking behind you, wondering if the ice was going to break underneath you. Nothing like the thought of plunging into a freezing cold lake to make you skate a little faster. Especially us goaltenders. If we broke through the ice, those leg pads would have dragged us straight to the bottom. It would have been spring before they found us! One of those things that my mother was better off not knowing. Times were certainly different back then.

"In skating over thin ice, Our safety is in our speed."
—Ralph Waldo Emerson (1803–1882)

A JUNIOR HIGH DANCE BREAKS OUT.

For many reasons, a lot of crazy things have happened during some of our visits to play Fergus Falls. Fergus Falls is forty-five minutes from Alexandria, and they were one of our main rivals. One bizarre incident happened after one of our games when I was in tenth grade. We would change and shower at the Fergus Falls Junior High School before and after our games. One of our players had found that the door to the school's pool was left unlocked. The pool was like our pool in Alexandria, it had two stories. The pool, locker rooms, and bleachers on the ground floor. On the second floor, there was a viewing area that was also used as a cafeteria and a room for meetings or dances.

After my teammates were alerted to the open pool door, we quickly entered the pool area without any clothes on, of course. There was an entire team of naked hockey players jumping into the pool and leaping off the high diving board, making sure to hold on to the important parts on the way down. Just having a hell of a good time. We were also making a great deal of noise. Suddenly the curtains up above came open, as it turned out, Fergus was having a Junior High dance that evening. I will never forget the look on some of those kids' faces as they saw us swimming naked in their pool. I am pretty sure the shock took a while to wear off for them. Yep, it took a certain breed to play hockey in Alexandria in the early years. I am sure the outcome would have been different these days, but back then, we quickly scurried off to the locker room, showered and changed. Amazingly we avoided any kind of punishment. I am still not sure if our coaches even were aware of what we had done.

""Spontaneity is the best kind of adventure."
—Unknown (Inspirational Quotes)

PLAYING HOCKEY OUTSIDE.

My good friend and fellow coach Denny Fermoyle once told a story on Facebook about trying to get an indoor rink built in Mountain Iron, Minnesota, and that same day, I watched a replay of the Gopher Men's Hockey team playing an outdoor game against Ohio State on Gopher Classics. It struck me as very interesting that we now treasure outdoor games as classic examples of the old-time hockey, whereas, when I was in high school, we wanted an indoor rink so bad, and we dreaded having to play our games outside, since it was so cold outside. Don't get me wrong, we were happy to have the opportunity to play hockey and often, after practice, you would find us at Noonan's Pond playing pick-up hockey. But it was playing our games in the bitter cold that was tough. Yet now it's fun to play a game outside. Well, for ONE game, that is.

Some of our craziest games came against Brainerd, who at the time, also did not have an indoor arena. Both teams had fans along the rink and there was no glass or wire fences along the top of the boards. It was not unusual to have fans from the opposing team "accidentally" grab or punch a player who was checked into the boards. When I was a sophomore, a minor (okay not so minor) skirmish broke out. Dave Kluver, our starting goaltender went after a Brainerd player who had punched his brother, A.J. Kluver, on the ice. All 12 players on the ice were going at it. Players from our bench, including yours truly, were trying to jump off the bench and join in the melee. I remember my coach Gus all but tackling me to keep me on the bench. He knew that Dave was going to get tossed out of this game and probably the next one as well, so he needed his backup goalie to be able to play in the upcoming games. Gus yelled at me to sit my butt down and sit I did. I am watching the poor referees try and get a handle on things when some fan reaches over and takes a swing at Dave Kluver. Suddenly, we saw Dave and A.J.'s dad, Arlo Kluver Senior, jump over the boards on the far side of the ice. He ran across the rink and grabbed the Brainerd fan who hit his son. This added a new dimension to the fight as now more fans were fighting than players. It was crazy! Finally, everything got sorted out. Dave was kicked out of that game, and subsequently suspended for our next game.

Our senior year we were once again back up north playing Brainerd. The rink was surrounded with wooden boards and chicken wire behind the nets to keep pucks in the rink. The chicken wire extended about 5 feet from each side of the goals. There wasn't any padding around the boards holding the chicken wire. Bobby Olson, who was really strong on the puck and tough as nails, was carrying the puck behind the net and a Brainerd defenseman lined him up and checked him into the board holding the chicken wire. Bob fell and hit his head on the board holding the chicken wire and a second time on the top of the rink board as he fell to the ice. The whistle blew for a face-off. Bob got up and staggered to the faceoff circle. The Brainerd kid says,

"Got you're a$$ that time."

Bob looked at the kid and says, "It will take a hell of a lot more than that to knock me out."

Play carries on and then there is a whistle for offsides. Bob skates to our bench and just stands about 10 feet from the bench and says, "Gus! I can't f@&king see."

Gus replies, "Bobby, watch your language!"

Bob says "Okay. But I still can't f@&ing see."

We lost the game that day and after the game is over Bobby comes onto the school bus and says, "Come on guys we can get 'em in the third period."

I looked at Bobby and said, "Bobby, we lost. The game is over."

I'm pretty sure Bobby played the majority of that game with a significant concussion. Back then, we didn't have the concussion protocols that we do today and as Bob said...it was going to take a lot more to knock him out of the game. He was one of the toughest competitors I have ever known in my entire life.

"It's hard to beat a person who never gives up!"
—Babe Ruth (1895–1948)

THE BUS GOES ROUND AND ROUND

We had some extremely long bus rides playing hockey, or any sport, for that matter, when we played for Alexandria. During my high school years our class was one of the best athletically to come through Alexandria up to that point. We were exceptional in basketball, wrestling, baseball, and in the relatively short history of the sport, one of the school's better hockey teams. In 1974, our football team was exceptional. We were the undefeated State Class A Champions. I played football until my senior year when I quit to concentrate on hockey. I attribute our winning the state title to me not being a negative influence on the team.

Our hockey team had some great trips, and several long ones as well. For example, it would be a good 6-hour bus ride up to International Falls. When we played teams way up north, Gus had set it up where we would stay over at opposing players' houses and then they would stay at our houses when they came down to play us. I remember one trip to Indus, which is thirty miles from International Falls. Bill Blanchard and I stayed with the Hasbargen family. They lived just outside of Indus on a big farm. They were great people and welcomed us like we were family. We played Indus at Bronco Arena in International Falls. After the game, we were paired up with one of our teammates and then the pair of us would go off with our host families. When Bill and I got to their house, the Hasbargen's had a big meal ready for us. On the table, were hamburgers, fries, salad and cake. All we could eat. The next morning, for breakfast, we had bacon, eggs, sausage, hashbrowns, and pancakes. I don't remember seeing so much food on one table, short of a team dinner. The two Hasbargen boys then took Bill and I snowmobiling all over their land. We had a wonderful time. When we got back to the house, we had Salisbury steak, mashed potatoes, fresh baked bread and green beans for lunch. Again, just a ton of food. Then the four of us hockey players took a nap, but before we left to catch the bus to our next game in Baudette, we had sandwiches and chips and more food. There was a reason those Hasbargen boys were so big and strong; they ate all the time. Now compare that to the experience our teammates Billy Anderson and Gordy Vipond had. They were woken up at 5:30 to chop wood and do chores. Their host dad was going to get some work out those boys. But most of our teammates had great experiences with the host families from other teams. It was a great way to get to know players from other teams.

On another trip, we traveled to Hallock and Crookston to play two games and once again we stayed with host families. We had a huge defenseman on our team by the name of Rodney Lorenz and during the game Rodney got into a fight with a player from Hallock. The dad of the Hallock player was leaning over the boards, yelling at Rodney. They served their 5-minute penalties and other than some extra physical play, the game ended with no further on-ice incidents. We showered and met up in the lobby to find out who our host families would be. Wouldn't you know it, the player Rodney and his partner were assigned to go home with was the player Rodney had fought. They ended up having a good laugh about it all, but I think Rodney slept with one eye open that night. I believe Gus' main reason for us staying with host families was for budget reasons, but the other side of the coin was a rich cultural experience for his players and the players we spent the night with. Generally speaking, it was a great deal of fun.

"If we live good lives, the times are also good. As we are, such are the times."
—Saint Augustine (354 AD–430 AD)

THE BUS GOES ROUND AND ROUND
AND ROUND AND ROUND AGAIN

Our out-of-town trips when I was in high school were usually on school buses. Anyone who has played high school hockey in Minnesota is well aware of the true comfort of a big yellow school bus. Okay, not so much. In fact, not at all. Occasionally, and especially for longer trips, we got to travel on the Alexandria Tech School's coach bus. A coach bus has more comfortable seats and is warmer than the typical school bus. Plus, the coach bus has a series of storage spaces for our equipment. In a school bus, all that equipment is usually stacked up in the rear of the bus or if you are fortunate, in a trailer that is hitched to the back of the bus. The coach bus was driven by an older gentleman by the name of Cecil. We didn't know his last name; he was just Cecil. On the trip home from an away game, we often would have a team sing-along. I think we were bored, and since this was before the invention of the iPod or individual music devices, we would just sing. We often changed the words to songs to include Cecil. Songs like "She'll Be Coming Around the Mountain" and "I've Been Working on the Railroad" were two of our favorites. I believe that Cecil really got a kick out of us including him. Some of the songs were kind of naughty. Somehow Gus let us get away with singing most of the way home late at night. Maybe he didn't hear us or, more likely, chose to ignore us. We were a little crazy back in those days!

"True wisdom comes to each of us when we realize how little we understand about life, ourselves, and the world around us."
—Socrates (470 BC–399 BC)

SOME CRAZY TEAMMATES

I grew up with some crazy teammates. You have heard about Bill Blanchard, the guy most instrumental in getting me to play hockey. Bill lived a block away from me and every season, fall, winter, spring, and summer you could find us outside playing football, hockey, basketball, and baseball. The ice on Noonan's Pond was one of our favorite hangouts in the winter and in the summer where we played baseball in the garden, next to the pond. It was also the scene of my first kiss. Kathy Stenso. She was in seventh grade, and I was in eighth. It was a Friday during Christmas vacation, and a light snow was falling. We were skating, playing Pom-Pom Pull Away, tag and other games. I had a crush on Kathy since school started that fall and I was really happy because she seemed to like me as well. As I waited with Kathy for her mom to come pick her up, we talked about Christmas plans and school. I moved closer to her and kissed her. It wasn't much of a kiss, but I remember both our lips being extremely cold. I mean, we had been skating all afternoon and the temperature was falling. I asked her to go steady and she said yes. All weekend I was flying high. She then called me on Monday and said that her mom told her that she was too young to go steady with boys. This was probably the shortest relationship ever.

Back to my teammates. Bill Blanchard and I played on the Varsity hockey team during our freshman year and since we were too young to drive, we would get a ride home from Scotty Thompson. Scotty lived out of town on one of the lakes. When he drove in the winter and particularly when we would arrive back in Alexandria late at night, he would scrape off just a small square to see out of the front windshield. He didn't want to spend too much time out in the cold clearing the frost away. The problem was that it was so cold out that the windshield would fog up on the inside. Bill and I would have to stick our heads out the side windows to keep Scotty in the middle of the road. Kind of made it cold in the car. Real cold!

Then there was the time Dave Kluver gave me a ride home from practice and when we were about a block away from my house, he told me to start throwing my gear out. I thought he was kidding. He wasn't.

He said, "Don't think I'm stopping, but I'll slow down some."

He did slow down to about 15 MPH when I jumped. Thankfully we had big snowbanks that year. Dave also was a bit crazy both on and off the ice. We had music in the locker room. One time Dave was up on top of the lockers and dancing in just his jockstrap. Everything was fine until as he was getting down, Dave slipped and scraped his butt on the way down. The look on his face was priceless.

Dave often came up with weird nicknames for some of the younger players on the team. To this day, I don't know where he came up with some of these, but he would just blurt it out one day and somehow the name would stick with you for your entire life. For instance, one day in the locker room, Dave yells out, "Hey Hertwig! Hertwig...throw me that towel." All of us in the locker room looked around in confusion, trying to figure out who he was talking to. This time it was me and of all the nicknames I have had over the years, that one stuck. Over time, the nickname was shortened to Twig or Twiggy, and I still have two or three friends from the hockey team that call me by this nickname. We did have a kid in school named Richard Hertwig, which is probably where Dave came up with it. How or why these names popped into Dave's head is still a mystery to all my teammates to this day. I learned a lot from Dave about how to play goal on ice and probably more on what not to do off the ice. He was an exceptional athlete and ended up being a golf pro at a golf course in Arizona.

We have lost seven of my Alexandria hockey family members over the years. Ray Devine drowned in 9th grade. Bill Theiss died in a car accident in Wyoming in 2003. Scotty Thompson died of cancer and then Gordy Vipond died in 2017 from a heart issue and Frankie Verdugt died a year later from unknown reasons. Brian Lynch died of cancer not long ago and the most recent one to leave us was Tim Fitzgerald, who had throat cancer. Rest in Peace my friends.

"There is nothing on this earth more to be prized than true friendship."
—Thomas Aquinas (1225–1274)

SOME DEDICATED HOCKEY PLAYERS

As I have written, I had some crazy teammates. But we were also extremely dedicated. We had to be to play the game in Alexandria. It was not for the weak of heart…not playing outdoors it wasn't. One of our more skilled players was A.J. Kluver. A.J. and I were Bantam goaltenders together and A.J. taught me as a novice goaltender a great deal about how to be an athlete. About three fourths of the way through our Bantam season, the Doctors discovered a cyst on A.J.'s knee and he had to have surgery to remove it. He was out for the season. So, the novice was now the starter, and I was scared out of my mind, but my teammates rallied around me, and even though it wasn't a Hollywood type ending, where we went to State and achieved the impossible dream, we did have a good finish to our season.

A.J. was recovering from the surgery and out of school for a while. So, every day after class let out, I would bring A.J. his homework and inevitably, we would end up playing knee hockey. Probably wasn't the best for the rehab of his knee but it was really good for his mental health. Mine too. You know, it's hard when you compete against a friend for a position. Especially as goaltenders, where only one generally plays. I can admit now that I struggled mightily in high school with the whole thing. It changed mine and A.J.'s relationship from Bantams to high school hockey. This experience was one reason why, when I started coaching, I had long talks with my starting goaltenders about making sure that the other goalies felt part of the team.

Dave Kluver, A.J.'s older brother, was the starter and justifiably so during my Freshman and Sophomore years. I backed him up and played JV. A.J. was such a good athlete that Gus could play him as a wing as a sophomore. Then it was A.J. and I during our Junior and Senior years. I was a spoiled brat our junior year and thought the starting job was just mine because I played goal for two years and A.J. could be a wing again. Gus had other plans and it was a good learning experience for me. A.J. had a great year in goal our junior year, and our friendship suffered further because I needed to learn how to compete and accept not playing as much as I would have wanted to. During the summer and fall leading up to

A Vagabond Life   61

our senior year I worked my butt off to get better. I ran, which I hated doing, and I lifted weights. I also had friends shoot at me with tennis balls and pucks on cement. That season A.J. and I split time in goal. The hard work paid off.

I remember one game against Willmar at home during our senior year, that the temperature, with wind chill, was minus sixty-three degrees below zero. The skaters from both teams would play a shift and then all of them would head to the warming house to thaw out, just like in the movie *Mystery, Alaska*. It was so cold that night, that at one point a Willmar player took a slap shot at me and I caught half the puck. Yep, the puck split in half. I wish I had kept that half of the puck. That was the coldest I have ever been. And of course, the goaltenders weren't going in and warming up. We stayed on the ice the entire game.

A.J. was a great athlete. He was a catcher in baseball and a half back and linebacker in football. He and Bob Olson were two of the best pure athletes that we had in Jefferson Senior High in the '70s. Looking back on those years, it was an honor to play with both. Together with a whole bunch of great people and athletes. The Class of 1975 was truly special!

"Sports do not build character. They reveal it."
—Heywood Broun (1888–1939)

MORE STORIES FROM FERGUS FALLS

I was talking to Bill Blanchard, and he reminded me about a couple crazier stories that occurred in Fergus Falls and Detroit Lakes. The first was during my sophomore year, we were playing Fergus Falls and we were down a goal late in the game. I was on the bench backing up our starting goaltender, Dave Kluver. There was a minute left in the contest when our coach Gus pulled Dave for an extra attacker. We got a couple shots at the goal and almost tie the game up. Fergus breaks the puck out of their end and their best player has the puck skating down the ice with a wide-open net yawning in front of him. One of our defenders cut over, forcing the opponent to skate wide along boards by our bench, and as he got to the end of our bench; he wound up to shoot at the goal, but Dave reached over with his stick and knocked the puck away before the Fergus player could shoot. Pandemonium reigned until the officials awarded a penalty shot. Today it would be an automatic goal, but back then it was just a penalty shot. Dave went back in the nets and the guy made a great move and beat Dave high to the glove side. The Fergus players swarmed off their bench to congratulate their players and there was Dave pushing his way through to get to the goal scorer. We all thought he was going to start a brawl, which very well could have happened. However, Dave wanted to congratulate the Fergus player on a great goal. You never quite knew what was going on in Dave's head.

The second story also happened in Fergus during our senior year, Bobby Olson hammered a Falls Otter player with an open ice check, causing the player's leg to bend backwards, breaking it. The Fergus player is lying on the ice writhing in pain, as an ambulance drives onto the ice. It started sliding towards the Fergus Falls player who turned white with fright as he thought that the ambulance is going to run him over. Thankfully the ambulance was able to stop in time. They carted the Fergus player off and we ended up winning that game.

That next fall, Bobby was hitchhiking up to Moorhead where he was going to school at Concordia College. He got picked up by Fergus Falls' head coach. Once he learned that Bobby was a hockey player from Alexandria, the coach started wailing about the cheap shot that broke his player's leg last season.

"Who was that guy?" He asks.

"It was one of my teammates" was Bobby's response.

For the record it was a clean hit by Bobby, who was built like a brick house and tougher than tough.

During another game, again in Fergus, Gus became outraged at some calls that went against us and he was going to go after the referee, which would have probably got him suspended.

Someone yells, "Grab Gus!"

So, I wrapped my arms around him. I'm glad I had a chest protector on because Gus pummeled me with about 15 elbows from both arms. Just another crazy moment at Fergus Falls. For some reason the Otters always seemed to bring out the competitive side in us!

"Life must be lived as play."
—Plato (427 BC–347 BC)

DETROIT LAKES SHENANIGANS

It seems like we, the Cardinals of Alexandria, created waves in every small town in Minnesota that we played hockey in. It was my freshman year when a fight started in a preseason jamboree in Detroit Lakes. I am fairly certain it was between Dave Kluver and one of DL's best players Tom Evans. Both players were kicked out of the jamboree, and I remember one of the cheerleaders from DL crying her eyes out. Now either Tom was her boyfriend, or he made an impression on all the Laker girls, I'm not sure which, he was a handsome guy so it could have been the latter. Anyway, the animosity between Dave and Evans didn't wane, and later that year Evans scored on Dave on our home rink. In response, Dave almost took Evans head off with his stick, swinging it through the air behind the net at him. Yep, another little brawl erupted. Dave did not like Evans and especially when he would score on him.

Another time up at Detroit Lakes, Billy Blanchard was playing defense and he fell to the ice next to our net. Dave was either trying to step over Bill or he was making a high blocker save and, since we were standup goalies at the time, we were taught to go up on one foot to get our blocker higher. At any rate Dave's skate comes down and slices Billy's neck. Thankfully it was the back side of his neck and not the front side of his neck. The puck headed down the ice and Billy skated to the bench. He was bleeding bad, not gushing, but still fairly bad. I tried to get Gus to take a look at Billy.

"Gus, Billy's bleeding. Billy's bleeding!"

I implored Gus to do something.

The play is going on, we have a 3 on 2 or something and I am yelling at Gus, "Gus, Gus...Billy's bleeding."

He threw me a towel and said, "Tommy, put some pressure on it."

In all fairness, Gus didn't know it was a bad cut because Billy skated back to the bench, and no one knew he was cut until he was on the bench. Gus had me put some tape over the cut and due to the length of time from the injury to Billy getting home, nothing could be done with the cut and because of that, Billy still has a scar on his neck.

I never had good luck against Detroit Lakes. Gus pulled Dave Kluver when he swung his stick at Tom Evans. I was put in the game and immediately victimized by a couple of quick goals. And when Dave was kicked out of the Brainerd game for fighting, I had my first varsity start and gave up 12 goals to Detroit Lakes. I wasn't very happy after that game. Actually, I remember being in tears on the bus ride home. I felt like I let the team down, when in reality it was a tough position to be in as a freshman goaltender against one of the best teams in our area. That was also the game that I took a puck to the mouth off the stick of Mike Neitzke, who, along with Tom Evans, played at the University of North Dakota. That shot stung a lot! It pushed my two front teeth almost flat in the top of my mouth and caused the nerves to die. They both turned black and ugly. I later had to have them removed. My mask took a bit of a ding as well, but it did its job, as I probably would have lost both teeth right there on the ice if I hadn't been wearing it.

Gus and my uncle Rod helped me make the mask. It was face formed, and it had no padding on the inside. Man, pucks stung when they hit you in the face, padding or, in this case, no padding.

"The pain passes, but the beauty remains."
—Auguste Renoir (1841–1919)

Thomas H Peart

MY FRONT TEETH

As I have mentioned, a slap shot from Detroit Lakes' Mike Nitchke hit me in the mouth and killed my front two teeth. My mask prevented me from losing them right then. My dentist, Dr. Blanchard, did root canals on the two teeth and dyed them a couple of times, but they kept turning black. I finally discussed the situation with Dr. Blanchard, and he thought that the best option was to take out the front two teeth as well as, the two teeth next to them. This would correct my large overbite situation. The overbite came from the fact that I had a huge problem with sucking my thumb when I was a kid. I also had a big gap between my front two teeth. This, of course, led to wonderful Nicknames like "Bucky," "Bucky Beaver," and "Piranha." I used to grab my sister's dish towels and hide behind the door in the dining room. The towel was used to dry my thumb off. My parents tried everything until my dad ascertained what I wanted more than anything in the world...cowboy boots. Not sure why, at 7 years old, I wanted them so badly, but I did. They promised me if I stopped sucking my thumb, I would be able to get cowboy boots. I stopped sucking my thumb in the summer and at Christmas the boots were under the Christmas tree. I was so excited! That was a great Christmas. I got my cowboy boots, my sisters didn't have to chase after me to get the dish towel back, and mom and dad stopped worrying about future dental bills.

Speaking of dentists in Alexandria, there was a dentist named Dr. Arendt that my parents sent us to see. He used to swear at our teeth,

" Come out of there you son of a b...!"

As well as other endearing terms.

I was scared of dentists for years. My sisters and I finally convinced my mom and dad to switch us to Dr. Blanchard. He was a far gentler soul.

After getting my teeth pulled, I had a flipper that you could take out to clean. A flipper is a temporary partial that fits in your mouth and looks close to your real teeth. I used to put my flipper in my empty glass at bars and restaurants just to see the reactions of the waitresses. I had such fun with that flipper. When I started teaching and coaching, my new dentist, Dr. Jim Scheller, convinced me to put a permanent bridge in to replace the flipper. That bridge lasted a good 35 years, which is far longer than expected. One of the anchor teeth for the bridge became abscessed and I had to have a root canal on it. Because of the bridge, the dentist drilled into the tooth and took the root out. About three months after the root canal, I was eating a slice of pizza, when I heard a crack and suddenly my bridge is loose in my mouth. I had fractured the tooth with the root canal, and this led me to a visit to the University of Minnesota Dental School to have it removed. In a couple of weeks or so, they fit me with a removable partial and bam...it was back to terrorizing waitresses.

"What hurts you today, makes you stronger tomorrow!"
—Unknown (From Quotespedia.com)

SOMETIMES COACH GOES A LITTLE CRAZY TOO

Another reminder from my buddy Billy Blanchard about some additional stories. In Hallock's old rink, the ceiling was very low, and the lights were old fashioned single hanging lights. One of our players, Jeff Schultz was really tall for the times, about 6'3 with skates on. We scored a goal and Jeff thrusts his arms up in celebration and "pop," his stick puts out one of the lights. We were all amazed and then had a good laugh about it later.

There was also a game where Billy took a stick to the mouth that laid his bottom teeth flat. The only thing that saved them were his braces. It was amazing that his orthodontist could save his teeth and realign them. And to add insult to injury, the errant stick was from one of our teammates, Bill Anderson.

Another teammate, Roger Conard, reminded me of our long bus trips and the Guess Who songs Steve Tillit wouldn't stop playing. We kind of got sick of the Guess Who songs. Maybe this is why the whole team would start singing silly songs about Cecil the bus driver and pretty much whatever else popped into our heads.

Gus had a tight budget and in the early seventies, we only received $1.75 for meals, which usually was enough to get a person fed with a little help from our own pockets. Gus loved Embers and his famous line was,

"Anything over $1.75, you pay."

Gus would get mad at a couple of us because we would run over to Burger King or some other fast-food joint, after eating our meal at Embers. I suppose, in retrospect, we should have told him we were going. Sorry Gus.

There was also the home game against Red Lake Falls. It was a close game and Red Lake Falls scored a hotly contested goal just as the final buzzer went off. Larry Then, one of the officials waved the goal off. Five of the Red Lake Falls players surround him complaining about the call. Larry came out from the scrum of opposing players and called it a goal. Gus went bonkers and all the players on our bench erupt in rage at the reversal of the call. My teammates jump onto the ice and go up to Larry to complain. Larry was done with all of us, he left the ice, and ran to his car in his skates. He took off driving with his skates still on. Larry was a decent official, but he never wanted people to be mad at him. That is the wrong profession to be in since fifty per cent of the time, one team or the other thinks you are wrong.

During another game in Fergus Falls, I was thinking about my life and my future in the game of hockey. I had decided that I wanted my life to be more meaningful from then on. I was on the bench with Billy Blanchard sitting next to me. I looked at Billy, and I said, "I don't want my life to be med-i-core!"

Billy turned, looked at me with this look of amazement on his face and said, "Mediocre."

I was confused, "What?" I asked.

He said it louder, "It's pronounced mediocre."

My reply? "Yeah, I don't want to be that either."

Billy was a great friend even when he was correcting my grammar. He still is!

"In poverty and other misfortunes of life, true friends are a sure refuge. The young they keep out of mischief; to the old they are a comfort and aid in their weakness, and those in the prime of life they incite to noble deeds."
—Aristotle (384 BC – 322 BC)

NOONAN'S POND...IT'S ALMOST LIKE HEAVEN

If you were a hockey player, or a skater of any kind, and grew up in Alexandria in the '60s, '70s and '80s, you were a lover of Noonan's Pond. It was developed and owned by Phil Noonan who then, together with his wife Mollie, donated the park and pond to the city of Alexandria under the condition that it remain a park. The Park Department has run it ever since. The Noonan's had a flower garden that they called *Little Bit O' Heaven*, but to me, Noonan's Pond was my sanctuary, my own Little Bit O' Heaven during the winter. If I had some issues at home, or with a friend, or with a girlfriend, or with Gus (Love you, Gus,) really anything that troubled me, you would find me skating at Noonan's. It was so peaceful late at night, just skating across the ice. I could think, feeling the wind on my face and listening to my skates cutting into the ice. I would feel myself becoming centered and calmer with each stride, with each lap. I recently heard the Simon and Garfunkel song and words of "The Sounds of Silence," and it inspired this story in my brain. It's a beautiful song and it just triggered memories of growing up. Noonan's was the place of many of my favorite childhood memories. Sometime in the '60s, budget cuts forced the park board to cut back on maintaining the flower garden over the summer. One of us in the neighborhood thought that the garden resembled a baseball diamond, and it became our playing field. After the Noonan's passed away, the Nodland's bought their house which was on the edge of the park, and they had a huge picture window that faced the former flower garden. It was a long poke to get the ball to their house and it was an automatic home run if you did it, so it was what we would swing for. Not any of us ever hit it, except Richie Nodland, who didn't play with us often, but one day he came out and hit a mammoth home run directly through the picture window of his own house. I don't know how much it cost to replace it, but his parents could easily afford it.

We spent many summer hours playing baseball in that park and then we would spend every evening in the winter skating, playing shiny hockey in the rink on Noonan's Pond with the ankle breaker boards. They came up to your mid shins or so. You learned how to avoid the boards unless you wanted to go flying out of the rink. We would also play Pom-Pom Pull away and Crack the Whip. And of course, tackle tag. We played tackle for a couple reasons, first we were boys and we wanted to be physical and tackling someone was more fun than just tagging them, and second, during junior high, when girls were playing? Well heck, of course you wanted nothing more than to tackle them into a snowbank. Of course, we weren't sharp enough to figure out that the girls always wanted to be tackled into the snowbanks as well, probably why they would skate close to us. We thought it was our excellent pursuit skills. There was a warming house at Noonan's Pond, and I remember going in to warm up, and the attendant Rudy would greet us with a smile and a kind word. Rudy lived two blocks away from me, but I never saw him anywhere except at the warming house.

Yes, Noonan's Pond was a special place, and it was my Heaven on earth. It was the springboard to my lifelong love of hockey and skating. It was a friend I ran to when I needed its friendship. Just like in Madonna's song *This Used to Be My Playground*.

> *"The true object of all human life is play.*
> *Earth is a task garden; Heaven is a playground."*
> —Gilbert K. Chesterton (1874–1936)

SUMMER HOCKEY IN BEMIDJI AND ST. CLOUD

We were always looking for ice in the summer since Alexandria didn't have an ice arena yet in the early to mid- '70s. Billy Blanchard and I went to Bemidji State Summer Hockey School after 8th grade. It was one of the first times that Billy had spent any time alone in a room with anyone other than his family. I guess I scared the poor boy out of his socks when he woke up one of the first nights and I was standing over him, mumbling to myself. He probably thought I was going to kill him. Thing is, I don't remember it. I tended to sleepwalk a bit back then. I guess he is lucky I didn't have to go to the bathroom as well.

There was a State Band Camp going on during the same week and one guy from somewhere up north was a really good drummer. He stole a pair of drumsticks and would play the drum solo from *Wipe Out* by the Safaris every night on the wall after the lights went out. The counselors were trying to find the drumsticks to confiscate them. To this day, we don't know where the kid hid them. The counselors searched and searched, but never found them. One day at camp, a whole group of us lifted one of the coaches' cars, a Volkswagen Bug, up onto the sidewalk from the street. It didn't matter to us that the coach would just drive it off the sidewalk onto the street. We just wanted to prank him. Bemidji was a fun camp. Larry Ross, the legendary coach from International Falls was one of the goalie coaches. I always respected him. And yes...Billy survived the week with his crazy roomie.

Later in high school, a group of us, including my teammates Bobby Olson, Frankie Verdugt and Bill Theiss would drive to St. Cloud to play in a summer hockey league once or twice a week. In this league everyone played equally, and teams were made up of a majority of players from the same school. The league director would then add players from other schools to fill out the rosters. This way players would not be playing against teammates, and it added a level of competition to the league.

In the first five games of the season, I started, and our other goalie, a very inexperienced goalie from St. Cloud would come in and play the second half.

We had a goal or two lead and then we would end up losing. One game, the poor goaltender gave up three goals on two shots and a missed pass.

Then a couple of things happened to swing the league in our favor. A player from St. Cloud Apollo named TJ Sauerer ran into me in one game, and we exchanged some not very nice words. I was feisty and competitive, especially during games. So, we got off the ice after the game, and TJ got in my face again. This time it led to a few punches. The officials broke up the fight, and we all went our separate ways. Before our next game, TJ's older brother Bob came up to me and told me if I had a problem with his brother, then I had a problem with him, and he would kick my a$$. I laughed it off as we were going into the locker room to get ready for our upcoming game. However, I did mention it to my teammates while we put our skates on. Games were played in two halves, with an ice resurface in between the two segments. Bobby Olson came off the ice after our game ended, we had lost so he wasn't in a great mood. He saw the older Sauerer brother playing foosball. Bobby went up to Sauerer and told him that if he and his brother had a problem with me, then they had a problem with him as well. The older Sauerer brother said something intelligent like F@&k you. Bobby then walked right across the cement on his skates and drilled Bob Sauerer in the mouth with a punch. Sauerer punched him back, but as Bobby took another swing at Sauerer, his skate slipped, and his punch hit the brick wall. I thought the wall was going to have a hole in it, he hit it so hard. Bobby punched Sauerer a few more times before the fight got broken up. Ironically, the next game we played was against the Sauerer brothers' team. During the game, Bobby saw Bob Sauerer carrying the puck behind the net and lined him up to drill him with a check. Bob Sauerer saw Bobby coming and tried to jump out of the way of the check. Bobby caught him perfectly in mid-jump and as a result he knocked Sauerer and the plexiglass completely out of the rink behind the net. It was the most awesome check I had ever seen. Sauerer always shied away from Bobby after that. Our team owned the league from then on. We began games starting our young goalie and played strong defense for the first half. Then I would play in the second half when we went total offense, which left me to stop numerous breakaways. The strategy worked and we won the league title. That was a fun summer league. Our coach, Mr. Tom Hoffman, was a man from St. Cloud who owned a dry cleaner shop.

He was a hell of a guy and encouraged us all to play up to our potential. It was a truly a great summer!

> *"Start by doing what's necessary; then do what's possible;*
> *and suddenly you are doing the impossible."*
> —Francis of Assisi (1181–1226)

THE UNITED STATES MARINE CORPS

After graduating from high school, I had planned on heading to Bemidji State University, both to go to school and to attempt to make their hockey team. Looking back, I don't think that I was good enough, but when you are 18 and hockey is your life, you can talk yourself into any manner of fantastic fantasy filled ideas. That is, until reality steps up and slaps you across the face. I didn't just get that slap this time around as another real situation changed the course of my life. I was at a bar called the Barn in Alexandria. It was around the Fourth of July, and there was a major softball tournament going on in Alexandria that weekend. My friends and I were drinking "Stump Lifters" which is essentially all booze. The ingredients include rum, gin, brandy, vodka, grenadine and either 7-UP or Orange Juice. It came in a pitcher and definitely snuck up on you. After one or two glasses, you were seeing stars. We had a couple of pitchers, and the stars were bright indeed. I was dancing with someone on the dance floor, when a hockey teammate Dave Kluver got into a fight with a softball player. A couple other softball players joined in, so I, like a great teammate, jumped in, and grabbed one of the combatants. The next thing I know, I am lying on the dance floor and there is absolute chaos going on above me. A guy from Lake Elmo was kneeling by me holding a rag to my head. I learned later that someone came up behind me and hit me with a beer glass and knocked me out. Another guy punted my head when I was out and broke my jaw. I ended up in the hospital with a bunch of stiches over my left eye and my jaw wired shut. It was a fun summer experience.

At the beginning of August, a man in a United States Marine Corps uniform showed up at my door. I am pretty sure that he either read the paper or had some contacts at the hospital, but he sat down and convinced me to change the course of my life. Marine Corps here I come. College was put on the back burner, and I left for the Marine Corps Recruit Depot in San Diego in October. I would have entered Boot Camp early, but my recruiter convinced me to wait until October. He told me he thought that I would make a good recruiter some day and wanted me to work with him for a couple of months before going to Boot Camp. I spent all of August and September helping in the recruiting office, doing paperwork and research projects for him. The only bad part was that he had lied to me. He said I would be home for Christmas, but I ended up spending Thanksgiving, my birthday, and Christmas in San Diego. I never saw him again. When I graduated from Boot Camp, he had transferred out to another duty station. He definitely changed my life though. I just wish I could thank him in person. Joining the Marines was the best decision of my life.

" In the midst of chaos, there is also opportunity."
—Sun Tzu (544 BC – 496 BC)

MY FIRST FLIGHT, MY FIRST DAY IN
BOOT AND THE FIRST NIGHT.

I had never flown before I got on the plane headed to Boot Camp that October. There were five of us from Minnesota all going to Boot at the same time. We were all eighteen years old and, in the fall of 1975, the drinking age in Minnesota was eighteen. Consequently, we were all nervous and decided to have a beer or two before the plane took off, just to settle our nerves. After we took off, I realized that I loved air travel, I still love the feeling of flying off to another destination. We each had a beer, or two, or three, before we had a stopover in Denver. We didn't have to leave the plane, and after we took off again, we ordered another beer. The flight attendant told us that the drinking age in Colorado was still twenty-one, so no more booze for us.

This was probably the best thing to happen to us. I am sure that it would have been even more miserable meeting our Drill Instructors for the first time had we been intoxicated. We were met at the airport when we arrived by a Marine Private and put on a bus to take us to the Recruit Depot. The first thing I noticed while looking out the bus window, were yellow footsteps painted onto the tarmac. As soon as the bus stopped...my whole life changed. What had been, up to that point, a rather pleasant journey, now turned into a living hell. A Drill Instructor hopped on the bus and started yelling at us to get our *&^% %*&# butts off his bus and stand on the yellow footsteps. We had thirty seconds to get off his bus and we had just wasted twenty of them.

For the next two plus months, someone yelling at us would be the norm and we did everything on the double. In other words, as fast as we could. First up they came around and corrected our stance as we stood at attention. Then it was off to get our hair buzzed. I swear it took the barbers about thirty seconds to shave everyone's head. I didn't dare move, as I was afraid of getting my scalp cut, as the barbers were moving so quickly. There were about eighty of us and we were out of there in a flash with all our hair cut off. Next it was off to the supply depot to get our GI issued clothes and boots etc. Then to the barracks to stow all our new gear. Next, we marched off to dinner.

Dinner was an interesting experience for the first three or four meals. But first I will give you some background about what made mealtimes so interesting. I had worked that previous summer at H. Boyd Nelson Brewery in Alexandria. I helped deliver beer and booze to resorts around Alexandria and the surrounding towns and lakes. It was a good job for the summer. However, we would tap a keg in the evening after our route was done and drink some beer together before heading home. Then, of course, I was off for half of the summer due to my broken jaw and concussion, so I had put on a few pounds.

Now, back at the Recruit Depot we were in line for chow. We had to do everything in the first phase of Boot Camp at attention. Which means your shoulders are back, your stomach is in, your chest is out, and your eyes are front and center. I got to the front of the line and stuck my tray in for bread, and suddenly there is a Drill Instructor in my ear. "Not for you, fat boy!" I yanked my tray back.

Meat? Okay!

Veggies? Okay!

Potatoes? "Not for you, fat boy!"

Dessert? Yep, you guessed it! "NOT FOR YOU, FAT BOY!"

For three months I ate meat, veggies, and no carbs. I lost 33 pounds in Boot Camp. Of course, we exercised a fair amount as well. As I sat down to eat that first dinner, I got in about three mouthfuls when I heard the Drill Instructor yell,

"Get UP! Get OUT! You're done!"

My first three or four meals were like this. I learned quickly to eat fast, or I wasn't eating at all. After dinner, I honestly don't remember what we did. I was kind of in shock from the whole experience.

We had a roster sheet on the bulletin board for nightly fire watch. Every one of us took a turn for an hour in uniform and walked the squad bay to make sure the barracks didn't start on fire. Really it was teaching us about guard duty for when we would be in the regular Corps after Boot Camp. I was lucky the first night as I was assigned the hour from four to five AM. Because at 4:55, the Drill Instructors burst into the Squad Bay and started screaming, yelling, kicking over garbage cans and pulling recruits out of their bunks. I was already awake and at attention. Thankfully. To this day, I can remember my Drill Instructors and how at first, I thought they hated us. Later, I realized that it was just preparation for life in the Corps and I am grateful for all they taught us. Pretty much every day for the first month was absolute chaos when they woke us up. It was so intense that I would wake up to the scratch of the needle on the record each morning that blasted out revelry to the entire Recruit Depot. As soon as I heard that scratch, I was out of the top bunk and at attention.

"The Marine Corps...Earned, Never Given!"
—Marine Corps Slogan

THE NEXT THREE MONTHS

There are three phases to Marine Corps Boot Camp. Basically, the first phase is all about tearing down the recruits' civilian ways and beginning to train them to be Marines. During this first phase, we spent a lot of time in close order drilling (marching in formation,) running, PT (physical training,) cleaning, shining, and cleaning some more. And, of course, time in the Pits. The Pits were a large area of sand front of the barracks, and they were large enough that all eighty of us could do bends and squat thrusts, often until the Drill Instructors got tired, or we got tired, or they…, well you get the point. Our DIs would send us to the Pits for anything they could think of. Coffee tasted bad?

"Get in the Pits!"

A recruit got a cramp running?

"Get in the Pits!"

Someone was out of step in close order drill? Yep…,

"Get in the Pits!"

On our first trip to the Pits, I was so gung-ho that I busted my hump and got there first. Of course, this put me in the back row. There were four or five lines ahead of me and for twenty minutes we did bends and thrusts. I ate sand and I was kicked in the hands, the shoulders, and in the face so much that from then on I was one of the last ones there, and thus in the front row. You had to be more precise because the Drill Instructor was right in front of you, but no more sand in the face, no more pain from boots to the hands, shoulders, and face. I remember that we had a few guys that always ran as fast as they could so that they could be in the back row. They never figured it out.

The second phase was all about close combat fighting, rifle and handgun training, and rifle qualification. Thankfully I was able to qualify as a Sharpshooter on the rifle range. Just a couple points short of Expert. One thing I did find out in boot camp is that I needed glasses and probably had needed them from the time of a couple of concussions when I was younger. At least that is what the eye doctor said. At any rate, I was able to see a whole lot better with glasses. We also had to go through different obstacle courses, one with full gear, helmet and rifle and we had to crawl over things, under barb wire, etc. All with simulated rifle fire and simulated grenades going off around you.

The third phase was all about finishing up. We became more precise on the parade grounds, we ran harder and faster, attended classes and learned how to be true Marines. And we were given shots for just about every disease imaginable. Some were with air guns that shot vaccines into both arms at the same time. There was one memorable time with the lovely penicillin shot. We were all in formation in our nice white undershirts, our skivvies, and boots. We filed into this building and stood in a line consisting of fifteen recruits. We were ordered to drop our skivvies down to our ankles exposing our butts. A Navy Corpsman came along on a rolling chair with a rolling tray full of prepared needles ready to stick into us. He was very efficient and not very gentle. He stuck me with the needle so hard; I thought the needle would come out the front. We then pulled up our skivvies and got into formation outside to wait for the rest of our platoon to get their shots. While standing in formation I started to feel dizzy (shots usually did that to me.) I suddenly had one Drill Instructor yelling in one ear and another yelling in my other ear. They said that if I passed out, they were going to kick the living &%$# out of me. Man, oh man, I saw every color in the rainbow, but through sheer will or fear or something, I stayed on my feet and didn't pass out. To this day, I don't know how I didn't go down that day.

The last test we had to pass before becoming a full-fledged Marine was the "O" course. The dreaded obstacle course. If you have seen movies like *An Officer and a Gentleman*, you know what I am talking about. We had to complete the course to graduate from Boot Camp. I had already seen a few recruits that were sent back to the previous phase because they either were injured or failed part of the requirements. I had one mental block. The rope climb. A single rope that you must climb up twenty feet to the top and touch the wood before lowering yourself down. For some reason, I had a big difficulty with that stupid rope. I was strong enough, but somehow, I would get halfway up and freeze. My Drill Instructors kept threatening me that they were going to drop me back a phase if I didn't get my a&& up that rope.

"Priv, you are going to spend another month here if you don't get up that rope!"

Geez I didn't want that at all. I was counting off the days until graduation from Boot Camp. My bunk in the barracks faced the San Diego Airport. Every night I fell asleep watching those planes take off and dreaming about my turn to fly off and leave the Recruit Depot behind.

It came time for our final Physical Training exam, after many times practicing the rope climb, I had one last chance to beat it. I finally did it. Due to sheer determination and fear, I finally got to the top and slapped the wood. I was so elated that I slid down the first 10 feet of the rope, before my brain kicked in and I used my feet to slow my descent. Let me tell you, the rope burns on my hands were worth it. I can't tell you how proud I was to graduate from Boot Camp and become a United States Marine. It was probably the proudest moment of my life up to that point.

"That which does not kill us makes us stronger."
—Friedrich Nietzsche (1844–1900)

FORT BENJAMIN HARRISON

My first official duty station was Fort Benjamin Harrison in Indianapolis, Indiana. This was where I attended Postal Operations School. After graduating from Recruit Training, every soldier is sent to a school for further Military Occupational Specialty (MOS) training. While all Marines are considered Riflemen first, and foremost, approximately eighty per cent are sent to Infantry Training. Twenty per cent of the recruits out of Boot Camp are sent to other support MOS schools. The school I was sent to trained us to operate all aspects of the Marine Corps post offices.

Fort Harrison was an Army base and was most memorable because my class and I were a few of the only Marines on the base. All of us were fresh out of Boot Camp and very full of ourselves. We actually held close order drill marches just to show off for the Army pukes around us. It was the Marine Corps brain washing and all of us Marines thought we were all the biggest, the baddest, because we were US Marines. It didn't last. Reality, in any branch of the military, sets in rather quickly.

Fort Harrison was memorable to me for a couple of reasons. One, it's where I attended my first ever live concert…Z.Z. Top. Man, it was so much fun. It was at what used to be called the Hoosier Dome. I believe it has been torn down now and replaced, as most stadiums of that era have been.

The second reason that Indianapolis was memorable to me was that one night we had a huge ice storm. The entire town was shut down. We had at least a good three inches of ice covering everything across the entire city. What was a fanatical hockey and skating nut to do? Why, go skating of course. I put on my goalie skates and started skating down the road leading off the base and into Indianapolis. It was one of the most incredible experiences in my life. Now, don't forget, I grew up skating on the lakes and ponds around Alexandria. I was used to feeling free with the wind whipping all around me while I skated. It is such an incredible feeling. On this occasion, I was the only person out skating on the city streets. In fact, I was really the only person who was out, period. It felt like I was all alone in a city of 830,000 souls. It was awesome. Well, that is until I was coming down a hill and hit a manhole cover! The heat from the sewer system melted the ice around the manhole cover. With the electricity across the city out, I didn't see the exposed steel cover. I flew a good 15 feet, landing on my knees. I don't think my knees have ever recovered.

I met some incredible friends at Fort Harrison. Friends whom I was close with throughout my time in the Corps. I will always remember Frank "Pink" Johnson, Ray Kane, David P. Iraci, Mike Kubiak, and all the other fellow "Postal" Marines from Fort Benjamin Harrison. OORAH Marines!

"Don't think too much. Just do what makes you happy!"
—Unknown (From Hearts143Quotes.com)

OKINAWA, JAPAN

After graduating from Post Operations School, I received my orders to my next duty station, in Okinawa, Japan. I was given a short leave of one week at home before shipping out. It's an interesting thing in the Armed Services…they tell you something, but often it's not the entire thing that you need to know. For instance, our instructors at school told us that the top two students in our class could have their choice of a duty station as a reward for finishing numbers one and two in our class. What they didn't tell us, was that the choice would be between stations where they needed us. The Corps needed two people in Hawaii and the rest of us would be heading to Okinawa.

The top two in our class did get their choice…between Hawaii and Japan. Dave Iraci was number one and he chose Okinawa. So, the second and third top students chose to go to Hawaii. I ended up in the middle of the class, so it was off to Okinawa for me. Had I known that Hawaii was a possibility, I think I would have studied harder. I still haven't been to Hawaii and desperately want to go. It is definitely on my bucket list.

Okinawa was interesting, but quite the culture shock in the beginning. It took us 23 hours to get there. I first took a bus to the Twin Cities from Alexandria, then I caught a flight to Los Angeles. From there I flew to Anchorage, Alaska. After a layover in Anchorage, Alaska, it was the long flight over to Japan. It seemed to take forever. Once the plane landed in Okinawa, I stepped off the plane and was shocked by the sweltering heat and humidity. I retrieved my gear and then got on a bus that left for Camp Butler, where I was assigned for duty.

Upon arriving at Camp Butler, the first stop was the infirmary for a physical and vaccination shots. I have never liked needles and have been known to pass out from them. This time the situation was exacerbated by fatigue from the long flight and adjusting to the extreme heat and humidity. At any rate, I passed out from the vaccination shots and fell into the weight scale, hitting my head and ended up with a huge knot on my head. I ended up spending time in the infirmary recovering from hitting my head. It was a crazy first day in Okinawa.

I remember being surprised with the entire culture change. My time in the Marine Corps up until then had all been positive. After graduating from Recruit Training and from Postal Operations school, I was a proud Marine, gung-ho and ready to be the best Marine possible. My first experience with more seasoned Marines sobered me to the reality of life in the real Armed Services. There was not much of the Esprit de Corps that the Drill Instructors preached about in Recruit Training. I was taken aback by the fact that many of my fellow Marines had the attitude that the Marine Corps owed them something or maybe it was just the fact that we all came from such different backgrounds and that tempered some of their attitudes.

After a few days I was able to use the pay phone to call home. I had to call collect. My mom and dad weren't really happy about that. Sure, they were happy to hear from me, but in their minds, it was time for me to pay my own way. The only problem was that I hadn't gotten my first paycheck yet. At any rate, I started in on whining about being homesick and my mom passed the phone to my dad. My dad listened for about a minute or two and said,

"Buck up Boy. Here's your mother!"

He later told me that it was extremely hard for him to do that, because he could hear the loneliness in my voice, but he said, "What was I supposed to do? You were thousands of miles away and in the Marine Corps. There was nothing your mother or I could do." All very true. It was time for little Tommy to grow up. I adjusted and I did grow up.

I actually made it to the number two position for enlisted men in the main post office under my boss Gunnery Sargent Ben Hildago. A fantastic man, he told me many stories about his three tours in Vietnam and all the craziness that went on there. One story that he told was about his first tour in Vietnam as an Infantryman. The Marines were sweeping through the country, only to have the politicians put the brakes on our advance. This gave the Viet Cong time to fortify their lines and build their tunnels. Unfortunately, the war in Vietnam then became a conflict of attrition and lasted much longer than it needed to.

It was fascinating to listen to his stories. Gunny Hildago was an incredible mentor to me, and I will never forget him.

"Never forget those who have impacted your life along the way."
—Anonymous (From Quotes'ndNotes.com)

TRUST THOSE INSTINCTS

Sometimes we have to follow our instincts. I am not sure if it is past experiences that pop back into our mind to help guide us or if it's divine intervention that shows us the way. Or maybe it's just gut instinct? I really don't know. I had an experience that has helped form who I am today.

As I have written, I spent a year in Okinawa, Japan. I worked in the Main Base Post Office, and we distributed mail to all the camps and bases throughout the Island. About 3/4 of my way through my year on Okie, I was assigned KP (kitchen patrol) duty up at Camp Schwab, way to the north of the island. When you are on KP duty, you are up at 3:30 AM and at the Mess Hall by 4:00 AM. And you work hard all day until 8:00 PM. Quite frankly, KP duty sucked. On the fourth day there, I did not have to be to the Mess Hall until 8:00 AM the next day. Bonus! I joined another Marine who was on KP duty with me that I met when I arrived at Camp Schwab. We went out to get a couple of drinks at the Enlisted Man's Club. My new friend had his eyes on a Navy Nurse, he got up to chat with her, while I went to get us a couple more drinks. The bar was packed and as I stepped around this big Marine, I ran right into this smaller Marine that I didn't see due to the large one. I knew right away that he had a big attitude about his small size. He pushed me and swore at me, as a bouncer moved over to settle things down. Things calmed down quickly, and I moved on to the bar, ordered our drinks and returned to our table. As I sat there drinking, I saw this little guy was very animated talking to his friends and pointing at me. I made sure that I kept one eye on him until he left a little while later. He kept glancing my way and I had a feeling that the night was not over yet regarding my interaction with this particular Marine. An hour later, my friend was still chatting up the nurse, so I sidled up to him and bid him farewell. As I was leaving the bar, I had this feeling in my gut. Something seemed off to me. I started walking back to my barracks and I had to walk next to some bushes. The odd feeling was still with me and just then, I heard a rustle, saw a shadow, and jumped backwards as an arm was swinging towards me. I reached to grab the arm. I missed and accidentally grabbed the knife that he was swinging at my stomach. It was the small Marine that I encountered earlier. I punched him hard in the face and he ripped the knife out of my hand, then he ran away. That was the end of KP duty for me and I was sent back south to my home base. After a trip to the infirmary and sixty-three stitches that is. That gut feeling, that little intuition, that divine intervention saved my life that night.

As for the Marine who tried to kill me, I never did see him again. I went to the south of the island and to my knowledge, the Military Police never identified him.

"Always trust your instincts. They are messages from your soul."
—Unknown (From Picturequotes.com)

BICENTENNIAL

I was in Okinawa for the Bicentennial on July 4th, 1976. It was a special day but one I wish we could have spent at home in the United States. We really will only see one celebration like this in our lifetime. A few fellow Marines and I had a case of beer, some snacks, and some fireworks. We spent the day down at the beach, thinking about home and blowing off firecrackers and cherry bombs that one of the guy's brothers had shipped to him from home. It was all fun and games until one of the guys lit a firecracker I was holding in my hand and did not let me know he had done so. Boom. It went off in my hand. I couldn't feel my thumb or my index finger for a month.

We got a little bored living on an island with not much to do, outside of work and physical training, and movies. We had a movie theatre on base where you could go to the movie, have popcorn and a coke for a dollar. We saw an average of thirty-three movies a month for a while there. And considering that Okinawa was a tropical island that was basically a jungle, it was hot. So hot, that you would take a shower, then walk down the hall to the squad bay and you would be sweating again. It was miserable. Especially during the monsoon season.

On the weekends we would head into town to "BC Street" or Before Christ street. Not sure who named it that, but it basically was the street where all the Okinawan bars were, along with many other rather nefarious businesses. It was wild, wilder and wildest. One weekend after we had been confined to the barracks for inspections by the Battalion Commander's office, we were finally released for a night on the town. We made our way to our favorite bar and started drinking. We loved this bar because they had a fairly good band made up of local Okinawans. I can't tell you the band's name after all these years, but they played a lot of cover songs including a couple that they played every night that we were there, one was *Closer to Home* by Grand Funk Railroad and the other was *Jesus is Just Alright by Me* by the Doobie Brothers. Both of those songs have a long solo, and they would play them when they needed a cigarette or drink break. They played other songs for sure, but for some reason, they loved those two songs.

On this particular night one of the Marines, I was with was quite drunk, and he made some negative comments about playing those songs again. An equally drunk soldier from the Army decided to get in my buddy's face. A minor skirmish broke out. Marines vs. Army Grunts. We were all really drunk by then and full of ourselves. All I really remember is carrying this guy outside above my head and dumping him in the gutter. He wisely decided to not have a further go at us crazy Marines. I can't go into some of the other stories that happened in town on BC Street. I am really trying to keep these stories appropriate for all readers.

"One must choose in life between boredom and suffering."
—Madame de Stael (1766–1817)

TYPHOONS

Another interesting experience of living on an island in a tropical climate is typhoons. During a typhoon we would be assigned to different satellite post offices to guard them. If you have never walked in typhoon just as it is starting up, it is crazy. Three of us were heading over to the Post Office that we were assigned to guard, leaning into the gale force wind, when a metal shed went flying by. It was like a real-life scene from the movie *"Twister."* We spent three days in that satellite post office, sending one of us out for food, but otherwise, we just had to entertain ourselves until the typhoon passed. We talked about our experiences, played cards, and generally kept busy until we were relieved. During a lull in boredom, I thought of a great story about some Marines who open the safe and steal money and the money order machine from the post office. It could be an interesting thriller. I never fleshed it out though. Living through a typhoon was definitely an interesting experience.

"In all things of nature there is something of the marvelous."
—Aristotle (384 BC–322 BC)

ANOTHER OPPORTUNITY TO TRUST MY GUT

After my year in Okinawa, I flew home for a couple weeks of leave. I was then assigned to Camp Pendleton in California, for my next duty station. I worked in the Separation Center there and did part of the work to discharge Marines after their time in the service was finished. There wasn't much to do on base at Camp Pendleton, so I would catch a bus and head to downtown San Diego. San Diego is a great town and there was plenty to see and do, including bars and restaurants, coffee shops, as well as some interesting book shops. One night I was hanging out in the downtown area, just enjoying the beautiful spring weather. A cabbie started chatting with me. He seemed nice and he asked me if I wanted to go to a party. He said that there would be some gorgeous girls at the party. I thought why not, and I hopped in his cab. He drove for a while and then suddenly he started driving out of town and he stopped talking to me. I tell you, the hair all over my body stood on end. It was that gut instinct again, but I am convinced that if I stayed in that car, I wouldn't be here telling you this tale today. I told him that I changed my mind and didn't feel like going to this party. He got mad and started yelling at me. I balled up my fists and told him,

"Pull this f'ing car over NOW!"

He did. I think I was so freaked out that my eyes were probably looking kind of psycho. He yanked the car over and yelled a string of obscenities at me and squealed the tires taking off. I had to walk about three miles back to downtown SD. It was worth the walk though. It's funny, I never saw that particular cabbie again. I also stayed away from downtown San Diego for a while. I guess the lesson is to trust your instincts. Trust your gut. Even if you are wrong and nothing happens, you are still safe.

"Always trust your first gut instinct. If you genuinely feel in your heart and soul that something is wrong, it usually is!"
—Unknown (From SayingImages.com)

APRIL 29TH, 1977- HONORABLE DISCHARGE

I was Honorably discharged from the Marine Corps on April 29th, 1977. My discharge day was a memorable day. It was the closing of one chapter and a door opening to a new chapter. I would be enrolling in college the next fall, the first person in my family to attend a four-year college. I remember while traveling to Phoenix, Arizona to visit my sister Diane, the thought came to my head that; *"I have nowhere to go and all the time I want to get there!"* I have never felt so free in my life as I did that day!

> *"Liberty is worth paying for."*
> —Jules Verne (1828–1905)

MESABI COMMUNITY COLLEGE- "DA RANGE"

After the Marine Corps, I wanted to get back into hockey and go to college, so you go where hockey is king, right? The Range is it! I did some calling around and Mesabi Community College had a hockey team, and it would be a good transition from the Corps to college. I loved and hated Mesabi. If you weren't born and raised on the Range, you aren't a Ranger, so you're always on the outside. Having said that, the hockey team at the time was very good and we ended up going to the National Tournament and lost in overtime in the Championship game. The entire team was inducted into the school's Hall of Fame in 2018.

Pat Finnegan (Finny) and Jim Matchefts were our coaches, and we had some really gifted players. Most were from Virginia or Eveleth. We had Chuck Clauson, Doug Schurr, Jim Hitti, Peter Finnegan and TP Harrington, the brother of John Harrington of the *Miracle on Ice* team, among others. It was a fun and crazy year.

Everyone on the Range knew everyone else and that adds a whole different dimension to hockey. One of the refs who worked a lot of our games was Cal Cossalter and he happened to be a relative of Coach Finny. Finny used to talk out of the side of his mouth and I remember him saying,

"Jeezus Cal! They're killing us out there!"

Spoken with a funny kind of Range accent and a slight lisp.

There was another game when we were playing Rochester Community College and Peter Finnegan gets into a fight. Cal breaks it up and kicks Peter out of the game for fighting and for then for swearing at him. Peter goes bananas! Helicopters his stick into the stands screaming,

"F you! F you! Just F you!"

Finny, knowing his son, followed him into the locker room and pretty soon we see Finny and Peter wrestling around on the floor of the arena. Turns out Peter was headed out to his cousin Cal's car to slash the tires.

I remember many other on ice and off ice fights that season. It was like the movie *Slap Shot* a lot of the time. There was one memorable fight during a game at Hibbing. Both players were ejected and as they left the ice, they started fighting again in the hallway leading into the locker rooms. I saw a group of fans running down there, so myself and a couple other players went down to assist. I remember Finny and Hibbing's head coach, Frank Catani almost coming to blows as they followed a whole group of us to the locker room. The police were called and somehow the game continued, with Hibbing winning. Since Hibbing and Virginia are only 29 miles apart, we all drove our own cars to the game and of course we ended up in a bar in Hibbing after the game.

I was surprised to see Finny and Frank Catani sitting together having drinks together like nothing happened. Once the game was over, all insults were pretty much forgotten. We were a little too young to do that and another fight almost started there in the bar between our players and the Hibbing players.

We had incredible battles against Hibbing. During one game at Miners Memorial Arena in Virginia, we were struggling mightily. I don't remember who started in goal for us, it could have been Robbie Benson or Danny Rodgers, doesn't matter, whoever it was that started gave up three goals on four shots. The second goaltender gave up four more goals on seven shots. Finny told me I was in at the start of the third. I gave up the first shot I faced, and we were down 8-4 before sieve number three finally made some saves that night. Well, we had about three minutes left in a very poor showing, and we popped in a goal. It was now 8-5 in favor of Hibbing. About a minute later, we score again and it's now 8-6. A couple penalties by Hibbing and we score again, 8-7. Forty-five seconds to go and we tie up the game. And with about ten seconds to go, we score the winning goal. It was the most stunning comeback I have ever been involved with.

It was a fun, crazy year topped off with a long, long bus ride through Canada to upstate New York for The Junior College National Championships. We won our first game and then lost in Overtime in the Championship Game and came home as National Runners up. On our trip out to New York, we had no problems going into Canada and again when we entered back into the United States. On our return trip, the customs into Canada was a breeze, but as we were coming back into the USA and stopped at customs, one of my bright teammates on the bus said quite loudly, "Don't worry guys, it's just a broad!"

The customs agent, of course, heard this, and took offense to being called a derogatory name. She insured that we would suffer a lengthy, two-hour search through everything we had on the bus, all our personal luggage and all of our equipment. Customs was finally satisfied that we had no contraband and that we learned our lesson, so they let us go. Uffda! Some of those guys didn't know when to keep their big mouths shut.

> *"Treat others with respect. How you treat others*
> *will be how they treat you."*
> —Buddha (564 BC–483 BC)

THE TRAP LINE-VIRGINIA, MINNESOTA

In many ways Virginia in the mid to late '70s and '80s was much like a lot of small-town America. Not much to do and a lot of time to do it in. Friday and Saturday nights were the time for cruising. The main street in Virginia is about six blocks long and there was an endless stream of teens cruising in their cars up and down the street, seeing and being seen by their friends. The drinking age at this time was eighteen, so all of my hockey buddies were of age, and they liked to spend their time in what many of us referred to as the "Trap Line." A trap line is a series of traps for game, such as mink or rabbits. I don't remember exactly, but there were at least fifteen bars and liquor stores on the main street of Virginia. Many tried, but few could make it to all the bars drinking one drink at each business before being so blitzed that they couldn't see straight. One of the bars was an establishment that, let's just say the women working there shed more and more of their clothes as the night wore on. This was a tough time on the Range with some of the mines closing, guys had to get new jobs, and it was a period of change across the Range.

I accidentally bumped into a guy in this bar of ill repute, and he proceeded to follow us from bar to bar, always staring at me. I finally had enough and went and sat by myself in a booth away from my friends and other customers. Sure, enough this guy comes over and sits down. He glares at me and says he wants to kick my butt. I told him that he could try, that I'd finish my drink and then we would go out back to settle things. Then I looked at him and said, "I do have to tell you that as a former Marine, once we start, we will end up with one of us in the hospital and it sure as hell won't be me."

The waitress then came over and I ordered drinks for both of us. We ended up talking for about 45 minutes about how he was just laid off, didn't know what he was going to do and what would happen next. We never fought that night. I don't know what happened to him after that night, as I never saw him again. I am certain that he was just a frustrated miner, who was down on his luck, and needed someone to talk to about his life. I guess I would have fought him if it had come to that, even though I was three inches taller and outweighed him by at least thirty pounds. I am glad it never led to a fight though. It was definitely an interesting experience. You just never know what things people are going through in life.

"When you look deeply into your anger you will see that the person you call your enemy is also suffering. As soon as you see that, then your capacity for accepting and having compassion for them is there."
—Thich Nhat Hanh (By Permission, from the book "Anger: Wisdom for Cooling the Flames." Parallax Press)

LUTHER PARK CAMP

I had finished my first year of school at Mesabi CC and I was looking for a job. My sister Margaret was working part time at Mount Calvary Lutheran Church in Excelsior, and she mentioned to me that their camp, called Luther Park, up in Danbury, Wisconsin, was looking for counselors. To me, it sounded like a great way to spend the summer. I had an interview and got the job. Luther Park is where I first met Sue Nygren who later became one of my dearest friends. We may not talk as much as we used to, but I still feel that if I needed a friend, she would be there for me, as I will always be there for her.

The camp is located on Lake 26, just outside of Danbury. Not quite sure why it's called Lake 26. There is no Lake 25, or Lake 27, just Lake 26. I arrived at this beautiful camp, and it really was incredible. It was on this day that I met Bill Kelly for the first time. Bill is an extremely intelligent and multi-talented person who has become one of my best friends for life. At this point in time, he had hair down to his shoulders, a huge black beard and piercing brown eyes. He looked like the Western version of Jesus. Bill was an incredible writer. He loved his poems, but my favorites were his children's stories, *"I Hate Big Birds Too!"* was my absolute favorite. It was a tale about how big birds bullied the smaller birds. It reminded me of growing up in my Alexandria neighborhood.

I was assigned to Cabin Pine, the very last cabin, of course. I have my arms full of my things and I am walking down the hill, stumbling over tree trunks and stepping into dips in the landscape. Bill was walking with me and asked if I needed help. I am trying to prove I that I am the big, tough Marine and hockey player, right? What a bonehead I was. Later that summer when we became better friends, Bill and I laughed about that first day.

We had a great time at LPC. Some of the people I worked with were Sue Nygren, Shelly Pelton, Laura Dahl, Bobby Jo Paige, Jenny Johnson, Russ Mayland, Julie Brown, Krissy Dale, Julie Gomoll, April Arvidsson, Julie Dalbec, and Linda Thompson. I still consider them all dear friends to this day. I ended up working three summers at LPC and they were three of the best summers of my life.

Every summer, someone new came into my life to enrich it. Some of the junior staff and campers that were instrumental at the camp included Nubby

Dale, Mary Claire Olson, Pete Sampson, Mary Treloar, Scott Reichert, and Lisa Reichert. The list literally goes on and on. Of course, the Camp Directors had a great influence on me as well, I worked with Stu Johnson in my first summer at camp and Randy Gullickson over the next two summers. Unfortunately, both of them have now passed away. RIP my friends.

There are so many great memories from Camp. We did a lot of skits and theme nights. We had the "Pittles of Peart" A band of four that rivaled the immortal Beatles. Only one of us actually played an instrument, Russ Mayland played guitar. Bill Kelly, Pete Sampson, and I stood around and sang. We were pretty cool with our shades and hockey jerseys though. We had "Disco Night," "Geek Night" and a ton of other theme nights. Of course, there was also a lot of prayers and counseling. We had incredible water polo games, intense capture the flag contests in the woods, great campfires and who could forget the weekend that the female staff decided to tease Bill and I by going skinny dipping during the middle of the day and not inviting us to join them. As Shelly Pelton would say, "How rude!"

One of my favorite times was our staff meetings. A chance during the day where we could let our hair down, drink coffee and touch base with the rest of the staff on what was happening during the week. This camp and the friends I made there truly changed my life. I love you all!

"A true friend is not a coincidence in our life. They were a stranger meant to come into our life and bring us priceless lessons and funny memories!"
—Unknown (From JoyofQuotes.com)

During my first year at camp, I worked with mostly younger campers. They were a great deal of work, but a great deal of fun as well, but my favorite weeklong camp was the Senior High Camp. I was the counselor in Cabin Pine and my guys were all incredible. We had a rocky beginning when on the second night I came back from a staff meeting and they were out raiding one of the girls' cabins. I was ready to strangle them in their sleep, but instead I thought fast, and came across the passage in the Bible about everything has a season...

Ecclesiastes 3:1-8

For everything there is a season,
and a time for every matter under heaven:
a time to be born, and a time to die;
a time to plant, and a time to pluck up what is planted;
a time to kill, and a time to heal;
a time to break down, and a time to build up;
a time to weep, and a time to laugh;
a time to mourn, and a time to dance;
a time to cast away stones, and a time to gather stones together;
a time to embrace, and a time to refrain from embracing;
a time to seek, and a time to lose;
a time to keep, and a time to cast away;
a time to tear, and a time to sew;
a time to keep silence, and a time to speak;
a time to love, and a time to hate;
a time for war, and a time for peace.

After reading them this passage, I sat down on an open bunk, and we had a deep discussion about why they were at camp and what my role was, as their counselor. From that point on, we bonded and had an incredible week.

And at the Talent Show on Friday, the boys picked a song from Charlie Daniels.

"A Long-Haired Country Boy" Still one of my favorite songs.

"We do not remember days, we remember moments."
—Cesare Pavese (1908–1950)

ST. CLOUD STATE HOCKEY AND MY FRIEND, COACH STEVE CARROLL

I have a very good friend, Steve Carroll. He is a former goaltender from Edina (Don't hold that against him.) He was an excellent goaltender and led Edina East to the State Tourney in 1977. He then went to Mankato State University and was cut from the team. Steve tells the story about always making the A teams growing up in youth hockey and the varsity team in high school. Consequently, he didn't know how to compete for a position upon arriving at Mankato State. Lucky for Mankato, a goalie got hurt and another dropped out of school, so Coach Don Brose called Steve back. He became a two time All-American and led MSU to their only National Championship in hockey, in the magical year of 1980, when the other *Miracle on Ice* team also did something extraordinary at Lake Placid. Steve had a phenomenal National tournament and was named the Most Valuable Player that season. Steve was also the first Division II player to be a candidate for the Hoby Baker Award as the best college hockey player in the nation.

Steve has gone on to train goaltenders for the past 40 years with his Carroll Goalie Schools and has been the Director of the Dave Peterson High Performance Goalie Camp since its start. I had the good fortune to work with Steve as the Assistant Director of the Dave Peterson camp for close to 13 years before retiring. I consider Steve to be the best goalie training person we have in Minnesota.

There are a lot of parallels between Steve's goalie career and mine although the path I chose was different. I first went into the Marine Corps and then I went to Mesabi Community College for a year before transferring to St. Cloud State. I, too, was cut my first year. Our coach was Charlie Basch and Charlie was an assistant football coach, along with being the head hockey coach. We were Division III at the time, though our games were against both Division III and Division II teams. I first met Charlie when I was enrolling in classes at St. Cloud State for the coming fall term. I stopped in his office at Halenbeck Hall and introduced myself. Charlie encouraged me to try out for the team. He gave me information about when try-outs would be held and when and where Captain's practices would be held. He informed me that they had one excellent returning goaltender in Doug Randolph and another one coming in, whose name was Rory Eidsness. I would be the only other goaltender that they were looking at.

When I stepped on the ice on the first day of try-outs, there were thirteen goaltenders on the ice. Wow! I wanted to ask Charlie if I was the only goalie that they were looking at, you know, on that particular day that I stepped in his office. I spoke with three of the other goalies, who all looked as shell shocked as I felt. They all heard the same thing from Charlie. On the second day of try-outs, we were down to seven goalies, six had decided to not try-out any further. By the end of the week, we were down to four, including me. That Friday, after the last try-out day, I was informed via a list posted on the bulletin board, that I was not on the team.

I was pretty upset because during the try-out week, Charlie only showed up one or two times, since he still was involved in football practices as an assistant coach. He let the captains pick the team. To me this was very wrong and unfair. I stewed about it over the weekend, as I knew I was good enough to make the team.

Now remember, although I was a sophomore class wise, I was twenty-two years old and was more experienced than most of my fellow student-athletes. I went into Charlie's office on Monday and laid my case out. I told him I didn't think he saw enough to cut me. I think he respected that and the next day I was back on the team.

I backed up Doug "Boots" Randolph and Rory Eidsness. Unfortunately, my career didn't turn out the way Steve's did as I really wasn't as good of a goaltender as he was. Plus, I had a rather inauspicious career, injury wise. Just before Thanksgiving during my first year at St. Cloud, I took a puck off the chest and while I was concentrating on catching the puck, my defenseman and the oncoming forward ran into me. I was knocked to the ice with both players on top of me. The collision drove my tailbone into the ice, breaking it. I spent all of Thanksgiving break in a lot of pain, sitting in my dad's recliner. That pretty much screwed up my first year.

During my second year, I tore ligaments in my right knee when a player fell on it in practice and that ended my season with the Huskies team.

And then in my last year at SCSU my left leg broke when it was pinned between a player and the ice, and another player fell across it. My leg snapped just above the ankle. I had surgery and a rod put into my leg to stabilize the ankle. And yep, you guessed it, season over once again. The funny thing was that all three injuries happened in late November right around my birthday. Nice birthday presents right? I guess it was the good Lord's way if saying,

"It's time to go into coaching, son."

So here we are 40 years later, and I am retired after a wonderful career coaching. I guess it all worked out for the best.

One other thing that defined my playing career at St. Cloud. I made the absolute, most outstanding save of my life. In practice. We were scrimmaging and Gary Stefano shot a slapshot that was coming to my left side. I kicked out and at the last second, Dave Reichel tipped the puck back to the right corner of the net. I did the only thing I could I dove backwards and threw my leg out in a desperate move. The toe of my skate blade tipped the puck off to the corner. Showed my luck, an ESPN Top Ten play and it happens in practice with no one watching. Reichel knew it though, he even slapped my pads and said great save!

> *"Always bear in mind that your own resolution to succeed*
> *is more important than any other.*
> —Abraham Lincoln (1809–1865)

LIFE HAS A TENDENCY TO CHANGE

After a year in Virginia, I decided to transfer to a full four-year university. I did some research and was told that St. Cloud had a ratio of three women to every one man. Great odds for the men, right? Actually St. Cloud had a great education department and I wanted to teach and coach, so I was St. Cloud bound. My teaching and coaching career was my third "decision" on a major. I was first going into law enforcement. That soon changed to psychology and from there to my true calling in education and coaching. I loved St. Cloud State University and going to school there.

As I have written earlier, during my third year at St. Cloud, I broke my ankle in a hockey game and had to have surgery. They put a long rod into my ankle and leg. This was my first experience with the Veteran's Administration Hospital after being discharged from active duty. And this was the first of 14 hockey or car accident-related surgeries in my life. I am all beat up. Thankfully, the VA Hospital has changed a great deal since 1981. Back then, I remember coming out of my room for a little walk and some exercise and there is a Vet smoking through his tracheotomy tube. Freaked me out. The halls were blue with smoke. I thought I had walked into a 3.2 Beer Hall up north somewhere.

The ankle surgery was in November 1981. I had a few more weeks of school remaining and one day I was making my way from Garvey Commons to Atwood Center on campus, hobbling along on my crutches when wham, I hit some black ice and went down just as a bus was bearing down on me. I'm seeing my life pass in front of my eyes, waiting to get run over by the bus. Thankfully the bus driver had the bus under control, and he stopped in time.

Once school was out for Christmas break, I headed to my sister Diane's house in Alexandria to rest up for a couple of weeks. I jumped in my car, a silver Satellite Sebring Plus (never did find out what the plus represented) and started the hour drive to Alex. We were having a huge snowstorm that day. I was on the street leaving campus, heading towards the freeway when my car died. Right in the middle of the street. Here I was, in a snowstorm wearing one shoe on my right foot and my left foot in a cast. Not a soul would stop to help. So, I did what any tough Marine would do. I started to push my car off the road. You know how hard it is to push a car while being only able to use one leg and trying to not get your cast wet? It took me forever and still no one would stop to help. I fell a couple of times as well. I was so mad. Where was everyone's Christmas spirit? Where was "Minnesota Nice?" Finally, after getting my car to the side of the road, I then had to hobble down a couple blocks to a pay phone to call my sister for help. Finally, my brother-in-law arrived from Alexandria to pick me up. It was a miserable day.

Speaking of that car, my Satellite, it had a weird function. It wouldn't start if you didn't have your seat belt on. Now this was in the late '70s, early '80s and seat belt laws were not yet in effect. In Minnesota seat belts weren't mandatory until 1986. Anyways, I would take a young lady out on a date and tell them they had to rise up off the seat or the car wouldn't start,

"Just thrust your hips off the seat." It was quite the conversation starter.

Of course, I could have said that they just had to put on the seat belt, but it was a lot more fun this way. Some of the looks I received were priceless!

"Sometimes what you want isn't always what you get, but in the end, what you get is so much better than what you wanted."
—Unknown (From Quotegate.com)

PARK WAREHOUSE LIQUOR-CASTAWAY'S
BAR-BEAUDREAU'S BAR

Because I was the third goaltender on a Division III hockey team and not playing in a lot of games, I needed some way to keep play goalie beyond the time I got in practices. I heard about a league that was put on by the St. Cloud Municipal Arena. I first checked around the dorms and, yes, there was enough interest from dormmates to field a team, so I started calling different bars and liquor stores to see if I could drum up a someone to sponsor a team.

The first year I found a bar that was willing to provide us with home and away jerseys, hockey socks and some other equipment. Do you know the saying that if something sounds too good to be true, it usually isn't true? Well, this was a living testament to that statement. I can't remember the name of the bar, but before we got anything from them, the bar burned down under suspicious circumstances. I don't have proof, but I suspect that part of their insurance claim were the jerseys, socks and equipment that they supposedly had in the back room when the place burned down. I think that their insurance got quite the bump from that, but like I say…I have no proof of that fact.

It was back to the drawing board, but I finally found a liquor store/bar in Waite Park called *Park Warehouse Liquors* and they provided jerseys for us. Unfortunately, we didn't make it out to the establishment much because our games were so late, consequently, they didn't want to sponsor us the next year.

Once again, I hit the phones and connected with the owner of *The Castaway's Bar.* He agreed to provide us with jerseys for the team. From a performance standpoint, we had a good year. Unfortunately, from an attendance in the bar standpoint, we didn't do as well. The owner of Castaway's didn't like our lack of presence at the bar. Once again, we were in search mode for a sponsor.

So I hit the phones and started calling more bars. This time I was fortunate to find *Beaudreau's Bar* on the east side of St. Cloud. The owner agreed to provide us with jerseys and the initial entrance fee to the league. This bar was a nice little neighborhood bar much closer to campus. It was easier to spend time and money there, which made the owner happy.

The team was a rag-tag bunch, mostly from my dorm combined with other players that I knew from hockey circles. John Thompson, Scott McPherson,

Scott Thompson, Jeff Marshall, John Selvog, Doug Kittrell, Russ "Chief" Larson, Lindy Jones, and many guys whose names I have forgotten after all these years. I think that we were the only bar league team that hit the road for games. I called a few MIAC schools and heard back from Whitey Aus at St. Olaf, so I asked him about a scrimmage. Whitey was up for it, so we traveled down to Northfield and played the Oles in a scrimmage during their practice time. Whitey was a bit nervous and made me promise that we wouldn't start or get in any fights as he was preparing for the upcoming MIAC season and in his words, "I don't want any shenanigans!"

I assured him that we were just a group of honest hockey players with suspect talent that wanted to skate more often and against better teams. On game day, we were in the locker room, getting ready for the scrimmage. We looked like a bunch of hooligans wearing all sorts of different jerseys, when I surprised the boys with our new jerseys from *Beaudreau's Bar*. This was in the days when the New York Islanders were at the top of the NHL and the owner of Beaudreau's just wanted his logo on the jerseys. The colors and style of jerseys was left up to me. So, I went with the Islander's jerseys. The boys were fired up and we took it to the Oles that day for most of the scrimmage including shutting them down on their power play and potting a couple of our own power play goals. The Oles began to get ticked off and started to run us a bit. One thing about college hockey players, they don't back down. On that day we gave the Oles as well as we got. To my boys' credit, we didn't get into any fights, but let's just say there was no lack of stick work or an elbow or two in the corners. Whitey became very frustrated and called the scrimmage with about a half hour left and I am fairly certain that he skated his team the rest of the practice time. It was a fun trip for the boys from Beaudreau's Bar. I think it was simply a case of the Oles overestimating us and we really had nothing to lose. We were just a bunch of college students who loved hockey and being on the ice.

I miss those days, even though most of our games were very late at night. I loved the comradery with the guys. I am still friends with many of them 40 some years later.

"Flying might not be all plain sailing, but the fun of it is worth the price."
—Amelia Earhart (1987–1937)

FIRST TRIP TO IRELAND/NORTHERN IRELAND

The year was 1979 and my buddy Bill Kelly was studying as a foreign exchange student in Dublin at Trinity College. Yeah, he's a smart one. Another friend from Luther Park Camp Laura Dahl, called me up at school I,n St. Cloud,

"Puck (my camp nickname) let's go to Ireland to see Bill!" she said.

"I'm in. Wholeheartedly!" I responded.

We decided to go during our spring break in late March. I had been working a bit and saved up some moola, so I could afford it. Laura made all the arrangements. We flew over to Scotland. Took a ferry across to Belfast, Northern Ireland, and then a train down to Dublin. There we met up with Bill and stayed at the house where he was living with his host, Mrs. Brunhild Hagenov, and her two kids Frankie and Nina. Some of the nicest, but craziest people I have ever met.

Bill was great, loving the fact he was getting to know the land of his ancestors. His mom's maiden mane is Mayes, so he had gotten a double shot of Irishness. We hung out in Dublin for a couple of days, then rented a Mini Cooper and headed on out to explore Ireland. Can you imagine? Three Yanks with backpacks, a tent and sleeping bags and food, driving all over Ireland? In a In a Cooper Mini? It was like bailing out of a clown car every time we stopped. We drove down through Wexford, to the Ring of Kerry, up to Kilkenny, then up to the West Coast and Connemara and Galway. (One of my favorites places in the whole world.) We went topless swimming in just our underwear at Inch Stand (yep…even Laura!) Boy the ocean was refreshingly COLD that day. We also stopped to kiss the Blarney Stone. We mostly camped out and one night we even slept in the ruins of a castle, which was really cool.

At Luther Park, the new camp director, Randy Gullickson had set up an arrangement with a program in Northern Ireland. This program's purpose was to get young kids away from the "Troubles" for a summer. The Troubles were the conflict between the Catholics and Protestants in Northern Ireland. The boy coming over to Luther Park was a ten-year-old from Derry, Northern Ireland by the name of Damien Hannaway. When Randy heard we were going over to Ireland, he contacted Bill and asked him if we wouldn't mind heading up to Derry to meet Damien and his family. So off we went. We somehow found our way to Derry and met the Hannaway's. Some of the nicest people on God's Green Earth.

Bill and Anne have 11 children. Yes, a good Catholic family and six of the kids were at home when we got there. Damien and his younger brother had to go to school and so we had a short visit with them. Then she walked down the stairs... older sister Rita! She was nineteen at the time and absolutely gorgeous. She had hazel eyes and her hair at the time was blonde. She also had that wonderful Northern Irish accent and I fell head over heels in about thirty seconds. Ah yeah, I am, or was, fairly predictable and somewhat pathetic. When I was younger, it seems I had a penchant for falling for women I ultimately didn't have a shot with. There's probably a deep psychological flaw in there somewhere, but we won't go there just now. Anyway, I did see the lovely Rita twice more in my life 1982 and in 2018, but those are stories left for another time.

We then drove back to Dublin for a couple of days, then took the train back to Belfast and the ferry over to Scotland, where we flew home. Unfortunately, I had caught some kind of bug and was deathly ill the whole way home from Dublin. Yuck! It was not a fun trip home, but it was an utterly fantastic trip overall. If you haven't been to Ireland and Northern Ireland, you need to go. It is a very beautiful country!

> *"Like all great travelers, I have seen more than I remember,*
> *and remember more than I have seen."*
> —Benjamin Disraeli (1804–1881)

STUDENT TEACHING

In 1981 I student taught at Irondale High School. I had two supervising teachers. Keith Engdahl and Bill Hesslin. Both were great teachers, but each with totally different styles. Both taught me a great deal about kids and teaching. And coaching is all about teaching. I wanted to do my coaching practicum at the same time as I was student teaching. Unfortunately, Dave Manley, the head coach at Irondale had his staff set. I was good friends with the Minnetonka Skippers trainer Nancy O'Connor, and she lined me up with Minnetonka and their new coach, Barry Lupovich. Barry was a counselor at the high school and came from Denver University where he was an assistant coach. Barry told me that I could come and work with the goaltenders at Minnetonka and learn from him. After the first scrimmage that I was with them, I told Barry that I would be happy to do anything to help the team, like scout upcoming opponents or tape the goaltenders etc. He told me that there is nothing to be learned from taping the goaltenders. And scouting high school hockey? "It would be a waste of time. Players just aren't that good."

This was my first clue that something was a bit off with him.

We had a game at Minnetonka Ice Arena against Hopkins, Barry came in after the first period and told the players what the plan was for the second period. As soon as he left the locker room, Lefty Larson and the other Assistant coach told the guys what they really needed to do. Second sign of a bad coaching situation. Then after about three days of practice where all I did was move pucks; I decided I was done with this craziness. I told Barry that I was going to concentrate on my student teaching.

Later that season Minnetonka was playing Jefferson and had a four-goal lead. Jefferson scored, then scored again, then scored a third goal and a fourth goal. By the third period Jefferson scored a fifth goal to take the lead. Back before they renovated Minnetonka Ice Arena, the walkway was right behind the benches, but was raised up, so a person could lean over the glass and talk to someone on the bench. A Jefferson fan came by and screamed, "Yeah, GO Jaguars!"

Good old Barry grabbed a stick and chased after the kid, hockey stick in hand. He never made a return to the bench that night. We don't know what happened to the kid. The next day at school, Barry didn't show up to work. So, the AD and Principal headed over to Barry's house. Barry had parked his car a couple of blocks away, towards school, they saw his car and so they knew that he was home. Not too subtle. After this incident, the Administration at Minnetonka found out that Barry lied to them and in fact he didn't have his Counselors license as he stated. Also, he lied when he stated that he was an assistant coach at Denver University, when in fact he was a volunteer assistant equipment manager and had never coached. Lefty finished out the year as head coach and Barry went off to parts unknown.

On the "Hockey is a small world" angle, I was living in Wayzata at my friend Bill Kelly's mothers house while I was doing my student teaching and there was a gentleman hitchhiking just off 694 and Long Lake Blvd, so I picked him up. He lived in Wayzata, so we drove the whole way together. We had the most fascinating hockey conversation ever. Turns out he was the Hamline University coach and was the conditioning coach for the 1980 Miracle on Ice Olympic team. Yep, I happened to pick up the one and only Jack Blatherwick. I learned so much in that 30-minute ride. It was unbelievable.

One last thing about student teaching at Irondale, there was a teacher that had his classroom right in-between Keith Engdahl's and Bill Heslin's classrooms, I have forgotten his name now, but every day, he played the song American Pie by Don McLean. I can't hear that song today without thinking about him.

"Our chief want is someone who will inspire us to be what we know we could be."
—Ralph Waldo Emerson (1803–1882)

MOOSE-RICHARD SALLMAN

During my first year at St. Cloud State, I lived in Hill-Case Hall. Hill was the women's side and Case was the men's side. It was here that I had the distinct pleasure of meeting a man who would become one of my best friends for life. His name was Richard Sallman, we called him Moose and he was in a wheelchair, due to three strokes he suffered shortly after his birth, leaving him with Cerebral Palsy. He would spend the rest of his life struggling to talk and he never was able to walk. But he was very intelligent, kind, and just one of the best human beings that I have ever come across. He got his nickname of Moose because he was a big man, he was about 6'3, weighing 275 pounds which made it difficult to lift him from his wheelchair to his bed. Moose and I were extremely close for the next four years.

During my first year, Moose and I would sit and talk, and he would gaze longingly at some of the co-eds that would go by. He so wanted to have a relationship with a woman, but he knew that under the conditions and with his aliments that it was unlikely to happen.

In my second year at St. Cloud, I moved off campus for the first semester, but then moved back into Hill-Case for the second semester. I was a Resident Advisor on Fourth Floor, but I would see Moose around the dorm and would help him study or just hang out with him.

In my third year, Moose and I moved in together and I was his personal care attendant. That is until Moose said that he thought we should just be roommates and he would hire another PCA. I had to work to make ends meet and I was gone most evenings right when Moose needed the most help. He also mentioned that he thought my being his PCA was straining our friendship. Again, he showed just how smart he was.

We continued being roommates during our last year in school and then we stayed close for the next 20 years until I went to Gilmour Academy in Ohio to coach the girls Prep hockey team. After I returned to Minnesota, I called Moose, but his phone was disconnected. I researched and found his parent's number only to learn that Moose had passed away a year earlier from a brain tumor. His mother had also died just a few months before Moose, and his father Ken was living in Wisconsin at their family cabin. I was devastated. Mostly because

I had lost touch with Moose, but also because he was now gone. I was hit with two thoughts. First, as human beings, we often take for granted that life won't change on us. We assume that someone younger won't die or even that our parents won't die. Yet, we know that it will happen, but we get so busy with life that we forget to keep living and loving the people that mean the most to us. Second, it struck me how cruel life is at times. Here, my friend Moose, had to live a life as a paraplegic due to unfortunate circumstances at birth, but he then spends his life as an incredible human being, only to have it cut short by a brain tumor. I miss you Moose and I am sorry that we lost touch. You were a very special part of my life. I love you, big guy! I hope you are doing all the things you couldn't do on earth, up in Heaven.

"I am more and more convinced that our happiness or unhappiness in life depends far more on the way we meet the events of our life, than on the nature of the events themselves."
—Wilhelm Von Humboldt (1767–1835)

THE WESTERN EXPLORATION TRIP-1981

In the summer before my last year at St. Cloud State I started dating a fantastic woman, Sue Krauser. She was a Resident Advisor in another dorm. At the time, I was also an RA in Hill-Case Hall. We met at a function for the campus Resident Advisors, and we hit it off right from the start. We got along extremely well, that is other than the fact that she was an Intramural Champion in racquetball and kicked my butt every time we played. At the end of the school year of 1981, we took a class together in the first part of summer school and we talked about our desire to go out west. I spoke with my sister Diane, who lived in Alexandria with her husband Jerry. They were thinking of heading west to visit sister Teri and family who lived in Beaverton, Oregon, a suburb of Portland.

So, my sister Diane, her husband Jerry, Sue, and I jumped in Jerry's car, a Datsun 280 Z and we started our trek west. Jerry was a paraplegic from a car accident when he was in the Service, but he still did all the driving. He had hand controls to accelerate and brake. He was really good at handling that car. I tried to drive the car once and let me tell you, your instincts are to use your feet, especially when applying the brakes. You tend to almost put yourself through the windshield when you use the foot brake and the hand brake at the same time. Anyways, since it was a two-seater, hatch back, it was an uncomfortable ride laying down in the back of that sports car for twenty-three hours.

Somehow, we survived, and arrived at my sister Teri's in Beaverton. We hung out there for about a week and then Sue and I started hitchhiking the eighty miles to the Pacific Ocean. We first were picked up by a family in Oregon, and they brought us home for dinner. Fresh fish caught that day, and vegetables from the garden. They were very nice people and even put us up for the night. It was a great evening of conversation. The next morning after breakfast, we got a ride to the Pacific Ocean. The ocean was gorgeous, and we had a great time playing on the beach. I remember being on a cliff looking out over the ocean, and the view was spectacular. The waves were rushing in and were incredibly violent, crashing upon the rocks. I could really feel the power of the ocean.

After our stint on the beach, we made our way south on the Oregon Coast Road, hooking up with Highway 1 in California. We got a few rides that brought us just south of San Francisco where we stopped at a restaurant for something to eat. We both decided to try the clam chowder. Oh my. It was so good. Now, even 40+ years later, I can remember the taste and the texture. It was wonderful. We visited the Redwood trees in Redwood National Forest. I was overwhelmed by the sheer size and magnitude of these massive trees. It is one of my favorite memories of our adventure. There was one tree called the "Founder's Tree." Talk about majestic, it was 350 feet high! Words can't describe how incredibly big this tree was. We then arrived in Pacifica and slept on the beach. We met a young guy, Kevin, who I think was attracted to Sue. She disagreed with me, but I saw how he looked at her. All in all, it was a beautiful night and one more thing off my bucket list, sleeping under the stars and on an ocean beach.

Then we made it down to San Diego and met up with a friend from school, Catie who together with her boyfriend, was kind enough to put us up for a couple of days of rest and a good shower at her boyfriend's apartment. He was friendly, but I got the sense that this was more a favor to Catie, and that he really didn't like having us in his apartment. It seemed like he spent a great deal of time at Catie's anyway, so it really shouldn't have been a huge deal for us to be at his place.

We spent the weekend in San Diego and then headed across California and into Arizona. We got a ride from Skip and Kris, a married couple who were two of the friendliest people that we met on our trip. They were awesome and put us up for the evening at their house. When you are on the road, staying in various places like campgrounds, or on the beach, or whatnot, you don't readily turn down an offer of a bed and a shower and a great breakfast in the morning. Our goal on this segment of the trip was to make it to Kingsville, Texas where Sue's brother Jack and his girlfriend Robin lived. Jack was a Navy pilot and flew jets. He had some training videos which I watched. It was amazing to watch the speed at which the jets could fly and still land on an Aircraft Carrier. It takes a special amount of courage to land a jet on a ship. I know I couldn't do it.

We stayed with Jack and Robin for a little over a week. At this point, we had been traveling for close to a month and so it was good to rest up for a bit. We explored all over Kingsville, Corpus Christi, Brownsville, and made a trip across the border into Mexico, which was a first for both of us.

After our stay with Jack and Robin, we headed north towards Minnesota. It took us another couple of days, but we finally made it home. We had been on the road for almost two months, and we had gotten fifty-six rides from strangers. Most of the people we met were great people. We occasionally ran into a trucker or two that liked to ramble on for long stretches. It appears that it takes a special person to be a long-haul trucker. The road does get a bit lonely. By the time we got back to the Twin Cities, we were more than a little tired and we really needed a break from each other.

Here are a couple of observations from our trip. Spending everyday with someone, no matter how much you love and care for them, takes its toll. Also, at the time, it didn't seem dangerous to us to hitch hike all over the west, but looking back on it, we were a bit naïve and certainly fortunate in our adventures. I can just say that I think the Good Lord was looking out for us. It was a fantastic adventure and quite the trip, all in all.

For Sue…my one–time traveling companion.

Remember the rain and the way it felt on our faces? And on our minds?

I always loved the rain and the dreary days with the thoughts that came with them. You always loved the sunny days and the happiness that filled your soul.

We complement each other in this way.
For you bring a smile to my eyes.
And I bring a thought to your heart.
—T.H. Peart

ANOTHER FANTASTIC JOURNEY-EUROPE

I graduated from St. Cloud State in April of 1982. My plan was to then go to Europe and explore for three months, all on my own. My parents bought me a Eurail Pass for graduation, and I had saved up to buy a plane ticket. I had just enough money to last me for three months, if I rationed it out carefully. I flew into Shannon Airport, in the middle of Ireland and caught a train to Dublin. My first stop was the Hagenov household. Bill Kelly stayed with Brunhild Hagenov and her kids Frankie and Nina when he was a foreign exchange student at Trinity College. Mrs. Hagenov was a wonderful woman, and we spent many evenings drinking tea and then walking the family dog Tia. We talked long into the nights about all the affairs of the world and the meaning of life. It was a magnificent week with her and the kids. I can still hear her yelling out the door in her high-pitched voice,

" Frank-ie! Ni-na! Din-ner!"

I will forever remember that voice. She was a wonderful person.

I then headed to Northern Ireland to visit Damien Hannaway and his family, Bill and Anne, their daughter Rita and the rest of the family. They graciously opened their home and hearts to me, and I forever will be grateful to them for their hospitality. Damien had spent the previous summer at Luther Park Camp, and I became really close to him. His sister Rita showed me all of Derry and this was a time in the middle of the Troubles. There was a heavy military presence in the streets. Bobby Sands, of the Irish Republican Army was imprisoned in the Maze Prison in Northern Ireland. Sands was right in the middle of his hunger strike in protest of the English and Protestant rule over the North. It was a hard time for the Catholics of Northern Ireland.

One of the coolest parts of my trip to Northern Ireland, was going to Easter Mass with Anne. It was a beautiful old church and majestic to see. It filled me with wonder and history. Here I was in Northern Ireland, during the Troubles and going to Mass in a Catholic Church. It was surreal in many respects.

Another interesting experience was the night I was hitchhiking and was picked up by three survivors of "Bloody Sunday." Bloody Sunday occurred on Sunday, January 30th, 1972. Thirteen people were shot and killed and at least fifteen others were injured as members of the British Army's Parachute

Regiment opened fire on Civil Rights demonstrators in the Bogside area of Derry, Northern Ireland, a predominantly Catholic area. I forgot their names, but they said that two of them were injured on that day. It's hard to verify as the injured weren't listed and it could be a situation similar to people stating that they were in an arena for a big event, but I had no reason not to believe them and their stories seemed real enough to me.

From Derry, I took a bus to Belfast and from there, the Ferry across to England, where I caught another bus to County Durham, England. This is the county right on the border of England and Scotland, and it's where the Peart's came from. I did some family history hunting and I remember becoming overwhelmed when I learned that the Peart's tended to name their sons and daughters the same name of their fathers and mothers. Thus, you had four or five John Peart's married to Nancy Peart or Thomas Peart married to Anne, etc. I took down what I could, but it was clear I was going to have to rethink how I approached finding out more about the family, as it would take more time than I had to research. After County Durham, home of the delicious Newcastle Brown Ale (my favorite beer), I caught a bus to London and then was off to the White Cliffs of Dover. From there, I took another ferryboat to France.

I made it to Paris with the intention of heading north to Belgium and on to Amsterdam. However, I couldn't find a train to Belgium anywhere on the board. I asked at the Information Desk in the train station in Paris, where I needed to go to catch the next train to Belgium. They acted like I was speaking Inuit. Finally, they told me that I needed to go to another train station, which was about two miles away. I had a map, so I started walking. I was standing in the middle of Paris, lost and getting frustrated, when this little old lady somehow recognized I was a complete dolt in need of help. She took mercy on me and pointed out on my map where I needed to go. She didn't speak English and I knew about two words in French, but somehow, she helped me out. I will forever remember her.

I finally made my way to the next train station, where I took the train to the Belgium and then on to the Netherlands. After two days in Amsterdam, I headed north through Germany to Denmark. The Eurail Pass I had allowed me to travel on any train, as well as some buses, any time I wanted. Some nights I would ride the train to one destination and then back to where I started, just to sleep for a few hours. I remember traveling on the train through Germany with a woman and a man from Australia. We stopped in Berlin and German soldiers got on and checked everyone's passports. They glanced at my passport briefly and then handed it back. With the Australian couple, they looked through their bags and patted them down. The Aussies definitely received a completely different experience than I did.

I arrived in Copenhagen, Denmark where I stayed with friends of Tim Smith, a friend from St. Cloud State. Tim had lived with Louis Goodwin and Clara Levetz as an exchange student in Copenhagen. They took me to Tivoli Gardens and showed me their beautiful city. Tivoli Gardens is an amusement park and garden in the center of Copenhagen. The park opened in 1843 and is the third-oldest operating amusement park in the world, after Dyrehaysbakken in nearby Klampenborg, Denmark and Wurstelprater in Vienna, Austria. Denmark, like much of Europe, was a very beautiful country.

After Denmark, I traveled back through Germany to the south and visited Munich where of course I had to stop at the Hofbräuhaus and enjoy a German beer. After my stay in Munich, I embarked on the hardest, most emotionally traumatic experience of my trip. I went to the Dachau Concentration Camp, just outside Munich. This place had such an impact on me that I can't even describe the effects of walking through that front gate, seeing the barb wired fences, the moat and guard towers. It was so surreal. I actually thought I could feel the souls of all the people that died there. It was overwhelming. I was incredulous that people could be so cruel to other human beings. The tour took us past where the barracks had stood. They were all torn down and only the cement bases were evident of something having been there. We next visited the killing showers and crematorium. Again, I was aghast at the insanity of this place. To think that there were over 1,000 similar camps throughout Europe was incomprehensible to me.

After the soul crushing visit to Dachau, I needed something to lift my spirits. Two years earlier, the 1980 Miracle on Ice happened in Lake Placid, New York. Herb Brooks was the architect of that incredible Olympic hockey success. Herb took some time off and then signed on to coach a Swiss team up in the Alps in Davos, Switzerland. Seeing as how Herb was one of my coaching heroes and since I was so close, I took a train to Davos just to see where Herb was coaching. Okay, I was hoping to see Herb as well, but I sort of knew that the chances were extremely low. But hey, you gotta try, right?

Most of the trains throughout Europe run 24-7 and if you need to sleep, you just take a train anywhere, catch a few hours of sleep and then catch another train to wherever you want to go. But not the train to Davos. It stopped in Davos and shut down at 10 PM. Everyone off the train. All right, not a big deal. I had a pup tent and a sleeping bag. I would just find someplace to pitch the tent. I found a nice park and put my tent up, tried to find a restaurant open for something to eat, and got back to the park where thankfully my tent was still there.

I went to sleep, planning on a big exploration of Davos the next day. Instead, I woke up at about 3:00 AM freezing my butt off. I couldn't feel my feet and I was cold and wet all over. A snowstorm blew in after midnight and my tent had a leak in it. I knew that I couldn't stay out in the storm. I needed to get warm again. I got up, threw on some clothes and my poncho, rolled up my sleeping bag and tent, then started walking around Davos. I finally found a heated commercial garage that allowed me to be out of the elements and warm up. I sat down in-between some cars and dozed, off and on, for the rest of the night. I woke up at dawn and went in search of coffee and breakfast. It was quite the night. I did explore Davos though, and it is incredibly beautiful. All of the Alps are.

At this point in my adventure, I had been gone from home for two and a half months and I was starting to get really tired. Plus, my money was running short. I decided to forgo exploring Italy and Southern France and leave them for another trip. But I did take a train through both Northern Italy and Southern France

stopping in Cherbourg, France, where I planned to catch the ferryboat back to England. There I ran into some English travelers who were also there to catch the ferry across to England. They were wonderful people, much like 99% of the people I met on this fantastic voyage, and they even shared their Gin and Tonics with me.

After walking around Cherbourg at dawn, I found some incredible fresh baked croissants and then I boarded the ferry to England, where I would take a bus to London. From London a train to Plymouth and then a last ferry to Ireland, where

I spent another couple of weeks in Dublin with Mrs. Hagenov and family. I then took a train back to Shannon airport, boarded a flight back to the USA and arrived home. In all I visited 11 countries, including, Ireland, Northern Ireland, England, France, Belgium, Netherlands, Denmark, Germany, Luxembourg, Switzerland, and Italy. It was a fantastic adventure and the trip of a lifetime.

> *"Live life with no excuses. Travel with no regrets."*
> —Oscar Wilde (1854–1900)

COACH BRUCE JOHNSON AND
ARMSTRONG HIGH SCHOOL.

I was fortunate to have coached at one of the best high school hockey programs in the 1980s. Bruce Johnson was my mentor, teacher, and friend. I owe him immensely for all the lessons, opportunities and effort he put into a young hockey coach. One who was long on ambition and enthusiasm and very, very short on experience.

I was hired for my first coaching job in the fall of 1983. I had applied to every school district that I could. I figured that I would do the blanket approach and see what came of it. Armstrong and Cooper had received an okay from the Robbinsdale school district to add a coach. Bruce Johnson (BJ) called me, and we set up an interview for a Friday right before the start of the season. I had just moved to Plymouth, ironically about a mile from the high school. I drove up to the school and Bruce met me at the front of the school. I remember thinking "Why did they have an assistant coach interview me?" Now, if you know BJ, you know that he still looks twenty years younger than his actual age. In the fall of 1983, he looked about twenty-five years old. The interview went well, and he told me that he had one other interview on Sunday night. They would call me on Monday morning and let me know the verdict. I was officiating at the time to make a little extra money and had a game Sunday night in Brooklyn Park. On Monday morning, I received a call from BJ and he tells me that they are offering me the job. I was elated. Oh, and he told me I missed a call in the corner the previous night. Turns out, one of the coaches of the game I was officiating was the other coach he was going to interview. Bruce came to the game to watch that coach in action and was able to see both of us in a hockey environment.

Bruce Johnson turned into my mentor, my friend and one of many people who have impacted my entire life positively in so many ways. I learned how to handle players, how to plan and run practices, how to schedule games, and the difficult task of how to cut players (part of coaching that everyone hates) He taught me all the behind-the-scenes things that many people don't know that go into coaching. So publicly, Bruce, thank you for taking a chance on a recovering goaltender who loved hockey and wanted to coach and work with players. You changed my life. I love you, my friend!

One other thing I got from Bruce was the start of a jersey collection. Bruce kept the number seven from each set of jerseys that he had as a head coach. I thought that was a cool idea, so I have kept the number twenty-seven (my college number and my favorite goalie's number Giles Meloche.) Since I coached so many teams, I have quite a few jerseys.

"I am a success today because I had a friend who believed in me, and I didn't have the heart to let him down."
—Abraham Lincoln (1809–1865)

THE PART OF COACHING EVERY COACH HATES

Now, lest you misunderstand, life with Bruce wasn't always rosy. I was hired as a JV coach/goalie coach. I stepped on the ice that first day, excited, nervous and amazed at the talent that was on the ice. Bruce skated up to me and said,

"You see that goaltender? He's been here skating the past week and we are moving him to Midgets. You're the goalie coach. Go let him know."

Yep, my first task ever as a coach was cutting a kid I had never met or seen play. Thanks Bruce. He later told me that it was a test and he wanted to see how I would handle it. I learned that no matter how difficult it is, you look a player in the eyes when you deliver news that is hard to hear. For a young player, not making the team is very traumatic, indeed.

"Do the difficult things while they are easy and do the great things while they are small. A journey of a thousand miles must begin with a single step."
—Lao Tzu (571 BC – 500 BC)

TALENT GALORE-ARMSTRONG HOCKEY

We had some extremely talented teams at Armstrong in the early '80s. In the six years I was an assistant coach, we could have gone to State at least four of those years, but we didn't, and that is one of my most painful memories from coaching. In 1984-85 we lost in the section final to Minnetonka. Todd Richards, who later would be the head coach for the Minnesota Wild, scored seventeen seconds into the game. Unfortunately, we couldn't maintain the momentum and ended up losing 7-3. Tough day at school the next day, as I was working at Minnetonka at that time. I had to put up with a great deal of comments from the hockey players and the students all day at school.

In 1985-86, we lost to Edina in the section semi-finals 3-2, when one of the referees waved off on an icing call at the last second. Edina picked up the puck and scored. That was also a very tough loss to handle. Bruce had a few choice words for the officiating crew that day.

The toughest loss, though, came in 1987-88, when we had eighteen seniors on the team. We lost the first game of the year to Minnetonka 3-2, and then won eighteen games in a row, beating the eventual state champs (Edina), runners up (Hill-Murray), and 3rd place winners (Jefferson) before we lost again. Once again, we lost to Edina in the playoffs. Even so, It was a special year. For six years, it was Bruce, Don Moore and yours truly. I loved my time at Armstrong and all the young men that were on our hockey teams. I was also fortunate enough to coach the softball teams and football teams during my years at Armstrong.

Besides the opportunity to coach hockey, Bruce paved the way for me to coach at Michigan Tech's summer hockey school. He also introduced me to Dave Larson of Hooter Sportwear. Dave has since changed the name to TOUGHJERSEY, as it is a better brand for his products. Dave made jerseys for us at Armstrong and for me at Roosevelt, St. Ben's, Gilmour Academy in Ohio, and Totino-Grace. He also helped me out throughout the years as a friend and eventually as a boss. He is a great person and opened a lot of doors for me.

"The eternal difference between right and wrong does not fluctuate, it is immutable."
— Patrick Henry (1736–1799)

ROOKIE HOCKEY COACH LEARNS
A VALUABLE LESSON

In 1983, I was in my first-year coaching at Armstrong High School, and we had a Junior Varsity scrimmage against South St. Paul. My players were not feeling it that day and they really were giving a half effort to the scrimmage. I lost it after 45 minutes and called the scrimmage. I told the South St. Paul coach, Paul Moen that we were done. I felt bad after I found out how far South St. Paul was from our home rink, New Hope Ice Arena. I was new to the Twin Cities and had no idea the length of the bus ride for them. Sorry Paul. Anyways, for the next 45 minutes, I skated the team. We skated laps at half-speed. 5 minutes one way, then 5 minutes the other direction. Not enough speed to make them exhausted, but fast enough to keep them always in a good skating position. Unfortunately, because I was a bonehead, and was so pissed off, I skated with them, yelling at them to keep their knees bent and their chest up. I informed them that if they wanted to waste scrimmage time by giving me only a half assed effort, then we will skate at half-speed for the rest of our ice time. It never occurred to me to just be standing and watching them skate. The next day was a day off, thankfully, because I could hardly walk. Oh, to be young again.

That first junior varsity team at Armstrong was a great group of guys. Later in my coaching years, I understood that players would sometimes test you to see what your boundaries were and how far they could push you. I believe that players want discipline and to know that you, as their coach, will control the team. It is all part of working young people. Especially when you, the coach, were new, and young. One of the many lessons that I learned along the way.

"Even the nicest person's patience has a limit."
—Anonymous (From PictureQuotes.com)

Thomas H Peart

SOME ARMSTRONG HOCKEY LESSONS

I learned a great deal from Bruce Johnson, but some things I had to learn on my own. During the 1985-86 season, I learned that you sometimes need to act mad before you really do get mad and ultimately, lose your temper. Oftentimes your own emotions cloud how you think, and you may overreact.

We were playing a Junior Varsity game vs. Anoka early in the season and we weren't playing well. We were down to Anoka after two periods. Bruce and the varsity assistant coach Don Moore said I needed to light a fire under the kids. So, I am ticked off and I am going to go in and light them up. No more Mr. Nice Guy, right? Now, my players are young, and they are used to me at practice. Positive, happy, welcoming and full of encouragement. So, when I slam the locker room door open, all eyes are wide open and staring at me, wondering who this crazy person was. I start in, very loudly, how we are playing horribly and what is wrong with us? I see a water bottle sitting upright on the floor and I kick that sucker as hard as I could. The water bottles at the time were big and fat and soft. The water bottle sailed across the room and nailed Tommy Reiswig right in the forehead. The whole room was quiet. Tommy's eyes were as big as saucers, but then he smiled at the look on my face. I laughed and said,

"Well, hell. That ruins a good tirade!"

The whole room broke up laughing and we talked about what we needed to do to win the game. Tommy was probably the one kid who had been playing his hardest out there the whole game. He even went out and scored the winning goal in the third period.

Tommy had a twin brother, Tim, who is a friend to this day and one player I wish I could have coached. He was a goaltender and unfortunately, we had better goalies that beat him out for the position. Sadly, Tommy died in a tragic work accident in 1995 at the age of 25. He was a wonderful young man, who was on his way to becoming an incredible adult. Rest in peace Tommy.

Bruce gave me the freedom to develop my junior varsity players for varsity. He gave me the autonomy to learn on the go. He encouraged me and gave me tips, but never complained or micromanaged me. One thing I believed in was that everyone on the JV played equally, even on power plays and penalty kills. During most years we had three different power plays. I figured that each group had different skills, so let's play to those skills rather than force them into one particular style of play. We still played fast and hard, we just tried to play to their talents. Thanks again Bruce, I love you, and I loved coaching with you.

"When life gets harder, challenge yourself to be stronger."
—Unknown (PictureQuotes.com)

ARMSTRONG/COOPER HOCKEY GAMES

The two games between the Robbinsdale schools, Armstrong, and Cooper each season were always a highlight during each of my six years with Armstrong. You could feel the excitement building in the practices leading up to the games and no matter what the talent levels of the respective teams were, the games were always hotly contested and always close. Also, the fans from both teams were always into it. We had some phenomenal teams when I was there and Cooper, coached by Ken Staples was always playing the "poor side of town" card. I remember in 1984-85, our two captains, Todd Richards and John Zimmer took an article from the paper talking about how good Armstrong was and plastered it all over the Cooper side of New Hope Ice Arena. They put up hundreds of copies of the article. Somehow, they got into the Cooper coaches' room and the Cooper locker room and put them up there as well. Those articles were everywhere, even in the bathrooms. It was awesome, though I don't think Ken Staples, or the Cooper players found it funny. Staples and Bruce Johnson were always at odds, one way or the other. Usually, it was Ken trying to use anything to motivate his kids.

Another time when we were playing Cooper during the 1985-86 season, the stands were packed with the usual combination of Armstrong and Cooper fans. The arena announcer began to introduce our starting line-up and suddenly hot dogs rained down from the Cooper fan section. There were a lot of hot dogs on the ice that night. The arena was always jammed to the rafters for these games and again, it didn't matter how good or bad each team was.

There was one game where we were winning by a goal or two and Cooper coach Ken Staples was mad at the referees. He always felt that Armstrong was favored because we generally had the more skilled teams. He played up the supposed disadvantages that his kids had or felt that they had. Again, it was Staples using anything and everything at his disposal to motivate his players. During this game, Cooper was called for three straight penalties and Staples jumps up on the dasher in front of their bench and proceeds to walk back and forth in his cowboy boots yelling at the referees as they skated up and down the ice. How he didn't fall or get a penalty, I will never know. Ken Staples was quite the character. Most every guy that I have met that played for Ken loved him. Ken was also a great baseball coach and coached in the Twins minor league system for a while. A story circulated around the rink about how a couple of coaches went down to watch a baseball game, somewhere in Wisconsin or Illinois. Ken was managing one of the teams and they arrived at the start of the second inning. The only problem was that Ken had already been ejected from the game. There was a dispute on a call at home and Ken laid down on home plate and wouldn't get up. Security had to carry him out. He was truly one of a kind.

Thankfully Armstrong won the bragging rights of New Hope Ice Arena more often than not. We had some great players. Todd and Travis Richards, John Zimmer, Dennis Vaske, Jim Rokala, Bill Rooney, Mark Merila, Mark Sundgren, Jim Koltes, Mike Wickman, Ross Larson, Steve Mateski, Jim Bode. The list goes on and on. I could spend days talking about all the wonderful players we had at Armstrong. Of course, I am also quite biased and Armstrong proud!

"Be more concerned with your character than with your reputation. Your character is what you really are while your reputation is merely what others think you are."
—John Wooden (By Permission– From the book WOODEN: A Lifetime of Observations and Reflections (McGraw–Hill).)

GREAT PARENTS-THE RICHARDS

In my thirty-seven years of coaching, I have run into a lot of different people. Some were really wacko, and some were absolutely incredible. One Armstrong family has become great friends to me over the years, the Richards clan, one of the most famous and successful hockey families from Armstrong. Todd Richards...yes, that Todd Richards, who coached the Wild and is still coaching pro hockey, was our best player during my years at Armstrong. Todd had incredible talent and was one of the best defensemen to ever play at the University of Minnesota. He still holds the career points record for defensemen with 158 points and the career assists record with 128 in his four years as a Gopher. During his senior year, Todd finished up as the runner-up to Tom Chorske of Minneapolis Southwest for the first ever Mr. Hockey award. Todd was drafted by Montreal 33rd overall in 1985.

Todd's brother, Travis was equally talented, but he had a different style of play. He was the motor that made us go in 1988 when we won 18 straight games at Armstrong. He was a great leader, on and off the ice. Travis also played defense at Minnesota and stands fourth in career points for defensemen with 133 points, fifth in goals with 35 and fifth in assists with 98. Travis was drafted by the North Stars in 1988 and played for the Dallas Stars. In addition, Travis played for the USA National Team in 1993 and 1994.

Then there are the two Richards girls, Heidi and Tracy. They both have kids that are good hockey players. Heidi's son Tyler Lindstrom played at Breck and went to Curry College. Tracy had two kids play at Benilde-St. Margaret's, Jonah Mortenson was a key player on the boy's team and played Junior Hockey after graduating. Last, but not least, is Lily Mortenson, who was a top player on the Benilde girls' team and attends Gustavus Adolphus College. She is smaller in stature but plays with a huge heart and the Richards competitiveness that won't quit. Oh yeah, their dad was a good player at Osseo back in the day.

Todd's son Justin was a two-time National Champion at UMD and signed with the New York Rangers after college. He then signed a contract with the Columbus

Blue Jackets and played in Cleveland in the AHL. The hockey genes run strong and deep in the Richards family.

Of course, it all started with Tom and Bonnie Richards. They are true rangers from Eveleth, Minnesota. Tom was a great hockey and football player for the Golden Bears. They were the type of hockey parents that made me proud to be a hockey coach working with their kids, but it went deeper than that. They always accepted me as a friend and opened their home to me. I learned a lot about defense and how to coach players from Tom, who was an incredible youth hockey coach in Crystal and was the key driving force in his sons' athletic careers. Bonnie was the glue of the family. She softened some of Tom's rough edges. Okay, well she was probably still working on that until Tom's last days. I used to make up excuses to go over to the Richards house just to drink coffee and talk Hockey with Tom. He always challenged me to be a better hockey coach.

Tom reminded me of my own dad in so many ways. After I left Armstrong and became the head coach at Roosevelt High School, I would consult with Tom about some of the decisions that I had made. He would look me in the eye and ask,

"Do you think that was a good decision?"

He had a way of saying things that definitely made you think. Tom taught me so many little things about coaching and about life. I am positive that he didn't even know that he was doing so because he could teach without making it seem like he was doing so. It was just natural to him. Another similarity between Tom and my dad was his love for his children. Tom adored his kids. He held them to high standards, but his love for them was evident in his manner and his demeanor. And he loved Bonnie with all his heart. I am sure she can tell stories of how obstinate Tom could be at times, but he was an incredible human being, and I am a better person for having known him. Tom died in 2020. He had some lung issues and was battling Alzheimer's at the end. The family arranged for hospice care, but thankfully Tom didn't suffer for very long. Sad times as a proper funeral didn't happen for several months due to COVID and all the stuff surrounding it. Rest in Peace my friend. I look forward to talking hockey with you once again someday.

I would be remise if I didn't mention Gaye Novack, Tom's assistant coach and friend. Tom and Gaye had coached the Crystal Bantams for many years. Gaye's son Joey played for us at Armstrong. He was a great person, and his dad is a good friend. Gaye and I would often talk hockey at whatever arena we would run into each at. He had a wealth of knowledge regarding the game. I have been so lucky in my career to know so many wonderful people like the Richards and Novack's among others. I will be forever grateful to them. Thanks for the years of friendship!

"I am not bound to win, but I am bound to be true. I am not bound to succeed, but I am bound to live by the light that I have. I must stand with anybody that stands right and stand with him while he is right and part with him when he goes wrong."
—Abraham Lincoln (1809–1865)

MARK MERILA-ONE OF THE GREATEST PURE ATHLETES AND PEOPLE, I HAVE EVER COACHED

One of the best, most talented players I have ever worked with in my thirty-seven years in hockey was Mark Merila. Mark was not the biggest player on the rink, standing 5'9" and weighing 180 pounds in high school. He wasn't the fastest skater, though he did have good speed. What Mark had was endless skill, fantastic desire, and a heart so big that it couldn't be measured. Mark set the career scoring record for Armstrong and held that record for fifteen years. I once saw Mark skate down the ice, then totally faking out the defensemen playing against him by slapping his stick on the ice on the right. When the defenseman leaned slightly to the right, going for the fake, Mark slipped the puck through the defenders' legs and to the left and then past the goaltender, into the corner of the net. He had the most incredible hands I have ever seen.

Mark was one of those athletes that could play any sport and excel at it. He was a phenomenal baseball player and received a full scholarship to the University of Minnesota. The U hockey team also wanted Mark to play for them, but he felt it would be too much. So, he concentrated on baseball. Turns out it was a smart decision. He was named the Big Ten Freshman of the Year in 1991. Big Ten Conference Player of the Year in 1994 and was a two time All- American for the Gophers. During his senior year Mark set single season (.452 BA) and career batting average records (.356) for Minnesota. He was drafted in the 10th round in the Major League draft in 1993. He decided not to sign and was then drafted by the San Diego Padres in 1994. He then played professionally in the Padres minor league system.

Sadly, near the end of Mark's senior season with the Gopher baseball team, he was diagnosed with a brain tumor. He went through radiation treatments and was cleared to play but was forced to retire after two years as a pro player due to the brain tumor. Mark was then hired as the bullpen catcher for the Padres. He was a valuable member of the Padres until 2005 when his health issues took another bad turn. The doctors found that the brain tumor had returned, and Mark then received an experimental treatment that saved his life. The owner of the Padres paid for the treatment, which was very expensive. This was a testament to the Mark Merila I know and love. He is known by many people, and I have yet to find anyone that doesn't think the world of Mark.

When his long-time teammate and friend, Trevor Hoffman, a pitcher for the Padres was inducted in the MLB Hall of Fame, he recognized Mark and what Mark meant to him. If you Google *Mark Merila Baseball*, you will find a story called Mark Merila's Sports Story. It is well worth the read. Mark has gone through more in his life than any ten of us, and yet he never lets that deter him and it never gets him down. He is a wonderful father to his three kids, and he is one of the most positive people I have ever met. He was an incredible athlete, and he is an even better person. I love you Mark, and it was a very hard decision to leave Armstrong before your senior year. It's one of my major decisions of my coaching career. One I wish I could have made after your senior year.

"When your back is against the wall. When it seems, there is no way out…you have to face your fears and never give up. Never back down. Never lose faith!"
—Anonymous (Quotes Gram)

CHRIS HANSEN, AN INCREDIBLE PERSON AND FRIEND

As I have said before, I was fortunate to coach many, many incredible young men, and women at Armstrong High School. One of the most impressive players I have coached over the years was Chris Hansen. Not because he was the best hockey player we had, but it was his heart and soul that made him inspiring to others. Chris was big, tough and could skate, and he had better than average skills. He was a great defender, but on a team that was led by Dennis Vaske (New York Islanders and Boston Bruins) and Travis Richards (Dallas Stars) and Mark Merila (U of Minnesota Baseball, All-American), Chris was a role player. However, he was a role player who played his role to the T. You always got 100% out of Chris no matter what the situation. Chris had a tough upbringing. His mom is a saint, but his dad was a bit rough around the edges. Chris played Junior Hockey and then went to Augsburg College, where his career was average. However, he would become an even more impactful person later in life.

Chris had a bad accident one day while rollerblading. He was skating with his two dogs on leashes, when they all got tangled up and Chris fell. He landed on his head and suffered a traumatic brain injury. He was in the hospital for a couple of months, and he came close to dying. His doctors did a phenomenal job working on him and saved his life. He still has some residual issues from the injury, but he is doing well. He married a wonderful woman and is now selling real estate.

One of Chris' most impressive contributions is taking military veterans to Gopher men's hockey games, and on Canadian fishing trips, free of charge. He calls his program "Time on the Water", and he holds various fundraisers in order to cover the cost of the tickets and fishing trips. He connects the veterans with former professional hockey players, which enhances the experience for all involved. His fundraisers include a golf tournament and a motorcycle ride.

Chris does this out of the goodness of his heart. Again, he has one of the biggest hearts of all the players that I coached in my life. As he has said, "Even though I am not a Veteran, I wanted to do something original for our Military Veterans."

Once again, I will tell you that my life has been enriched beyond calculation by all the wonderful men and women that I had the pleasure to coach as I watched them grow into incredible human beings. I truly feel like the luckiest man alive. Thank you, Chris, for your friendship and for all that you do to help veterans find more enjoyment in their lives. I love you buddy!

"Stay close to anything that makes you glad you are alive."
—Hafiz (1325–1390)

ARMSTRONG SOFTBALL

I was asked to be an assistant softball coach at Armstrong by head coach Bob Brinkman. Bob was the long time Armstrong coach, and we had two of the most balanced and talented teams in the 1988 and 1989 seasons. We made it to state both years and had a chance to win the title but fell short both times. We had talent, power, speed and desire. I've always believed that our infield was the best I have seen in high school softball during those two seasons. Kerby Norman was behind the plate, Michele Sumstad at 1st base, Kelli Sibet at 2nd base, Mary Steiner at shortstop, and Nikki Campbell at 3rd base, with Chris Hartman and Kelly Norman sharing the pitching duties on the mound. Our outfielders were Kelly Norman (when she wasn't pitching,} Tracy Olson, Laurie Edwards, Jenny Hanson and Marla Kottke. We routinely turned double plays and on more than one occasion I would see Kelly Norman purposely mishandle a ball causing the base runner to try to advance, then she would gun the runner down with a phenomenal throw. Many of our players went on to play college softball with twins Kelly and Kerby heading to the University of Minnesota, where they played four years for the Gophers. Both ended up marrying future pro hockey players Trent Klatt (Kelly) and Ken Gernander (Kerby.)

We took 3rd place in the 1988 state tournament, and we took 2nd place in 1989, losing in the championship game to Mankato East. Bob ended up winning a state title in 2000 and then he retired on top. Congratulations Bob!

We had all the pieces to be state champions both years. Mary Steiner was an incredible shortstop, and she was the motor to our team. I am not sure I ever saw a better 3rd, Baseman than Nikki Campbell. She was fearless, competitive, and had the reflexes of a cat. It was a great three years with the softball team and my first experience coaching girls.

My first year was marred, however, by the death of one of our top Junior Varsity players, Allison Musich. We came back on the bus from an away game and Allison seemed down and depressed. We were walking down the hill to put our equipment away and I asked her if she was okay. She said that she was fine. I told her that I was always open if she wanted to talk. Her response was,

"I don't talk to anyone about my problems."

Allison went home, wrote her adopted parents a letter and then closed the garage door, turned her car on and laid down behind the car's exhaust pipe. She died that night and I have wondered over the years if I should have pressed her more to talk and if that would have changed the ultimate outcome. Somehow, I don't think it would have, but I will never know. Rest in Peace Allison.

"Some souls are too beautiful for this world, so they leave early."
—Unknown (From Yourquote.com)

After three good years at Armstrong, I was hired as the head softball coach at Cooper High School.

I took over at Cooper in the 1991 season. We had a core of really good players, led by one of the best pitchers in the state of Minnesota. Her name was Kristi Windsperger. She was an exceptional player. The only problem was the fact that she was pregnant during her senior year. When I was hired, she was very upfront about her condition. I made a tactical decision and hired her dad, Jim, as an assistant coach. I knew Jim from summer ball, and he turned out to be an excellent assistant for the team. We had the added benefit of him working with Kristi and managing the effects of her condition. We got through the year, as we developed our team.

The next year, Shelly Sawyer took over the bulk of the pitching duties from the graduated Windsperger. She was a junior and an incredible athlete, lettering in three sports in high school. Erin Brophy was behind the plate, and she went on to play for the Minnesota Gophers in college. We also had some other good athletes that filled out our team, but our problem was depth and that we didn't have a quality player at every position. My two years at Cooper were definitely up and down years.

The best thing that happened for me at Cooper was meeting Shelly Sawyer and her parents Sharon and Jim. They have been great friends for the past almost 30 years. They are great people and have supported me through thick and thin. And Shelly ended up marrying Mike Smith, my boss when I coached girls' hockey at Totino-Grace. The world is truly a small one indeed.

"Open your arms to change, but don't let go of your values."
—Dalai Lama (1876–1933)

ARMSTRONG FOOTBALL

I was hired to coach 9th grade football at Armstrong High School in the fall of 1988. Don Moore was the varsity head coach; Bruce Johnson was a varsity assistant coach. The three of us spent a great deal of time together that fall with the football team and in the winter with the hockey team, when they would reverse their roles with Bruce being the head hockey coach and Don his top assistant.

Another assistant coach and I oversaw the freshman team. We also were assigned to scout our next week's varsity opponent. Then on Sundays we would go over to Don's for a snack and the entire coaching staff would review the tape of last week's varsity game. I, or my partner, would give the scouting report on our up-coming varsity foe and then we would all plan out practice for the week.

I hated football practice. I did as a player, and I did as a coach. With hockey, practices are ever changing. Yes, there is repetition, but there are dozens of different drills that you can do that replicate the same skill. I loved hockey practices as a player and more so, as a coach. Football just has plain old repetition.

"Good…run it again." Is a common phrase.

We did have some great kids there though. They were fast and tough and fun to coach.

"Success is a science; if you have the conditions, you get the result."
—Oscar Wilde (1854–1900)

BRIAN BOEDER

There are many great things that happen to you when you are a coach of young people. It is, to me, the greatest feeling in the world to have former players tell you what you meant to them when they were younger. It just fills your heart.

There are, however, things that break your heart as well. By chance, in 2020, I came across a story about a man who shot and killed two young men at Montana State in 1990. The story stated that he was denied parole for the third time for the murders. This hit home with me because one of the young men that he killed was Brian Boeder, a varsity football player at Armstrong High School in the 1988-89 season. Brian graduated in 1989 and was excited to go to Montana State University in Bozeman, Montana. Brian was a great athlete at Armstrong and one of the captains of the football team his senior year. I was coaching the 9th grade football team, but Brian and I hit it off somehow, even though I wasn't directly coaching the varsity team. I remember talking to him about some of his frustrations with how the season was going. The team was struggling, and he took his responsibilities as a captain seriously. I was in a unique position where I could give him advice without any pressure on either of us, as outside of scouting upcoming opponents, I had no contact or influence over the varsity. Brian could listen to what I said, knowing it was completely meant to help him and was not an attempt to manipulate him in any way.

It was a sad day when I got the news that he had been shot in his dorm room. There were rumors that it was about a girl, but that was refuted later. It turned out that the guy who shot him thought that Brian and his friend James had vandalized his truck. This wasn't true, but the guy was high or drunk and walked into Brian's room at 2:00 AM and shot each of them twice. They both died later that morning.

The killer was convicted and sentenced to 165 years in prison. Three young men's lives were shattered that night. Three families were changed forever. And for what? A moment of stupidity? A moment of passion? A moment of I don't know what. It just makes you wonder why bad things happen to good people.

I haven't had the pleasure of having my own children, so my players were like my children. I just want to tell all my players, over thirty-seven years, just how much you meant to me, how much you still mean to me and how much you have enriched my life. I will be forever grateful.

RIP Brian.

And to the reader, you never know when tragedy may strike, so give your kids an extra hug and tell them you love them!

"It matters not how a man dies, but how he lives."
—Samuel Johnson (1709–1794)

THE BANTAM FESTIVAL

When I first started coaching hockey at Armstrong, a man named Ralph Goldhirsh got me involved in the Minnesota Amateur Hockey Association (MAHA.) This acronym was a bit problematic because both Michigan and Massachusetts went by MAHA as well, so the leaders of our association changed the name to Minnesota Hockey. This was right around the time that The Amateur Hockey Association of the United States (AHAUS) changed their name to USA Hockey. It was so much easier all around.

At any rate, Ralph was an administrator for a camp that was a precursor to the High-Performance programs. It was called the Bantam Festival and originally was held in Duluth at the University of Minnesota-Duluth. By working this Festival as a coach, I met a lot of great players over the years and was exposed to many of the best coaches in the State of Minnesota. Coaches like Don Olson, Brad Buetow, Ted Brill, Mike Sertich, Doug Woog, Paul Moen, and David Hendrickson, just to name a few. It was an incredible camp and so much fun. We would be given a roster of players on Sunday and then we would scout practices and scrimmages from Sunday to Tuesday. On Tuesday night we would hold a draft where we would pick our new team and then we would coach that team from Wednesday until Saturday. You really learned to spot talent in this type of set-up.

It was interesting to see the type of players that certain coaches liked. I tended towards blue collar, tough players who could skate well and were good teammates. Other coaches only liked the top end skill players. I also tended to lean towards the northern players, though I always tried to draft the best goaltenders early. As the years progressed, we did away with the draft. The advantage to the later system was that you had less chaos with having to move kids around the dorms and we could spend a couple more days focusing on team building.

We had most, if not all, of the best players in Minnesota come through the Bantam Festival. It was so much fun. One of the most incredible parts of camp was hanging out with the coaches at the Movillas (Mobile home student housing) at night once the players were in bed. We would have a few beers (okay, more than a few) and listen to hockey stories from legends of the game. We would talk hockey and coaching for hours. I really miss those days.

One of the coaches that I really admired was Mike Sertich, the UMD head coach at the time, I told him how much I respected him and loved the opportunity to work with him and learn from him. Mike looked at me and said, "Tommy we're peers out here. You are going to be a good coach."

I can't tell you what that did for my confidence, being a young, relatively inexperienced coach. Hearing this from a man of Sertich's legendary status was incredible. Of course, I then proceeded to skate backwards watching a drill and one of the kids had left the door open to the bench. I ran into it and fell flat on my backside. Mike skates over to check on me, laughing, he said, "You might want to make sure all the doors are closed on the rink Coach!"

Ah, coaching is a lot of ups and downs.

Later, Minnesota Hockey moved the Festival to St. Cloud and since St. Cloud State was, and is, a dry campus (no alcohol allowed), the evening hockey talk sessions were moved to DB Searle's in downtown St. Cloud. Still a lot of fun, but there was a special magic about the Movillas that couldn't be recaptured in a bar.

One note, Ted Brill also had a great impact on my life, as he did with many people involved in hockey. Ted was from Rice Street, a tough neighborhood in St. Paul. He then moved to Grand Rapids and was instrumental in helping many terrific players come out of there. Many of those players became fantastic college players, and some excellent pro players over the years. Ted passed away from cancer at the young age of 65 in 2003. He was a great man and a straight shooter. I respected him immensely.

"A man's friendships are one of the best measures of his worth."
—Charles Darwin (1809–1822)

SUMMER HOCKEY CAMPS-
MICHIGAN TECH HOCKEY SCHOOLS

My mentor Bruce Johnson, the head coach at Armstrong High School was also instrumental in many of my summer hockey jobs. The first was Michigan Tech Summer Hockey Camps in Houghton, Michigan. Houghton is located on the Upper Peninsula and is a gorgeous spot in the summer. In the winter? They get a lot of snowstorms that dump an average of 202 inches of snow per year. I worked at the summer camp for 10 years starting in 1985.

We had an Assistant Camp Director that was responsible for the coaches during the on-ice training sessions. We called him the Hawk because he watched everything we did on the ice from up in the stands, like a hawk. One night, a group of the coaches had met downtown at one of the bars and enjoyed a few adult beverages. I was a little hungover on the ice the next day. Now, seeing as I was young and spent most of my life stopping pucks, my puck handling skills were limited to begin with. On this day in between sessions, the Hawk comes down to the locker room and says, "Pearty, the next time, when you're demonstrating a drill, do it without a puck!" Really, you can't expect a lot from a recovering goaltender to begin with. The boys had a good laugh at that one. I have a lot of great memories from the camp.

"Do all the good you can, by all the means you can, in all the ways you can, in all the places you can, to all the people you can, as long as ever you can."
—John Wesley (1703–1791)

NOTRE DAME HOCKEY CAMPS

In the summer of 1995, I worked as a coach at a USA Hockey camp in Lake Placid, N.Y., where the 1980 "*Miracle on Ice*" Olympic team won the Gold Medal. One of the other coaches working the camp in Lake Placid was Tom Carroll, a longtime assistant coach at Notre Dame University. Tom encouraged Ken Pauly and I to come to Notre Dame for a week or two and work at their summer hockey camps. I had worked at Michigan Tech's hockey camp for ten years, so it was a nice time for a change. I told Tom that I was in. He hooked me up with Andy Slaggert who was the Director of the camp, he would become a good friend of mine. Later that summer, I was off to South Bend for a couple of weeks.

The 1995-96 hockey season was Dave Poulin's first year as head hockey coach at Notre Dame. He had incredible physical skills and certainly could play the game. He rarely passed up an opportunity to let the campers know about his NHL playing days. Andy Slaggert was the camp director, and through this camp I met Andy's brother Jim who has become a brother to me in so many ways. Both Jim and Andy have added greatly to my life over the past 25 years.

In addition to Andy and Jim, I also met JJ Bamberger, another coach, at Notre Dame's camp. All three of them are from Saginaw, Michigan. Who would have thought that I would meet the only three hockey big shots that Saginaw produced all at one place?

The Notre Dame camps were always fun and full of laughs. I remember one incident where a young local camper had mouthed off to Tom Carroll. Tom brought him in to Dave's office and Dave gave the young man a lecture about respect and not talking back to coaches. Dave went on to tell him about his playing days in the NHL. The little guy looked at Dave and said,

"You're a liar! You never played in the NHL!"

Tom was trying to not laugh as Dave almost blew a gasket. I would have loved to be a mouse in the corner that day. We also had Notre Dame players that would work on the ice, assisting with the camp. These players included Ben Simon, Joe Dusbabek, Sam Cornelius, and John Wrobeleski.

With Ben, you always had to get to the rink early for your session because you might have your skate laces in knots, or your gloves all taped together. Ben, together with Joe, were always looking for ways to prank the other coaches.

Before Notre Dame built Compton Arena, the team and camps skated in the Fieldhouse. There were always various camps going on. Sometimes girls' basketball or girls' volleyball. Do you know how hard it is to keep Bantam age (13-15 yrs.) boys minds on hockey when there is a plethora of teenage girls playing right next to them? We were always warning them to keep their eyes on our side of the fieldhouse. Camp was always fun and, of course, there are a few stories that wouldn't be prudent to tell!

"There is nothing in the world so irresistibly contagious as laughter and good humor."
—Charles Dickens (1812–1870)

Sports, in general, provide a unique outlook on life. I often marvel at what a small world we live in at times. The hockey world often seems to be even smaller. I have written about some Notre Dame hockey camp stories, as well as the fact that I met the two Slaggert brothers Jim and Andy. Jim, at that time was living, and working in the San Francisco Bay Area of California. He would plan his vacations so that he could come to South Bend to work the hockey camp. I started to plan my time at camp so that I would be there during the same time as Jim. Andy, a full-time assistant coach at Notre Dame, served as the on-ice director. He is a very intelligent coach and truly dedicated to the hockey program. Jim, Andy and the Slaggert family are like an extended family to me. I consider both to be my brothers.

One of the fun aspects of the Notre Dame camp included scrimmaging at night with the Notre Dame players that were staying on campus taking classes or working at the camp. They would skate with us for an hour or so and then scrimmage at quite a bit of a higher pace amongst themselves after us old guys would get off the ice. We would then all have a few beers in the locker room before heading out to The Linebacker, a local watering-hole. Sometimes we would then head downtown after socializing at the Linebacker. One night it was Ladies' Night at a nightclub on Main Street of South Bend. I don't remember the name of the club, but it was packed, and we were drinking our share of alcohol. A few of us jumped up on the stage dancing to *'Da Dip* by Freak Nasty. It was a crazy night. As Jim Slaggert, JJ Bamberger and I were driving back to the dorms, Jim said let's go to Burger King and get some food. So, I pulled into the drive-up window, and I told the young guy what the boys wanted. Then I told him I wanted a Whopper meal with milk. He said that we couldn't get milk with the meals. I started arguing with him and I said, "This is Burger King; we can get it our way."

Which was their slogan at the time. The kid started to argue with me, and I may have said some, let's say, not so nice things. The young man told us we had to leave with no food. We took off and before we left the parking lot I said,

"To heck with this, we're getting our burgers."

I pulled back to the drive-up. This time I got a diet pop with my Whopper meal, and we got our food. As we were leaving, I told the kid that the next time I come to Burger King, I want my damn milk! Oh, we were very fortunate at times. We pretty much hung out at the Linebacker because it was within walking distance of the dorms. Lots safer. It's best if I don't get into some of the other nighttime stories. You know, to protect the guilty!

Now, this is where the hockey world gets smaller. Andy is married to a Minnesota woman. Her name is Tara and her brothers Tadd and Tray Tuomie worked at the camp. One year the Tuomie's cousins Anna and Maria Richardson came to camp. This started a lifelong relationship with both. Anna played for me at the College of Saint Benedict and Maria later coached with me at Totino-Grace. I treasure both to this day. They played at Irondale High School and, ironically, are the nieces of Ric Schaefer who played at Notre Dame and was the Irish head coach from 1987-1995. I recruited Anna to come play for us at St. Benedict's. She had a solid four-year career. Maria opted to travel her own path and went to St. Olaf. After one year she transferred to St. Thomas, finishing out her college career with them. Anna had the heart of a lioness and more work ethic than anyone on the ice. Maria had the greater skill and ability and ultimately had a better career. Years later, when I was coaching at Totino-Grace, Maria started teaching in the Physical Education department and became my assistant coach. She would later succeed me as head coach but hung up her coaching whistle after giving birth to her third child. She was an excellent coach, with a great feel for the game and players. I hope she takes up coaching again.

I could go on and on about how one dot leads to another dot and so on. Years later you look back and you find yourself amazed at the people you have met, the places you have been and the experiences you have had. I can't begin to tell you how blessed I have been in my life after falling in love with the game of hockey. But it really begins with the feeling of freedom and excitement when you are skating on the ice in an arena or, even more so, outside on a frozen pond. Just the feeling of the wind rippling your jersey and hearing the sound your skates make cutting into the ice. It's almost Heaven!

Thomas H Peart

"Be silly. Be fun. Be different. Be crazy.
Be you, because life is life is too short to be anything but happy!"
—Anonymous (From Daily Inspirational Quotes)

SUMMER GOLF

If you are a hockey coach, chances are you have golfed at a summer hockey camp or in summer alumni golf tourneys. When I was coaching at Armstrong, we had the Lake Conference Golf Tourney every summer. It was an incredible time. I was out on the golf course with legends of high school hockey, including Willard Ikola-Edina, Tom Osiecki-Burnsville, Jerry Peterson-Kennedy, Tom Saterdalen-Jefferson, Bruce Johnson-Armstrong, and Ray Dahloff-Osseo. I had never golfed when I was young. My dad wasn't a golfer and only a few of my friends golfed, so I just never spent much time around the game. Besides that, it costs a lot of money to golf and it's something you need to do a lot to get good at. In addition, I thought it took way too long to golf.

Anyways, I started golfing once I started coaching and I can say that I have probably done something that a lot of coaches haven't. I accidentally hit two people on the course with my ball and nearly beaned a third person, who happened to be a very prominent coach.

The first person I accidentally hit happened during my second year at Michigan Tech Hockey Schools. Chris Limbeck, another coach at the camp, and I were golfing one beautiful morning. After my first shot, my ball was slightly left of the fairway. Chris was on the right edge of the fairway, maybe 50-75 yards ahead of me waiting to take his next shot. Somehow when I hit the ball, I sliced it terribly. The ball headed straight for Chris. I yelled fore. He watched the ball coming at him, it skipped once and glanced right off his elbow. I felt so embarrassed and horrible. We golfed again later in the week. I stopped at Chris' room to pick him up and the smart a$$ answered the door in full hockey gear, including helmet. I guess I deserved that one.

The next person I accidentally hit was while I was golfing up in Brainerd. I was working at the Minnesota Hockey Camps. For some reason the Beer Cart guy decided to drive across the fairway right when I was hitting the ball. This time, I hit the ball on a straight, hard line-drive. The ball skipped once and nailed the kid right in the leg. I ran up to check on him. He looked like he was going to drink a few beers off his cart to dull the pain, though he acted tough and said he was alright. The pain on his face told a different story.

My near miss at beaning someone happened during the Lake Conference Golf Tourney. The tournament would rotate around to different courses and during the summer of 1985, we were in Bloomington at the Minnesota Valley Country Club. It was a shotgun start with my group of four teeing off on the first hole, which was north to south. Another group, including Tom Saterdalen, the Jefferson head coach was starting on the tenth hole tee box, which was west to east. I teed off and hit the ball hard. Once again, my nasty slice took over and the ball hits one of the wooden poles next to the tee box, separating the golf cart lane from the course. The ball then flies backwards and hits a golf cart and deflects right past Tom's head as he was teeing off on the tenth hole. Tom yells,

"Who the hell hit that ball?"

I quickly looked down my fairway, like I was looking for my ball. It all occurred so fast, no one knew what just happened and thankfully they didn't know that it was my ball that almost nailed Tom. If my ball had hit him, he might not have been around to win those State Championships. Sorry Tom.

"I never make the same mistake twice. I make it three or four times,
you know, just to be sure!"
—Anonymous (Cool Funny Quotes)

MORE SUMMER HOCKEY CAMP STORIES

When you coach sports and work with kids, lots of funny things happen. One summer at Michigan Tech hockey camp, we had a week of first year squirts on the ice. These are players who are the age of 10 and under. If you have ever watched these cute little buggers on the ice, it's like watching the game PAC Man. All of them chase the puck in a swarm. Well, during one scrimmage, a little guy's cup falls out of his breezers (hockey pants.) It was black and he kicked it into one end of the rink, which caused half the kids to start chasing after the cup like it was the puck, while the other half was in the opposite end chasing the real puck. When the kids chasing the cup caught up to it, they stopped almost as one, and you could see the confusion on their faces as they realized that this was not the puck. Then they took off as one towards the other end where the actual puck was. The little guy who lost his cup didn't realize it till later. After our ice session he skated up to me and with a straight face says, "Coach, I lost my nuts."

I laughed so hard; I was almost crying. He looks at me like I'm crazy and yells, "I don't get why you're laughing; I can't find it!"

Cracked me up again. I was able to reconnect him with that oh so important piece of equipment. He never did see the humor in the situation that I did though.

Communication is important as a coach. I was working up at Minnesota Hockey Schools in Brainerd one summer and the owner Chuck Grillo (Gringo) had the Japanese National Team at camp for some training. Gringo was connected with the New York Rangers as a scout and often had pro players hanging around the camp. One of the coolest that I met was goaltender Mike Richter, who played at Wisconsin and won a Stanley Cup with the Rangers in 1994. Anyways, I was working with the Japanese goaltender, who didn't speak English and I don't speak a whole lot of Japanese. Okay, in fact none. The other problem was that the English interpreter for the Japanese team couldn't skate. During a break in drills, I was on my knees trying to explain how the goalie, Ichie, should handle a 2-1 break. I am using hand signals and holding up 2 fingers. It seemed like he understood what I was talking about and trying to show him. When practice ended, I skated off the ice and the interpreter found me. He looked at me and said, "Ichie wants to know what he is supposed to do at 2 o'clock?

I realized then that my sign language was about as ineffective as my Japanese. Remember, I spent a year in Okinawa, Japan and the best I could come up with when I left was "Domo arigato, ne." Which means thank you very much. I wish I had an aptitude for languages, well other than English that is.

"The single biggest problem in communication
is the illusion that it has taken place."
—George Bernard Shaw (1856–1950)

EVEN MORE SUMMER HOCKEY

There was a great article in the Minneapolis Star Tribune, written by Patrick Reusse about how the great Russian goaltender Vladislav Tretiak came to work at International Hockey Schools in Detroit Lakes. I also worked at that school one summer. A friend recommended the camp and told me to call John Erickson, the owner. I arranged to work for a week at the camp, and when I got there, John asked me what I usually was paid for the camps I worked at. I told him the going rate for the camps I worked. But, one thing we didn't discuss was how many hours I would be on the ice each day. The first day I was on the ice for 9 1/2 hours. At the end of the day, I could hardly walk! I talked to Scott Oliver, the coach from the Roseau/Warroad area about it that night. I told him that I didn't understand how it was that we could skate all day when we were kids without feeling tired. Why did I feel that I just went 15 rounds with Muhammad Ali? Scott looked at me and said, "Tom, we weren't as heavy back then. It makes a difference." Good point. Scott and I were about the same size, we both were six feet tall and well over 200 pounds.

Later that week, I spoke with John about the schedule, and he told me for the price I quoted him that at his camp that was a double shift. Thus, the long hours. It got better once we started playing the evening games, but those first couple of days I was hurting.

I met a goalie coach named Bill Manuel a few years later at the Dave Peterson Goalie Camp. Well, it was quite a few years later actually and as it turns out, Bill's sister Lyn was married to John Erickson. There is probably a good chance that I actually first met Bill at the International Hockey Camp, when he was a young coach just starting out. I never got to meet Tretiak though. That was a bummer. I would have loved to talk hockey with him. It never ceases to amaze me how small the hockey world is.

Bill Manuel is a great coach who is passionate about coaching goaltenders and is the boy's goalie coach at Buffalo High School, He also works with Steve Carroll at the Carroll Goalie Schools. In addition, Bill helps Steve run the Dave Peterson

Goalie Camp, taking over as General Manager after I retired. I was a coach the first year of the Dave Peterson Camp and then became General Manager, a position I held for ten years. Bill also came down to Kent State University in Ohio with me for the Mid-Am District Girls camp which was run by Yvette Anderson. We worked with some great people down there. Bill Switaj ran the arena and was the supervisor of all the summer hockey camps. Brianne Brinker oversaw the goaltenders. Former Swedish National Team coach Christian Ygnve ran the on-ice drills. In addition, we were lucky to have Eva Maria Verworner, an Austrian National team player and coach at the camp lending her expertise. I spent some great summers from 2010 to 2014 down at Kent State. Great facilities and great hockey people. First place I ever saw black squirrels as well.

"Let us be grateful to people who make us happy, they are the charming gardeners who make our souls blossom."
—Marcel Proust (1871–1922)

WALLY ODELL

Wally Odell was a very good friend of mine. He was the sole reason that I became involved with USA Hockey. Wally passed away in February of 2018 at ninety-four years young, as Wally loved to say. If you knew Wally, you knew he had a great many sayings. He was the one that got me into the habit of referring to my sisters not just by name, but by sister Lynda or sister Teri, etc. He always referred to his kids as son Rob or daughter Sue. It seemed to me a great way to delineate between family and friends.

I met Wally in 1983. I was at a Gopher Hockey game with my girlfriend and Wally and Dan Hofstrom had season tickets right behind us. We chatted during every game, and it turned out that Wally was a big shot with both Minnesota Hockey and USA Hockey. Because of Wally, I met Mike MacMillan, Bob O'Connor, Ken "Buddha" Pauly, Barry Ford, Bill McClellan and a great many friends from other states at the USA Hockey Camps that were held in Lake Placid and The Olympic Training Center in Colorado Springs.

I was also fortunate to work for USA Hockey in their development camps at Northern Michigan University, St. Cloud State and Kent State University in Ohio. These camps were just incredible opportunities to work with many of the greatest coaches and players to skate for USA Hockey over the years. Wally was the person that made decisions on which kids and coaches from Minnesota would attend these camps. He spent a great deal of time going to games and even practices scouting players. Wally used to come out to Colorado Springs and take the coaches and team leaders out to dinner at Zev's Restaurant or to Anton's Wharf in St. Cloud, as a thank you for our working with the players.

Wally grew up in Chaska and helped develop the Minnetonka and Wayzata Youth Hockey Associations. He was a lawyer and worked for Darkenwald Realty until he retired in 2016 at ninety-two. Wally liked to say that work wasn't really work if you love what you are doing. In addition to his love of hockey, Wally loved history and spoke often about one of his favorite politicians, Winston Churchill.

Wally served in the Army during World War II, and he was an avid reader. He read anything on World War I and World War II that he could get his hands on.

For a good thirty years, Wally, Dan Hofstrom, Bill Blanchard, and yours truly would spend Thursday of the Boys State Hockey Tournament together both at McGovern's and at the games. Wally loved to have a beer and talk hockey. One of Wally's famous sayings was, "Life is good, but you have to work at it!"

Here's to you Wally. Thanks for taking a young coach under your wing and helping me to become a better man through years of guidance and many great opportunities.

Love and miss you, my friend!

"A good character is the best tombstone.
Those who loved you will remember you.
They will carve your name on their hearts, not on marble."
—Charles Spurgeon (1834–1892)

MIKE MACMILLAN

In the late 80s-early 90s I met a coach that would have a huge impact on my coaching career. I first met Mike MacMillan (Mac) through USA Hockey. Mac and I worked at USA Hockey camps along with Barry Ford, Bill McClellan, and Ken (Buddha) Pauly. Mac and I would later coach against each other in the 1992 State Tourney, I was the head coach at Roosevelt and Mac was an assistant coach at New Ulm. Over the years, we have become best friends.

Mac was instrumental in hiring me at Buffalo High School, to work with his boy's program and then helped get me hired as the first head coach of the Wright County Blades girls' team. Later Mac and I worked together for Minnesota Hockey with various Select 16 teams. At one time in the late '90s USA Hockey would allow each District to choose their own team and we would play a National Tournament in Ann Arbor. There are twelve Districts in USA Hockey that represent every state in the United States. These include Minnesota, Michigan, Massachusetts, Pacific, Northern Plains, Rocky Mountain, Central, Atlantic, Mid-Am, New England, New York, and Southeastern. The tournament was held in Ann Arbor and the teams were housed at the University of Michigan. Teams were put into divisions of six and would play a round-robin segment with the teams playing off at the end of the week to determine the National Champion.

For our Select 16 teams in the late '90s, Mac was the head coach and Dick Emahiser was an assistant. I was the team leader and an assistant coach. Together, we won the National Championship two of the three years and took second in the last year. It was an incredibly fun time and brought a great deal of pride and prestige to Minnesota Hockey. We had some tremendous hockey players on those teams, including many who went on to play Division I college hockey and Pro hockey, including Jordan Leopold, Keith Ballard, Adam Houser, and others. USA Hockey then changed to their current format of having players from different states playing together. Later Mac tapped me to be the Director of the Girls High Performance Program. I owe a tremendous amount to Mac.

Mac has dedicated a large portion of his life to boys' high school hockey in Minnesota and to Minnesota Hockey. The Minnesota Hockey High Performance programs would not be the success that they are without his dedication and leadership. Mac takes criticism from others because he has so much influence in what goes on in Minnesota Hockey and now in USA Hockey, as he is the current Coach-in-Chief for all of USA Hockey. He is an incredible person. I can say that he is stubborn and opinionated, but he is extremely devoted to hockey in the state of Minnesota and across the nation.

Thank you for all you do Mac. I love you buddy!

"Hold a true friend with both hands."
—Nigerian Proverb

One of my greatest pleasures with being involved in hockey has been the Minnesota Hockey Coaches Association annual fall coaches' clinics. Over the years we have had some incredible speakers and great discussions at these clinics. I remember when a state championship coach from the previous year spoke about his power-play. He said to us, "For a successful pp, take your best puck handling defenseman and put him on the right side. Put your best shooting d on the left side, put your strongest tipper in front of the net and your best two passers down low." Just then a coach from a small school raised his hand and said, "That's great, but what do we do if our best puck handler and our best shooter and our best passer are all the same guy?" The room cracked up at that one.

During another clinic, we had Pierre Page as one of the featured speakers. Pierre was the new Minnesota North Stars head coach. He brought along a handout with ninety-nine different plays for the power play. Almost all of us agreed that our players could maybe execute three or four of those plays, most of the handout was way over our players heads.

At one clinic, there was a state championship coaches panel and someone asked Willard Ikola, Edina's legendary coach, "What is the key to your success?" Willard looked at the coach and said simply, "Get off the bus with the best players." Willard was always humble and always gave credit to his players.

At another clinic, Jeff Whisler had won the state title the year before at Hill-Murray. He was talking about the season. He told us about his wife's twin brothers Mark and Mike Strobel, who played for him. One game Jeff said that his wife had a stopwatch in the stands. When he asked her about it, she said that if her brothers don't get enough playing time, than Jeff wasn't going to get play time at home! Some of my friends have the greatest sense of humor.

I have also been fortunate to attend the American Hockey Coaches Association convention in Naples, FL on numerous occasions. My earliest memory of the

Thomas H Peart

convention was when they would have roll call and every coach in the room would stand up, state their name and what school they coached at. Every year, Mike Sertich, the UMD head men's coach would always come up with some name like "Elmer Fudd, Utah State" or something just as crazy. The whole room would crack up.

Much like the MHCA clinics there would be general discussions on various things happening in the game of hockey. One time two coaches from the state of Michigan both ridiculed Women's college hockey. One went as far as saying, "What's next, will my players have long hair and earrings?" Obviously, he forgot about the seventies and shortly after that convention, many male players started sporting various earrings and piercings. Both coaches stated that no girls would play varsity hockey at their schools as long as they were coaching. To this day, neither school has stepped up to the plate in spite of the popularity of girls and women's hockey. Proof that dinosaurs still roam the earth.

At another clinic one of the featured speakers was Mike Smith, who at that time was an assistant coach with the Detroit Red Wings. The Red Wings had the Russian Five, five extraordinary players from Russia including Sergei Fedorov, Vladimir Konstantinov, Slava Kozlov, Slava Fetisov, and Igor Larionov. Scotty Bowman, who was the head coach at Detroit, had them all on the PP together. They were working on the pp and every time one of the five had a chance to score they shot the puck wide. Scotty watched this happen four or five times when he finally blew his whistle and lost it. He yelled for a while, then called the five in and asked them, "Why are you guys missing the net on wide open shots?" Fedorov replied in his Russian accent. "Coach, we pass, we shoot, we score. You then take us off ice. We like to play!" Way too funny, but it goes back to what I have always said, it doesn't matter the age of the player, we all play hockey or other sports because they are fun.

The AHCA coaches' convention includes holding a Saturday night awards ceremony. This is when the NCAA coach of the year award is presented along with dozens of other coaching awards. It is a huge formal affair with a great meal served. When I first started going all the award winners were introduced by a friend of his or hers. This understandably got to be too lengthy as the introductions turned into a speech and then the winner would give a speech. It made for a long night. The AHCA board decided to have an MC and then limit the speeches to five minutes. Well, if you know hockey coaches, why take five minutes when you want your fifteen minutes of fame. One year, Jackie Parker was the MC and he introduced Brush Christiansen from Alaska for an award. He knew Brush from many years of coaching and Brush took his full fifteen minutes and then some. When he finished the lengthy speech, Jackie said in a deadpan voice, "Not many people to talk to up there in Alasker, eh Brush!" Yes, the room cracked up. On a side note, I have always wondered why Bostonians say "Minnersoter" or "Alasker", words that are spelled with an A at the end of the word and then say "Parkah" or "Lobstah", with words that are spelled with an er at the end of the word. It totally baffles the mind.

My last story about the AHCA clinic involves my good friend Laura Halldorson. Laura had just won her first National Title coaching at the University of Minnesota following up Shannon Miller's three in a row for the University of Minnesota-Duluth. After the Saturday night awards ceremony, the coaches would all meet at the Naples Beach Clubs outdoor bar. Shannon had convinced Laura that the winning coach was on the hook for a round at the bar for all the Women's coaches in attendance. Laura thought it would be just one round. Turns out Shannon was telling everyone that Laura was buying. Let's just say, that coaches can drink, and Laura was a bit overwhelmed when she got the bill.

"Be happy for this moment. This moment is your life."
—Omar Khayyam (1048–1131)

TIM MORRIS

I have known Tim Morris pretty much since our college days. He is a native Chicagoan and claims Chicago is the best city ever, even though he has lived in Minneapolis and Minnesota longer than his days in Chicago. I usually tell him he was a putz until he got smart and came to Minnesota. Tim and I both went to St. Cloud State. Our paths would cross many times over the years.

Tim's coaching career started in Roseville, Minnesota where he coached the Bantam A team. A team that included Winny Brodt, a pioneer in women's hockey in Minnesota. He also had a brief stint in the Fridley, Minnesota hockey program before his career took off in girls high school hockey. Tim was the first head coach at Torino-Grace High School, starting the girls' program in 1994-95. He coached at Totino-Grace for seven years. He was then named the girls head coach at Eden Prairie High School. He worked hard at Eden Prairie and turned that program into a metro powerhouse, winning two State AA Championships in 2006 and 2008 and having a fifty-three-game winning streak. Eden Prairie went to the state tournament four times, adding a third-place finish and a fourth-place finish to go with the two championships. Next, Tim went to Blaine, where as an assistant coach he helped Steve Guider lead the Bengals to two state tourney appearances. He is now back at the helm, this time with Lakeville South, where he is turning another team into a state powerhouse.

Tim's true legacy, however, is his off-ice leadership. It is his steady handling of the Minnesota Girls Hockey Coaches Association (MGHCA) and all its programs that make him one of the most influential leaders of girls' high school hockey in Minnesota. Maybe even the most influential leader. Under his guidance as Executive Director, the Minnesota Girls Hockey Coaching Association has started The Senior Classic, the highly successful fall Premier Prep League, the U-18 Festival, the MGHCA High Intensity Training Camp, the High Performance 18 Festival in conjunction with Mike Macmillan and Minnesota Hockey and the MGHCA Hall of Fame. I am proud to say that both Tim and I have been inducted into the MGHCA Hall of Fame. Tim has also been instrumental in many awards and scholarship opportunities for the young women involved in girls high school hockey, two of which honor exceptional people and coaches who have passed away. Charlie Stryker from St. Paul United and Brano Stankovsky from Blake School.

Now, life with Mr. Morris isn't always rosy! Just ask his family, fellow coaches or virtually anyone on the Minnesota Hockey Board. Tim can be very stubborn and very opinionated. I once sat at his house as he spent almost an hour trying to find a dime that was missing in the association checkbook. I was amazed and said, "Tim! It's a dime. Put a damn dime in the bank!"

In response he stated,

"No, it's here somewhere."

He stuck with it until he found the missing dime. Tim is one of the most honest people I have ever met. However, anyone who knows him, will say that some days he can be downright cranky. A real curmudgeon.

The truth is that Tim Morris is a very loyal and dedicated man to the game of hockey. He sincerely wants what's best for the game and works tirelessly to accomplish his vision for girl's high school hockey and for the association. He is also a loyal and dedicated friend to those few people that he considers close friends. He has stood behind me in the past and I appreciate that more than I can say. He also loves his family and though he has been going through a great deal with one of his grandkids battling cancer, he doesn't let that affect his coaching and his work for the association. In all honesty, Tim personifies professionalism as a coach and administrator.

Thank you for all that you have done for girls' hockey in Minnesota Tim. And guess what buddy? I love you too!

"No one who achieves success does so without the help of others. The wise and confident acknowledge this help with gratitude."
—Alfred North Whitehead (1861–1947)

MINNEAPOLIS ROOSEVELT

My first hockey head coaching job was at Minneapolis Roosevelt. I started in the 1989-90 season after I spent six years as an assistant coach at Armstrong High School. I was really excited to be a head coach. That first year started off rather auspiciously. In the summer, we lost our starting goaltender when he severely injured his knee in a car accident. He never was able to play for us. We had one remaining goaltender, a senior, and I asked the captains who on the team would make a good goaltender? They told me that Brett Olson was a great athlete, and he would fit the bill. I asked Brett to put the pads on and try playing goaltender. He gladly accepted the challenge. He eventually took over the full-time goaltending duties for the varsity team.

Before the school year began, I was invited to the Roosevelt Alumni golf tournament in August of 1989. All the players were in foursomes and the tourney began with a shotgun start. After finishing nine holes, the entire group met and had a few beers (some of them had a lot of beers.)

Next up was a barbeque for the group and a chance to meet me, the new head coach. Steve Reiter, an alum and the guy instrumental in getting me hired, introduced me to the group and asked me to say a few words. I spoke for about 5 minutes, outlining my playing and coaching background. I also told the alums that if there was anything I could do for them, let me know. Just then I hear a voice loud and clear, "How about win some more games!"

Less than a month into the job, I hadn't even met all my players yet and I was already getting heckled. Nice crowd.

That first year was a difficult one. We had seventeen players suspended throughout the season for all sorts of transgressions including drinking, chewing tobacco, and harassing girls in school. We struggled to win consistently that season due to the suspensions. Some of them were suspended by me and some by the school. I knew I had to draw a line in the sand and take control. The team culture needed to change.

One day I told my assistant Bill Taleen to run the practice, while I did something that probably wasn't 100% legal. I checked every player's coat for chewing tobacco. All but about eight guys had a tin in their pocket. Now I was faced with a conundrum. I couldn't suspend every player and really, how would I explain in the first place how I knew that they had chewing tobacco in violation of the rules, without admitting that I checked their coats? I sat down and thought about the situation for a bit. How can I make the biggest impact using my knowledge? If I simply take the tins, they will think that someone came into the locker room and stole them. If I leave them, then they won't learn the lesson. I thought about what my dad would do. My dad always had a clever way of handling these types of situations. So, I decided to dump the chew out of every tin that I found into the garbage and then put the empty tins back in their pockets. I didn't tell the players what I had done and instead waited to see how they would respond. Two weeks later I checked their pockets again while they were on the ice. Not a tin was to be found. Was I naïve enough to think that they all stopped chewing? No, but at least they were smart enough not to bring tobacco into the rink anymore. Who said that South Minneapolis boys couldn't learn things?

"What we do in life echoes through eternity."
—Magnus Maximus (335–388)

CITY KIDS ARE TOUGH

There are some stories from my time at Roosevelt that I choose to not tell, and some stories with names that I have changed to protect the innocent. Or in the case of some stories, to protect the guilty. Anyways, in addition to the seventeen suspensions during my first year, we were pulled over in the school bus twice by the police. Once when we were leaving Mound after a couple of my players used their sticks to fend off some unruly Mound-Westonka fans. A second time leaving Austin after one of my players decided it would be fun to break into the quarter toy display at McDonald's and steal some toys. Not sure why this was fun or intelligent, but there you have it. It was crazy. Thankfully, the police were fairly understanding in both situations. The team ended up doing some extra running as an attitude adjustment for these transgressions.

During a game against Southwest High School, we had one young man, Sean Lynch a sophomore, get checked into the boards awkwardly in our end. He got up and attempted to skate across the ice to our bench. When he finally got back to the bench, our trainer checked him over. As I turned to the trainer Kelly Flynn, she said to me, "His leg is broken. He is done for the game."

I looked Sean in the eye and asked him, "Sean, why did you come back to the bench? Your leg is broken. You should have just stayed down."

Calm as could be, he looked at me and says, "Coach, we had the puck on a rush, I didn't want the ref to stop the play."

Tough as nails that one. The Lynch brothers Chad, Sean and Scott, were part of the core of players that helped to turn our team culture around. All three were incredible players, with hearts as big as Minneapolis. Once the team culture changed, the winning started to happen. Our team culture before I came to Roosevelt was selfish and players didn't care about one another or winning, really. They cared about their playing time and just having fun. I needed to instill discipline and show the players that we could have fun, work hard and win, all if we bought into the team first atmosphere. Now that wasn't true of every player. We had guys like Nick Rey, Max San Roman, Brett Olson, Nick Mulvey and Derek Reiter who cared about the team and their teammates, but we needed to get the entire team moving in one direction to succeed and win consistently.

Not only were my players tough, but our cheerleaders and team managers were not someone you messed with. One night our team was playing in Hudson, Wisconsin in a game just before Christmas. The local fans were rowdy, loud and boisterous. Turns out a group of Hudson girls were harassing our cheerleaders and managers in the women's bathroom after we won the game. A group of Hudson boys joined the girls to create quite a crowd outside. With Nick Rey and Max San Roman making a path, the whole group of our girls made it out through the crowd and onto the bus without incident. Not too many people wanted to mess with Nick and Max. However, one bully from Hudson went around the outside of the crowd and decided to come onto our bus. One of my managers, we'll call her "Joy" (and she was a joy) told this idiot to get off our bus. The girl responded by swearing and carrying on. Joy told her again to get off our bus. The girl refused and so Joy punched her in the face. The girl left our bus on her backside. You do not mess with South Minneapolis women! When I got on the bus, Joy was shaking because she thought I would be mad at her. I just laughed and said, the girl had no business being on our bus. Sometimes as a coach, you have to use a little common sense when dealing with these types of situations. Joy's hand was banged up, but some ice and ibuprofen, not to mention pride at defending our team, helped ease her pain.

> *"Champions are made from something they have deep inside of them—*
> *a desire, a dream, a vision."*
> —Mahatma Gandhi (1869–1948)

THE SWEDES AND JAN THE CZECH ARE COMING

At the end of the 1989-90 season, I was talking with Steve Reiter and his son Derek, who was going to be a senior in the 1990-91 season. We were discussing a way to add to our program and give the current players a little cultural experience. Given that raising the money and going on a European trip was a bit out of reach, we decided to bring Europe to Minneapolis Roosevelt. We came up with the idea of hosting a foreign exchange student or two. Obviously, the exchange students needed to be hockey players and we needed host families to start the process. We found some parents who were willing to host a player. Both the Poepping family and the Rowland family agreed to host. Now, we just needed to find a couple of European hockey players. And find them, we did. Henrik Svensson from Linkoping, Sweden, was a big, tough, great skating defenseman, who could move the puck really well. He was also a smart, heads-up player with a terrific shot from the point. The second player was Johan Svensson from Sundsvall, Sweden. Johan was a smaller but quick player who could read the game well. He was a playmaking forward who had a good shot and was a great passer.

In my second season at Roosevelt 1990-91, we improved to 12 and 12 from a record of 8-12-1 the previous season. I was selected as the Section 5 Coach of the Year. I would like to take credit for this award, but it was really due to two things. First, the players bought into our system of play, which included playing with more discipline. Secondly, Henrik and Johan added to our depth and to our team culture of playing hard, fast and with discipline. It was a great cultural experience for my inner-city boys to meet someone new, from another country. I am sure that the Minneapolis boys introduced the two Swedes to rap music and city living.

Both of the Swedes were quiet and shy at first, at least around me, although Henrik really came out of his shell quite a bit as the season progressed. They both were great to become acquainted with and taught us about the Swedish culture that they grew up in. On the ice, Henrik had thirteen goals and nineteen assists for thirty-two points and Johan had thirteen goals and seventeen assists for thirty points. As I said, they added to our team a great deal both on and off the ice.

The next year 1991-92, Per-Erik Karlsson arrived from Sweden. He wasn't as skilled as his Swedish predecessors; he was just happy to be on the team and get a shift every now and again. This was the year we made it to the Minnesota state high school tournament. Unfortunately, Per didn't get in the first state tournament game due to the circumstances of the game, a 2-1 loss in overtime to Rosemount. Before the second game of the tournament, he forgot his maroon socks at home. I asked him if his host family could bring them, but they were busy, so he didn't suit up for that game. Alas, he didn't get into the consolation championship game either. A 4-3 overtime win over Mahtomedi. He told me he had fun anyway with the whole experience.

In my fourth and fifth years 1992-93 and 1993-94, we had a foreign exchange student from the Czech Republic, Jan Skorepa. (Jan the Czech) Jan was a highly skilled, great skating player from a little town outside of Prague called Vsestudy. He was a very good scorer for us and had thirty-one goals and forty-seven assists for seventy-eight points in his two years with us. He stayed with Scott and Barb Godin, who I became great friends with. Scott and I even had the chance to go visit Jan the Czech and his parents in the Czech Republic. I was coaching in Guildford, England during the 1994-95 season and we went after that season was over. It was an awesome trip. I also had the chance to go visit Henrik and his family in Sweden in 2017. Another fantastic trip. My Roosevelt teams certainly benefited immensely from having these foreign exchange students skating for us, but the experiences off the ice were just as great, especially getting to know the players and many years later, their families.

Ha en bra dag. (Have a nice day) A little Swedish for my boys in Sweden.

"My country is the world, and my religion is to do good."
—Thomas Paine (1737–1809)

A GOOD TEAM STARTS IN THE GOAL

I was working at a USA Hockey camp in Marquette, Michigan in the summer of 1990. It was a national goaltender camp with the best goalies from all over the USA meeting for a week of training. Jeff Jackson, who now is the head coach at Notre Dame University was the head coach of the camp. I was one of the assistant coaches. Jeff asked me to meet with him. In our meeting, he told me that he had a high school age goaltender from Ohio who was exceptional and needed a place to play. Did I know of a school that was looking for a goaltender? Ironically, Minneapolis Roosevelt needed a goaltender. Andy Kruppa was the goalie's name. He lived in Bowling Green, Ohio where his dad Richard was a professor at Bowling Green University. Andy enrolled at Roosevelt and moved in with the San Roman family. He helped take the Roosevelt team to new heights. He was an incredible talent and an even better person, but probably the best thing he did was take our two young goaltenders, Mike Grover and Shawn Haroldson, and help teach them to be better goaltenders and better people.

Since Andy had transferred in, by Minnesota State High School League rules he had to play on the junior varsity for most of that season. He became eligible for varsity towards the end of the regular season and into the playoffs. We played Benilde-St. Margaret's in the Section 5 playoffs that year. And as fate would have it, Andy forgot his skates at home. Ken "Buddha" Pauly, a very good friend of mine, agreed to delay the start of warmups a few minutes until Andy's skates arrived. Holy Angels had beat Willmar 10-2 in the earlier game and went into running time, so we had some extra time for Andy's dad to rush to the San Roman's and get his skates. We were the last game on that day and that gave us some leeway. I told Andy that he owed it to his teammates to stand on his head in goal. He did just that, playing one of the best games I had seen him play up to that point. We beat Benilde-St. Margaret's 3-1 to move us into the quarterfinals where we would face Jefferson. Buddha still kicks himself for that game, saying that he shouldn't have allowed us to delay the start of warm-ups by a few minutes.

We ended up losing to Jefferson to end our season, but we had eight players finish with twenty or more points that year. During my first year we only had three. The next year we made the state tournament. Andy had the game of his life in the Section 5 Championship game, and he played phenomenally in the state tournament, helping us win the consolation title. Andy left us the next year before his senior year. He decided to attend Northwood Prep School in Lake Placid, New York. This school is known as a hockey factory, providing a great number of players with an opportunity to play Division I hockey and has had at least thirteen players make it into professional hockey. The school also had a schedule that included sixty plus games a year. This was a chance for Andy to improve his game and move up the hockey ladder. He attended Colby College in Maine and was a four-year letterwinner.

We had a lot of success in my five years at Roosevelt. We won a Section 5 title, a State Consolation title, a City Conference title, and a great number of games. However, the thing I am most proud of is how we did academically. We won the Section 5 Academic Championship twice and took second a third year by a fraction of a point. And before you say it's easier at Roosevelt than it is for our competition at Blake, Breck, Southwest, Jefferson, or Benilde-St. Margaret's, think about the motivation necessary to be successful academically in an inner-city school. My players faced adversity everyday they went to school, including the adversity of people not believing they could be good students, classmates who didn't value studying or going to class and some teachers who didn't give them credit for working hard. I was damn proud of my boys. I still am. Andy Kruppa is a successful lawyer in Miami, Chad, Sean and Scott Lynch were all pilots in the United States Air Force. Mike Grover is a chef out in California, Tony and Max San Roman became a policeman and a fireman respectfully, in Minneapolis. Tony Rich is a fireman in St. Paul, Chris Chelberg spent 30 years in the Navy and Henrik Svensson is back in Sweden where he has a beautiful family and still skates. I really could go on bragging about my boys, but you would all get bored.

> *"One secret of success in life is for a man to be ready*
> *for his opportunity when it comes."*
> —Benjamin Disraeli (1804–1881)

THE MAGICAL THIRD SEASON

On the first day of school in 1991, I received a call at the elementary school I was teaching at. It was my athletic director Eric Magdanz and he said, "Tom, please come over to Roosevelt as soon as you can."

I asked what was going on, but he told me that he would explain when I got to the school. I drove over to Roosevelt and met Eric and Barb Belair, the school Principal in her office. They told me that one of my players, Shawn Haroldson, a fifteen-year-old freshman had just been shot and killed on the way home from school. He and a twelve-year-old friend were playing with a handgun when the friend accidentally shot Shawn. As a coach, you deal with a lot of heartaches and ups and downs in a season. One thing you aren't prepared having to deal with is the death of one of your players.

We had a team meeting that weekend and the players decided to honor Shawn by wearing a patch of his number on our jerseys and by hanging his jersey on our bench during games.

That season we started out a little slow, going 3-3 in our first six games, and then won twelve out of the next sixteen games. We co-hosted a Holiday Tournament with Edison that December, and at the end of the tourney, the Edison statistician Steve came you to me and said, "Mr. Peart, when you go to the state tournaments, can I do your stats?"

Now, it's Christmas and we were 5-3 at the time, so I said, "Sure Steve." I thought he would forget by the time the Section tournament came around and who knows how good we would be by February, but the team turned things around and we ended the regular season with a record of 14-7-1.

This was the first year of the Tier I/Tier II setup in the Minnesota boys high school hockey. In this system, all schools would be seeded by the Sections coaches from 1-8, this would be the schools that competed in the Tier I tournament. The rest of the schools from 9-17 or 18 would compete in the Tier II tournament. We were seeded 10th in Section 5.

We played Minneapolis South in the quarterfinals and beat them 5-1. We then played Minneapolis Washburn in the semi-finals, and we had a 3-0 lead in the third period. It was a very physical game. We took a penalty late in the period. I kept my best players on our bench during the penalty kill, as I thought we could kill it off and didn't want any of my top players getting hurt and potentially missing the championship game. Washburn scored and shortly thereafter, we were assessed another penalty. I again kept my best players on the bench and Washburn scored again. Great coaching, right? My top line of Sean and Scott Lynch and Chad Bennett jumped onto the ice before their bonehead coach could say a word. They kept us ahead the rest of the way, and we won the game 3-2.

We then played Holy Angels in the section finals the next Wednesday at the Met Sports Center to determine who would go to the state tournament. One thing about coaching is that you have just as many nerves as the players, but not as many tangible ways to expel those nerves. It was very exciting to play at the Met Sports Center, big enough to seat 15,000 fans. The kids were in awe and played with more nerves than skill through the first half of the game. We would have gotten run out of the building if not for our goaltender Andy Kruppa. Andy, who had dedicated his season to Shawn, played the game of his life.

We were a young team that year with only four seniors. We basically played two lines, spotted a third line and played three D spotting two sophomores. One of our senior captains, Jason Bennett, had a tough game, giving up the puck on several occasions and falling on a three on two opportunity by Holy Angels. Jeff Burton and Rob Anderson, but of course Andy Kruppa were there to back him up and keep the puck out of the net. At the midway point in the second period, we were trailing 3-1. I noticed that our whole bench was quiet, including the coaches. This was not good. I felt that if Holy Angels scored again, we would definitely lose the game. I grabbed my assistants, Bill Taleen, Mike Mulvey and Mark Bergum and told them that I didn't care what they said, just keep talking positively to the kids. Keep them up. We started to gain momentum scoring a second goal towards the end of the second period to make the score 3-2 in favor of Holy Angels.

In the locker room between the second and third periods we talked to the kids about leaving everything on the ice in the third period, that our whole season was dedicated to Shawn, and it was time to win the game. We went out, tied up the game and scored the winning goal, not once but twice. The first goal was called off because the referees determined that the puck was directed in off a skate. When I complained to the referees, Sean Lynch turned to me and told me, "Don't worry coach, we're going to score again!"

I knew right then that destiny was on our side. Confidence definitely was. And sure enough we did score again off a beautiful passing play between Sean and Scott Lynch, who always seemed to know where the other was on the ice. The third member of that line, Chad Bennett crashed the net to put in the game winner and the whole Roosevelt section went crazy.

I remember thinking of the 1980 Olympic "Miracle on Ice" game against the Russians and the guys on that team saying how long the last 10 minutes felt like. Ours was only a little over 5 or 6 minutes, but it felt like a lifetime. When the final horn went off and the celebratory hugs were going on, I looked up in the stands and was amazed at the size of the crowd. Sure, it wasn't a full house, but my boys had never played in front of that many people ever before. It was an incredible feeling and really, one of the greatest nights of my life. I know my players carry that win with them to this day. It was one of my proudest moments as a coach, maybe the proudest. We had won the Section 5 championship 4-3. I remember thinking about the whole season and how tough it had been. I really feel that both Shawn Haroldson and my dad. who died the previous February were looking down on us and imagined that they both gave us a big emotional push.

As I walked off the ice there was Steve from Edison,

" Mr. Peart! Remember, you said I could come with you to the state tourneys as your statistician."

I just laughed and said, "Yep Steve, I remember. You're coming with us!"

We then played in the big show, the Minnesota Boys high school hockey tournament. The dream of every kid growing up playing hockey in Minnesota. We made it!

The South Tigers followed us in 1993 and Edison in 1994. And twenty-eight years later, it was 2022 and the Minneapolis boys were heading to state not as an individual school, but as one combined team for all the Minneapolis schools. Maybe there is hope for Minneapolis hockey yet.

"Every great dream begins with a dreamer.
Always remember you have within you the strength, the patience,
and the passion to reach for the stars to change the world."
—Harriet Tubman (1822–1913)

THE TEDDIES PLAY AT THE CIVIC CENTER

The week leading up to the State Tourney's was incredible. We were so giddy, and our practices were sharp and upbeat. The school was buzzing. It had been fourteen years since Bucky Freeburg, the awesome long time former Roosevelt coach had brought the last Teddie team to state. Although, this would be the ninth state tournament appearance for Roosevelt, sadly it almost certainly will be the last, as all seven of the Minneapolis schools are now combined into one team representing the city.

As I have written earlier, this was the first year of the two-tier system for boy's high school hockey. Many of the traditionalists across the state wanted the Minnesota State High School League (MSHSL) to keep the previous system of eight sections and all the teams in the state competing in one state tournament and for one championship. There was a group of coaches and parents however, who lobbied for more opportunities for their players. The MSHSL decided to let the Minnesota Hockey Coaches Association come up with a plan. For the first two years, the Tier One-Tier Two system was in effect. The top eight teams, as ranked by the coaches in each of the eight sections, would play for the Tier One championship. The teams ranked nine through sixteen or seventeen would play for the Tier Two Championship. Now before anyone poo-poos our tourney appearance as being less meaningful than the other appearances by Roosevelt teams, to my boys and coaches, this was an incredible experience. No different than if it was only eight teams playing. And we had never played in front of so many people. My boys never once said, "Oh look, the arena is half empty!"

They were excited to play their hearts out at the St. Paul Civic Center.

The first game against Rosemount was a classic goaltending battle between Andy Kruppa and the Rosemount goaltender Corey Jorgenson. Play was up and down the ice. Chad Thier opened the scoring for us in the first and we led 1-0 until about forty-three seconds left in the game. With about one minute to go, I called timeout and instructed the boys to go to a one-man forecheck. Unfortunately, we were always so aggressive that two of my guys got caught deep and the third player got beat at our attacking blue line. Then, to further complicate things, one of our defenders caught an edge in the ice and fell in the neutral zone. Rosemount had a three on one. Andy initially saved the puck, but it then slowly rolled down his arm and into the net. At that same moment, I heard a whistle from the referee right next to our bench. I thought he saw that Andy had the puck secured in his equipment and had determined that the play was dead. The referees then conferred and called it a goal. When I questioned the referee, he stated that they now blow the whistle when goals are scored. Still doesn't explain why he, the referee furthest from the goal, blew his whistle as there was no way for him to see the puck go in the net and make that call. That play stood as the tying goal. I have called referees blowing the whistle when goals are scored "The Teddie Rule" from that point on, as this was the first time, ever, that they blew the whistle on goals.

We lost the opening face-off to start the overtime and the Irish broke in on a three on two. They scored 20 seconds into OT to win the game. I didn't watch the replay of that game for ten years after that tournament. When I did, I was amazed at how well we played. We basically outplayed Rosemount for all of the game with the exception of the final minute. It all came down to two plays that unfortunately didn't go our way and plays that did go right for Rosemount. The Irish had a great tournament, they made it to the Championship game where they lost to Greenway-Coleraine.

My Teddies came back to beat New Ulm 5-1 in the first game of the consolation bracket. We then beat Mahtomedi in overtime to 4-3 to win the Consolation championship. It was the perfect end to an extraordinary season, one that started with heartbreak, but culminated with an incredible lifelong experience of making it to the state tournament.

I had tremendous leadership on that team, starting with goaltender Andy Kruppa, my top two defensemen Jason Bennett and Jeff Burton, and my top line of Sean Lynch, Scott Lynch and Chad Bennett. However, this season was a success because it was a total team effort all the way through the lineup. Guys like Ron Starr, Rob Anderson, Tony San Roman, Derrick Rollins, Justin Anderson, Dave Byhre, Mike Ogdahl, Tony Rich, Chad Their, Dave Farwell and Ryan Kriech.

Even our backup goaltender, Mike Grover kept pushing Andy all year to be the best goaltender he could be. It was a true joy to coach that team.

There was one incident that demonstrated the kind of leadership I had on this team. One of my players, I'll call him "Harry", took a needless penalty in the first period of our game against Rosemount in the state tournament. He was just over excited, I believe. We killed off that penalty and as Harry came back to the bench, I told him we didn't want to be killing penalties against this team, so stay out of the box. On his next shift Harry jumps over the boards and skates straight across the ice and runs the player carrying the puck. He gets his second penalty in just over four minutes. We again kill the penalty off and when Harry comes back to the bench, I say in a much louder voice, "Harry! Stay out of the box!"

Harry turns to me and starts mouthing off. Before I can say another word, Scott Lynch pivots, punches him right in the face mask and yells, "Stay out of the box and don't talk back to coach!"

I thought, *"Yep. What he just said."* No more penalties out of Harry that day. By the state tournament, the leaders on our team had handled a lot of team issues before they ever got to me. They were a remarkable group of young men. Jason Bennett had a phenomenal state tourney and made the All-Tournament team. Also on the All-Tournament team was Scott Lynch, who led the Tier II tournament in scoring with four goals, and five assists for nine points in the three games.

"A team is a group of people with different abilities, talents, experiences, and backgrounds who have come together for a shared purpose. Despite their individual differences, that common goal provides the thread that defines them as a team."
—Andrew Carnegie (1835–1919)

THE TEDDIES VS. THE JAGUARS

After our extraordinary run to the state tournaments the previous year, we had another good season in which we won the Minneapolis City Conference Championship and were primed for another run at the State Tournament. It would come down to the Section seed meeting. This would be the second year of the Tier I-II system. After this experiment was completed the Minnesota State High School League then decided to go with a Class A and Class AA system with school enrollment being the determining factor in which class every school would fall into.

The seed meeting for Section Five was always held at Parade Ice Gardens in Minneapolis. During the meeting, before the seeding each individual coach could talk about their team, good or bad. Most coaches talked up their team, but occasionally a coach would sandbag the other coaches to try and get a different play-off opponent.

There was a coach, who I will call "Don Penguin." Don always, and I mean ALWAYS, complained, and whined about how his team was better than where he anticipated that they would be seeded, during those meetings. He did this year after year. During the 1992-93 season, we ended up being seeded eighth, the bottom team in Tier I. Don's team was ninth. During that season, Don's team not only beat us, but they won their conference. They also had a better overall record than we did. Add in that they won the head-to-head game and logic would have it that Don would have something positive to say about his team, right? Nope. Not a peep. He kept his mouth shut because he wanted the number one seed in Tier II, with a chance to go to the state tournament. Of course, the number eight team would be facing the number one team in the section in the Tier I section tournament, which was the undefeated Jefferson Jaguars. An unenviable position, to say the least.

When it came my turn to talk about my team, I looked at Don and said, "Hey Don, aren't you going to say anything about how your team is better than mine?"

He just looked down. I refused to put my team down and I talked about how we were getting better, peaking at the right time, etc. We ended up eighth and Don's team ended up ninth. A couple of my friends asked why I didn't make a big stink about it, but what coach wants to shoot his kids down and not give them a chance to play the best team in state, right? Karma intervened though. Don's team lost in the section tournament and did not make it to the state tournament. Minneapolis South went on to play in the big show in St. Paul.

On the way home, I started to plan how to face the Jaguars and I panicked. I mean we are taking Nick Checco, Mike Crowley, Joe Bianchi, Brian LaFleur, Mark Parrish, Josh DeWolf, their whole lineup was awesome. My greatest fear was that we would get blown out 20-0. When I arrived at home, I called all my coaching buddies, Bruce Johnson, Ken (Buddha) Pauly, Mike MacMillan and Larry Hendrickson. How should we, how could we play with them? After getting my friends input, I came up with a game plan. I told my guys,

"Honestly, we can't skate with them. If they get skating full speed, it will be ugly. We need to do something to disrupt their flow."

The plan I came up with was to keep the puck out of the middle of the rink. Every puck should be played on the side boards and if you don't have a play, ice the puck. In the first period we iced the puck at least 19 times. Jefferson was frustrated, and completely out of any kind of flow. Head coach Tom Saterdalen was glaring at me, while assistant coach John Bianchi had a knowing look on his face. He knew why we were doing what we were doing. The Jaguar players were slamming their sticks on the ice and on the boards. They were downright angry. It was incredible to see my boys battling so hard under adverse conditions.

We got out shot that day 63-7. But we held the mighty Jags scoreless until halfway through the game. They won 6-0, but that was a moral victory for us, one we could live with. My buddy Nick Checco had a hat trick in the first period all waved off because each time the goal was dislodged before the puck went in. Very fortuitous for us. And my goaltender, Mike Grover stood tall with 57 saves.

Nick and Mike Crowley were two of the greatest hockey players I have ever seen play high school hockey. The Jags finished the season undefeated and won their second of three straight state championships. On that team from 1992-1993, 10 players played DI, one more played Major Juniors. 5 more played DIII and 2 played Juniors and then ended their careers. 9 players on the team played Pro Hockey at some level. They were incredible.

Although I was happy with how we played against Jefferson. It was still a sad time for me, as Scott Lynch and Jeff Burton both finished their high school playing careers that day. But I was extremely proud of all my boys and extremely happy that my biggest nightmare didn't come true.

"Our greatest glory is not in never falling, but in rising every time we fall."
—Confucius (551 BC – 479 BC)

PARENTS ARE TRULY UNBELIEVABLE

Okay, I was being a bit facetious with the title of this one. I ran into Herb Boxer at the State Tournament. I met Herb at Michigan Tech Hockey Schools. He was the former Head Coach at Tech and was doing some scouting for the pros the year we won the Section 5 title. Herb came to our Section title game and since he was staying at the Thunderbird Hotel next to the Met Sports Center, he stopped in the bar for a couple of cocktails. While he was there, he ran into a couple of Roosevelt parents celebrating our win. He started talking to one mother and in Herb's words, she ripped me up one side and down the other because her son, who was a senior, should have played more or so she felt. She said that I certainly didn't know what I was doing or how to coach. Now, I know what you're thinking. I was thinking the same thing. We had just won the Section title for the first time in 14 years, something that no one expected when I took over the program just three years before. Herbie laughed and told me that he started to defend me at first, but then he said to himself, "*Why should I do that? This could be fun!*"

Instead, he said, "Yeah, he sounds like a jerk." Ah, good friends love to rip on each other.

One of my first lessons in coaching when I started at Armstrong was that certain parents would rip on the coaches if they were unhappy about playing time or what position their kid was playing. This led me to always deliver a major message to the players' parents at the beginning of the season meeting. "A parent's focus is their son or daughter. That's good, but as a coach, my focus is on all of my players and that will always be the first factor when I am making decisions." I always factored all players into my decisions that effected the team.

"Don't be afraid of losing people.
Be afraid of losing yourself by trying to please everyone around you."
—Unknown (From fabquote.co)

SOME EXTRAORDINARY PEOPLE

I was extremely fortunate at Roosevelt, to be able to build a program and have some success while doing so. And I have been lucky throughout my life to work with many, many great people. They far outweighed the people that made the job difficult. At Roosevelt I met a man who has remained a friend for the past thirty-four years. His name is Steve Reiter, and he is an Alum who helped get me the job. Steve was one of the parents on the committee chosen to select the new coach and he had the principal's trust and the ear of the athletic director. They listened to him, and he believed in me. He felt that I was the best choice of the seven coaches that applied for the job. Steve bleeds Roosevelt maroon and gold. He even got after me when I had our white jerseys made and he believed that there wasn't enough gold in the jersey. Steve's son Derek was a good player for us. He played with a lot of heart and was a good leader on and off the ice. Derek played college hockey at Augsburg. Steve was a great player back in the late '60s and early '70s, earning All-City Conference honors in 1970.

My first year at Roosevelt was tumultuous, and an up and down year. We had a lot of unique things happen to us that year, but the best thing that happened to me was meeting the Lynch clan. Laura, Denny, Chad, Sean and Scott. All three boys were Captains at one point in the careers with me. Laura, their mom, was an exceptional nurse and Denny, their dad, was a Viet Nam vet who worked at the VA Hospital. The boys? Well, I can't say enough about how skilled, driven and tough all three of them were. They are the kind of men you want with you if you are in in a difficult spot. They are loyal and never give up. They were three of the most competitive players I have ever had the pleasure of working with. They were incredible. All three attended the University of St. Thomas and went into the ROTC Program. All three were pilots in the Air Force after graduating from UST. I remember talking to Laura just after the terrible events on 9/11 and she was nervous that her boys could be in harm's way. Sort of a *Saving Private Ryan* situation. If you remember the movie, A group of Army Rangers are trying to find Private James Ryan after three of his brothers had already been killed in action. At the time, Sean was flying an AWACS plane, Chad was flying troop transport planes and Scott was flying something so secret that he couldn't tell his folks what he was flying or where he would be going. Laura worried about her boys, but thankfully they all made it through that period of time safely and are thriving in their personal lives. Sean is now a commercial pilot and lives in Florida, Chad went into coaching and lives in Iowa and Scott, I believe, is still in the Air Force. Incredible people and a family, I hold in high esteem.

In addition to the Lynch brothers, one of my best players and captains was Jason Bennett. I have always respected Jason for his dedication, desire and toughness. He currently is married and lives on the east coast. The last I heard, he was in some form of sales and loved going fishing and golfing. He was an exceptional player for us. His mother Kris was one of those incredible parents that make hockey worth coaching. She was instrumental in helping us build the kind of culture I wanted by assisting with anything the coaching staff needed. She was a great supporter and a great person.

Don't get me wrong, we had a great deal of additional talent on that State Tournament team along with the two younger Lynch's Sean and Scott, we had Jason Bennett and Andy Kruppa. We had one of the best D around in Jeff Burton, who is now coaching Juniors in Montana. We also had a defenseman that played solid for us all year in Rob Anderson, a bright, young winger named Chad Bennett (no relation to Jason) who helped make us an incredible team and a group of sophomores that rounded out the team. Ron Starr, Mike Ogdahl, David Byhre, Justin Anderson, Tony Rich, Mike Grover and Dave Farwell. We also had one of the toughest kids around in Tony San Roman, who is now a Policeman in Minneapolis. And Derek Rollins, who was one of the most intelligent players on a very intelligent team. We won two Section 5 Academic Championships and missed the third by .3 % points. It was the most incredible experience of my coaching career. Mostly because no one gave these boys from South Minneapolis a chance or any credit. But we proved to the world that we could compete and win!

> *"Do what you can, with what you have, where you are at."*
> —Theodore Roosevelt (1858–1919)

ROOSEVELT SOCCER

I had the distinct pleasure of coaching soccer at Roosevelt during the fall of 1993. My players were an incredible group of young, ordinary soccer players. My athletic director, Eric Magdanz asked me to coach the girls' soccer team on an interim basis. We had a very inexperienced team. Our best overall player was an 8th grader, but our leadership came from a couple of great seniors including one of my favorite people of all time, Sarah Cedarblade. If this was a Disney movie, we would have lost until we came together to first win the City Conference Championship and then make it to the state tournament, right? The Mighty Ducks deal and all that. But you know what? This wasn't a movie and, though we did come together and played with intensity as a team, it didn't show with wins or goals on the scoreboard.

My buddy Bill Kelly was my assistant coach, and he ran the practices. He assessed our talent and summarized our team strategy. We played defense and had a floater, who could score if she got loose, but that was the extent of our offensive prowess.

My main responsibility was to do team building and deal with some of the crazy issues that tend to arise in South Minneapolis kids' lives. Have you seen the Keanu Reeves movie "Hardball?" It was about a compulsive gambler who kept struggling with his need to make the big score. He ends up coaching a youth baseball team in the projects of Chicago. It was a very touching movie, and one line really moved me. It reminded me of my one time soccer crew. Reeves is talking to the team, and he tells them that he is blown away by their ability to just show up day after day. And that's how I felt about my girls. They weren't going to win; they definitely weren't going to the state tournament. Yet they showed up. Everyday. They showed up and worked hard, had fun and pulled for each other as if they were the best team in the world. They were incredible and so much fun to be around. I was sad it was such a short season. I have lost touch with all of them, save for Sarah, who went through some tough times when she lost her husband. However, I knew she would pull through. She is awesome and tough and a true blue South Minny gal. I Love you kiddo!

Thomas H Peart

"The way you see people is the way you treat them, and the way you treat them is what they become."
—Johann Wolfgang von Goethe (1749–1832)

BRITISH ICE HOCKEY LEAGUE

I realized in the spring of 1994 that with my class of seniors about to graduate, the Roosevelt hockey cupboard was going to be quite bare. These seniors were the group of sophomores from our state tournament team from 1991-1992. Coincidently that summer I ran into a good friend of mine from my time at Michigan Tech's hockey school. His name is Mike O'Connor, and he played professional hockey in England. I explained how I was looking for a new experience in my coaching career. Mike sent me some information on teams in England and I contacted several of them inquiring about their coaching openings.

I ended up connecting with a team that was supposedly starting that fall in Leeds, which is in the Midlands of England. My coaching contract was going to be for three years, but things were a bit discombobulated from the start. They said that they had sent the contract in the mail, but no contract arrived prior to my flight over to London. Next, the General Manager of the team said he would meet me at the airport with a work permit and a check to reimburse me for my flight over there, but that didn't happen.

On the flight to England, I met two Canadian hockey players, and we got to talking. It turns out that they were going to play on the team I was going to coach. However, they didn't receive their contracts prior to leaving either. The three of us were new at this, so we trusted that things would work out. Boy, were we wrong.

After we landed, we all were in line at customs. I let the boys go first in the line, following right behind them. The agent asked them what their reason was for coming to England and they said that they were there to play pro hockey. But there was no one from the team meeting us, nor any work permits from the team. The Customs Agent told both of them that they had to leave the country on the next plane out of London. Next up was yours truly. What does any intelligent hockey coach do when posed with the same question after the two ahead of him get booted out of the country, knowing there is no work permit for him either?

The Customs Agent looked at me and asked, "Why are you here Mr. Peart?". I responded with, "I'm visiting!"

It was quite disconcerting to be in the airport and wonder what was going on with the team from Leeds. I called the number that I had for them, and it was disconnected. It occurred to me that I was now in England, and I would need to sort things out for myself. I didn't find anything else out about the group from Leeds. Supposedly they couldn't get an arena built, but I never heard from them again.

I had some friends in Plymouth in the southwest corner of England, so I rented a car and headed to Plymouth. Once there, I contacted Mike in Sheffield, and he introduced me to his coach Alex Dampier. Alex was a well-known coach in Canada and England and had contacts all over Europe. Alex lined me up with an interview with the Guildford Flames, a team located in County Surrey. By the time that they hired me, the team was into their second month of play and was losing quite regularly. I signed on for a salary of 125 pounds per week. At that time, it was about $250. I also had use of a team car and a flat in rural Godalming, about fifteen minutes outside of Guildford. It was a tremendous year of growth for me and an incredible experience.

"If there is no struggle, there is no progress."
—Frederick Douglas (1818–1895)

COACHING IN ENGLAND-THE GUILDFORD FLAMES

I spent one year with the Flames. After taking over the team in the second month and close to fifteen points out of a play-off spot, we started out on a positive note with a 26-5 win over Lee Valley, a team on the north side of London. I felt like Dorothy in the Wizard of Oz. You're not in Minnesota anymore Toto. The imports all had incentive bonuses built into their contracts. Goals, assists, points and plus/minus stats. Thus, when you have a team down by five or more goals, you kept firing the puck and scoring goals. It would put more money in their pockets.

Plus, the supporters loved lots of goals. They would rather have a 9-8 win, than a 2-1 win. It was so hard for my goaltender, defensive minded, mentality.

During my first home game with the team, I came into the locker room. I looked around and I asked one of the lads,

"Where's Andy? Where's Nicky?"

"Oh, they are out back having a fag." *What?*

I went down the hall to the back door to the arena and there's my two guys, three guys from the opposing team and the referees, all smoking cigarettes. Geez Louise, it was a weird culture shock.

Hockey in England was certainly different than what I grew up with and was used to. In the 1994-95 season there was three divisions with the Premier Hockey League being the top league with twelve teams, the British Hockey League was next with fourteen teams and the English Hockey League, the lowest league had twenty-three teams. Teams were located all over Great Britain from Scotland to Wales and all places in-between. The interesting thing was that the Premier League which had the oldest, most skilled players mostly played in the older arenas. The British League which I coached in, had newer and nicer arenas. The English league was more of an adult hockey league. Another fact that was different than the USA, was that practices were late at night, from ten to midnight, as all of our British lads had other jobs to supplement their hockey careers. They didn't make enough playing hockey alone. All the imports were paid well and worked in some capacity for the club. They either worked in the front office, coached youth teams or worked in promotions. Some of the promotions included classes for the supporters, theme nights for games and merchandise sales.

We had five imports on our team. That is, three actual imports that were working with work permits and then two that had been living and playing in England for over ten years, so they no longer needed a work permit. The challenge for a coach was that at that time you had to always have three British players on the ice. Usually, your goalie was British. When you were given a penalty or two, then things got interesting. I only was caught once during the entire season with too many imports on the ice, which resulted in another penalty. We were playing one of our rivals in Swindon and we took a penalty, then we took another penalty, so we were down by two men. I sent out an import. And sure, enough, we received another penalty. I think we lost that game 5-3 that day and two of the goals came during that 5 on 3 situation.

We had a few great players at Guildford. Our best was Fred Perlini from Sault Ste. Marie, Ontario. He was big, fast and had an incredible shot. Freddie played in England for over ten years and had seventy-eight goals and fifty-seven assists in forty-four games during the time I coached the Flames. Certainly, Wayne Gretzky like numbers. He was phenomenal and any time we needed a goal Fred seemed to get it for us. Fred had played for the Toronto Maple Leafs for parts of two seasons prior to coming to the United Kingdom. Fred and his wife Vickie had two sons. Brett who played at Michigan State and is back living and playing pro hockey in Europe, and Brendan who has been playing professionally for four years and is currently playing in the American Hockey League.

I remember one game we were playing on a Sunday afternoon and those of you who know me, know I have a cup of coffee or two before the game and then another one in-between periods. Of course, with water on the bench, I usually had to use the bathroom between periods. After the first period, I talk to the boys, they head out to the ice, and I stop in the bathroom. I hear a noise at the door, but I don't really register the noise. I washed my hands and wouldn't you know it, the door is locked. No way to open it. I pound on the door for about two minutes and then hear over the loudspeakers,

"Will someone please free the Guildford coach from the loo? (British for bathroom) Thank you." The lads and the fans had quite the laugh as I made my way to the bench. Needless to say, I was a little quicker on potty breaks from then on.

One of the greatest aspects of coaching in England was the traveling. As the reader can tell from my stories, I love to travel. With Guildford I was able to journey a great deal throughout the British Isles. We played games in Scotland in Dumfries, Paisley, a suburb of Glasgow, and Murrayfield, just outside Edinburgh. We also played in Billingham, which was close to the boarder of Scotland and England. We traveled to the northwest often, to Manchester, Blackburn, Telford, and Solihull. We had a number of our contests right around the London area, including Bracknell, Medway, Chelmsford, Lee Valley, Slough and Swindon. I made it to Wales when we played the Cardiff Devils and the Isle of Wight, which is south of the metropolitan area of London. You take a ferry across the English Channel to a quaint island that is a prime vacation spot for many people from England.

"Do not go where the path may lead,
go instead where there is no path and leave a trail."
—Ralph Waldo Emerson (1803–1882)

A TRIP TO EASTERN EUROPE

I was finishing up the season in Guildford, England when my good friend, Scott Godin (RIP Scott.) contacted me and indicated that we should go see Jan the Czech in the Czech Republic. Jan played two seasons for me at Roosevelt, and he then attended Hamline University, where he played his freshman season as a varsity hockey player for the Pipers. He was heading home to the Czech Republic for the summer. We decided to go see him and Scott made all the arrangements for the trip.

Our first leg was taking the train through the Channel Tunnel which runs underneath the English Channel. It runs from Folkstone, England to Coquelles, France. The Chunnel, as it is known in England, is a bit over thirty-one miles long and the train can travel at speeds up to a hundred miles per hour. At its lowest point the tunnel is 250 feet below the seabed and 380 feet below sea level. It was fascinating to be on that train knowing that you were under the English Channel. Other than that amazing thought, it actually was kind of boring. It was thirty-one-mile train trip, although this time there was nothing to see.

Once we arrived in Coquelles, France we transferred to a train heading north to Amsterdam, Holland. In Amsterdam, we took in the sights, picked up our rental car, an Alfa Romeo, and headed east towards Germany. We stayed in a small Bed and Breakfast just outside Hiddenhausen in central Germany. We had a great meal in town and went back to the B & B for a good night's rest, because we would have a heavy day of travel ahead of us the next day.

The next morning, we woke up and had a nice breakfast before hitting the road again. Scott started out driving. After we stopped for lunch close to Hanover it was my turn to drive. We were on the Autobahn, which has a loose speed limit of around eighty, though no one actually abides by that speed limit. Most cars are flying by you going upwards of a hundred miles per hour. While Scott was driving, he pushed us up to eighty miles per hour. When I took over, I wanted to see what this Alpha Romeo could do. I was going 110 miles per hour and loving it. When I hit 115 miles per hour, Scott started to get a bit nervous, so I backed it down to 105. In the rearview mirror, I saw a car coming at us and the driver blinked his headlights at me. This is the international sign for *"get the heck out of my way!"* Which I did, very quickly. A Mercedes buzzed by us and had to be going 125 MPH. I love the Autobahn!

That night we stayed in Berlin. After dinner, I asked Scott if he wanted to walk around Berlin some, but he declined. I believe he was still recovering from our second leg on the Autobahn, my driving had maybe stressed him out some. I ended up heading out by myself. If you have never been to Berlin, you need to go. It is a fascinating city. All the history and statues, just the majesty of the city is incredible. Our hotel was not far from the old Iron Curtin and one of the gates that separated the East German side from the West German side of Berlin. It was just a few blocks away. I walked into what was East Berlin during the Cold War. The architecture and roads were so different between the East and West sides of the city. The buildings were less ornate and plain on the East side. Other than the Linden trees, the roads on the East side were also stark. It was a marked difference from the West. I loved walking around this historic city.

It was getting dark, so I started walking back to the hotel. I couldn't quite remember the way and ended up heading back on a different street than the one I had traveled on. I walked by a bar, where there was a guy out front soliciting customers, trying to get people to come in the bar. I thought it might be fun, have one drink and call it a night. When in Rome, or more apt when in Berlin, right? I was told that there was a two-drink minimum, and I had to pay for both when I ordered. I ordered my drinks, as I quickly figured out that this was more than just a local bar. Just then, an Asian woman sat down next to me and grabbed my arm. All doubts left my mind as to type of bar this was. Plus, I was in Berlin; it was kind of strange to have an Asian woman trying to pick me up. I expected some native German woman, but not a woman from Asia. Anyways, she started speaking in German. I informed her that I didn't speak German, so she smoothly switched to English. Just then another Asian woman sat down on the other side of me and put her hand on my leg, as the waitress brought my drinks. The waitress pointed at the two women and said something in German. The first Asian woman nodded her head and replied to the waitress in German. I was totally confused but I had an inkling that it involved me buying the two women something to drink. The first Asian woman smiled at me and told me that she and her friend wanted to take me upstairs. I could hardly hear as the music was extremely loud. I looked at her and said, "What?"

She looked at me and said very loudly, "We want to go upstairs with you. For two hours, both of us. 650 Deutche marks."

This was around $940 at that time. Wow!

I looked at this beautiful woman and I said, "Two hours? I am going to last about a half hour with the two of you. What are we going to do for the rest of the time? Watch television?"

I am fairly certain that she took this as a major insult. Just then the waitress came up to us with two small bottles of champagne for my new friends, which would have cost me $120 each. When I told the waitress that I didn't order the champagne and wouldn't be paying for them, the two women stormed off. The waitress waved at a bouncer, who came over. He spoke to the waitress in German and told me I had to pay for the drinks. I laughed, drank down my two weak drinks and stood up. I was at least two inches taller and had him outweighed by forty pounds. He decided not to stop me as I walked out. I am sure I wasn't the first patron that these women tried to run this scam on. He told me to never come back, so I was officially 86'ed out of a bar of ill-repute in West Berlin. It was an interesting experience to add to an already fantastic trip.

The next day we left Berlin, driving through the old East Germany to the Czech Republic border. We stopped at customs and there we were told that we couldn't drive the rental car into the Czech Republic. Something to do with insurance issues. We were not real clear about that as we were pretty used to being able to move freely from one country to the next no matter what car we were driving. At any rate, we ended up parking the car at the German/Czech border and leaving it there for three weeks. We called Jan the Czech at his home in Vsestudy. Jan and his dad drove three and a half hours to pick us up.

Upon arriving in Jan's hometown of Vsestudy, we visited with his parents, had dinner, and then went to sleep. The Skorepa's house was a wonderful, large farm style home with four bedrooms, so we all were quite comfortable.

The next day Jan showed us the hockey rink that he grew up playing on and then took us all around the countryside area by his hometown. Since his village only has 400 inhabitants, a great deal of the land surrounding the town is farms and fields. It is very rural and extremely beautiful. We stopped at a small bar that Jan favored. Scott and I had a Budweiser beer each and Jan had a Top Topic (Czech version of Sprite) and a pretzel that was big enough for all three of us. The cost for all of that? $1! Yep, a dollar. The Czech Republic is very cheap in regard to products and food.

We spent a week at Jan's parents' house in Vsestudy. Then Jan's mom set us up with a Czech rental car so that we could explore the rest of eastern Europe. We rented the car for two weeks and spent less than half of what the Alfa Romeo that was still sitting on the Czech border, cost us for one week. Jan, Scott, and I first set off to the north to Poland. I had always wanted to see Poland, but unfortunately the Polish security police wouldn't let us into Poland with a Czech car. We certainly had not experienced this anywhere in Western Europe. Jan took it all in stride and said that this was not unusual in this area of Europe. So, we turned the car around and went back to Jan's house. It was a ten-hour trip to Poland and back, so we spent the night at Jan's, Scott and I then headed out the next morning for the southern leg of our tour.

We first went to Slovakia, passing fields and fields of gorgeous yellow flowers. It was amazing. We drove into Hungary and stayed in a hotel just outside of Budapest. It was a wonderful, old hotel with small, but comfortable rooms. The next day would be a fun exploration of Budapest and the Danube River. We also had plans to see the historic Hungarian Parliament building and the famous Szechenyi Baths. This was 1995, so we didn't have cell phones with GPS on them. Instead, we had good old-fashioned maps and some of them weren't easy to read. Understandably, we were a bit lost once we got into Budapest. We took a right down a street and a policeman standing in the street, pulled us over. He started speaking to me in Hungarian. I unfolded the map on the hood of the car and started pointing out where we were trying to go. The policeman looked at me, totally uncomprehending what I was trying to ask him. So, he just waved us on. It was kind of funny since he and I didn't understand a thing each of us said. We drove on, making random turns and trying to figure out the difficult streets of Hungary's capital city. As we took a left, another policeman pulled us over. This one spoke English and asked for our Passports. He took our documents and went back to his car. Close to five minutes later he came back, and he told us that we had to pay ten dollars each to get our Passports back. They had a nice shakedown scam going on for cars with foreign license plates. Scott figured that I had successfully confused the first policeman and thus, we avoided the *Foreigner Tax* with him, but the second policeman was a bit more experienced at shaking down foreigners.

We escaped Budapest and drove to Vienna, the capital of Austria. Another beautiful city which lies in the eastern part of the country also on the Danube River. We explored the city for a day and stayed there for the night. Vienna's artistic and intellectual legacy was shaped by many famous former residents, including Amadeus Mozart, Ludwig Beethoven and Sigmund Freud. After exploring Vienna, we drove to Bratislava, Slovakia which is on the Slovak/Austrian border. Bratislava became the capital of Slovakia when the old country of Czechoslovakia divided into two separate countries. We stayed in Bratislava overnight, and we returned to the Czech Republic and the city of Brno the next day. This experience was incredible. The countries and cities we explored and the different foods we ate, make this already fantastic trip even better.

The next day we drove back to Prague and on to Jan's home in Vsestudy. After another week in Czech Republic, we drove with Jan and his dad back to the Czech/German border where we picked up the Alfa Romeo. We then made our way back to France to catch the Channel Tunnel train back to England. Scott then flew home from London, and I finished out my contract working for the Guildford Flames. I had some scouting duties and other things to clean up before I headed back home to Minnesota. All in all, my year in Europe was a fantastic one. I met some life-long friends in England and throughout the world.

"Wherever you go, go with all your heart."
—Confucius (551 BC – 479 BC)

ED SAUGESTAD AND THE AUGSBURG AUGGIES-MEN

When I came back from England, I was looking at different coaching options when I received a call from the Augsburg men's head coach Ed Saugestad. He told me that Mark Wick was leaving his staff and going up to St. Scholastica to be their head hockey coach. He needed someone that could come in and coach with him. He had a young guy that was enthusiastic, but not very experienced, coaching wise. Would I like to come and join him? I jumped at the opportunity. Ed was a legend in the hockey coaching world, and it would be an honor to work with him. So, I became an assistant coach at Augsburg.

The 1995-96 season didn't quite go as well as we would have liked. We had good talent on that team, but we didn't gel, and we couldn't seem to find our way most of the year. We played well against the better teams and would stumble against the weaker teams. We did have a phenomenal last weekend of the season against Gustavus which prevented them from winning the Minnesota Interscholastic Athletic Conference title outright. We came back after being behind by a couple of goals to tie them 6-6 at St. Peter and then destroyed their title hopes by beating them 6-3 on Saturday at home. It was an awesome weekend and as it turned out, a fitting end to Ed's phenomenal career, as he was forced to retire at the end of the season because of health reasons. I miss my hockey talks with Ed. He died in 2014. I miss his big smile and his enthusiasm for life. Rest in Peace my friend.

That year I also met a man who has become a great friend over the years, Steve Houge. Hougie, as he is known, has been coaching for a long time. He worked part time at Augsburg with the men's team, coached at St. Paul Johnson, and ran the Steve Houge Goalie School. He also worked in the Minnesota Hockey/CCM High Performance 15's Program, as well as the Dave Peterson Goalie Camp. Hougie is one of those coaches who does all this not for money or fame, but because he is passionate about hockey. He simply loves helping kids, making them into better hockey players and people. He has made players and programs better wherever he has coached. I can't remember meeting a more dedicated, enthusiastic, and passionate person. He has been a great friend to many coaches and to me for years. From all of us Hougie...thank you and love you buddy!

Thomas H Peart

"I am not afraid of an army of lions led by a sheep;
I am afraid of an army of sheep led by a lion."
—Alexander The Great (356 BC–323 BC)

A TRIP TO THE SOUTH

As I said earlier, after coming back from England, I coached one year with Ed Saugestad at Augsburg with the men's program. Sadly, Ed had a lot of medical issues that year and it would be his last season of a wonderful career. Most colleges plan a big trip each year and ours that season was to the University of Alabama-Huntsville. Ed couldn't fly so it was just the other assistant, Troy Zangs, and I coaching the team. Huntsville was just transitioning from Division I to Division II. It was a bad weekend for the Auggies, we lost like 12-1 on Friday night, and 13-2 on Saturday afternoon. The public address folks at their arena played the song *Sweet Home Alabama* after every home goal, before the game, after the game and in between periods. I couldn't listen to that dang song for months. Hearing it now, twenty-six years later, still reminds me of that weekend.

We were playing in our second game and getting homered pretty bad by the referees. Troy, who had been with the Auggies for a couple of years and was *technically* in charge, came to me and said, "If we get another penalty, I am sending everyone to the penalty box."

Sure enough, the referee called a ticky-tacky penalty on us. Wouldn't you know it Troy sends all the players to the box. I am fairly certain Alabama had never seen anything like that happen before. Heck, I was in my 13th year coaching, and I had never seen that happen. We ended up getting penalties for having Too Many Men on the Ice, Unsportsmanlike Conduct and probably making a mockery of the game, I don't really remember all the penalties we received that afternoon. I bet we were the talk of the town for a while after that series.

On Saturday night we watched a minor league game in Huntsville. The Huntsville Channel Cats of the infamous Southern Pro Hockey League were taking on a team from Florida. The Channel Cats had a former NHL player, Craig Coxe who played in the big leagues with Vancouver and St. Louis. Coxe was a big fighter in the NHL, racking up 100 to 200 penalty minutes per season in the years that he played. Now, I watched him skate on the ice while he was looking up at the ceiling and into the crowd. It looked like he was still in shock that somehow, he went from playing in NHL arenas with 17,000-19,000 people in the seats to the Southern Pro Hockey League in Alabama, in front of about

5,000 people at the most. Quite the letdown, I'm sure Of course, he was still playing the game that he loved, so there was that side of it.

"To succeed, jump as quickly at opportunities as you do at conclusions."
—Benjamin Franklin (1706–1790)

I received a call from a former Augsburg men's hockey player, Ben Cole. Great guy and working his tail off in the coaching profession down in Florida. We were just catching up on old times and it all reminded me of a couple of stories from my time at Augsburg. First, I must tell you when I first met Ed Saugestad. I had graduated from St Cloud State University with a Teaching degree in Speech Communications and Coaching. There were no jobs open in that field, so I ended up substitute teaching for a year, then I was hired for a job at Minnetonka where I worked with physically challenged kids. This led me to go back to school at Augsburg and finish up my Physical Education major and my minor in Health. Ed was my Kinesiology teacher and he and I would talk hockey every chance we could. My classmates knew my history with Ed and prior to tests would beg me to stop in Ed's office and start talking hockey with him. This would delay the start of the test and give them more time to study. We would be talking, and Ed would lose track of time as he would be telling me a story. Suddenly he would remember that he had a class to get to.

"Oh geez! We gotta go. We have a test." He would say.

Ed was one of my favorite people in the whole world. Both a world class person and coach. He knew more about the game of hockey then almost anyone I knew.

We had a few crazy Canadians on our team. I was the defense coach that year. Chris Bruce, from Trail, British Columbia played defense for us and was probably our most talented defender. Ed would get frustrated when we would have shots blocked from the point. He would come down to my end and say no more slapshots. We are getting too many of them blocked. I would relay the message to all the defenseman and the next shift the crazy Canuck would go out and wind up, blasting the puck way wide. Ed would come down when Chris would get back to the bench yelling at him, "I said no slapshots!"

With just an absolutely innocent look on his face, Chris would reply, "But coach, it didn't get blocked."

Ed would shake his head and walk away. One day at home, we had a very contentious game against St. Thomas. We had a few scuffles, a fight and finally one of our crazy Canucks, forward Mike LeDuc 1) took an errant shot 2) Made a very, very high pass or 3) The puck slipped (take your pick) right at the St. Thomas bench. The puck just missed hitting the Tommie's head coach Terry Skrypek in the head. This led to another scuffle. Incidentally, LeDuc heard Skrypek earlier lobbying the refs to toss him out of the game during one of the scuffles, So, I am going to go with the puck slipped. Gotta trust in my players, right?

It was a crazy year. It was also the year that I met a few people who became lifelong friends. The aforementioned Ben Cole being one of them. Jason Houge who played defense for us. He was a hard worker and had a lot of heart. All three of his kids were great players as well. Kennedy played at Hill-Murray winning a girl's state title, then she played at St. Scholastica in college. His two boys turned into good high school players.

There was also Chad Norman, a defenseman that was a quiet player, who came to the rink every day with desire, and dedication, ready to work hard. He was skilled and tough and a wonderful human being. Chad went on to coach for many years and emulated the skills Ed taught him.

My year at Augsburg was a mixed year. It was great working with Ed and Hougie, but it was also the year my mother passed away, so it was also a tough year. But, as always, the sun came up and life went on. Unfortunately, I only got one year with Ed, as he retired after that year. I applied for the head job, but Augsburg made the right decision and hired former player and longtime coach, Mike Schwartz. Schwartzie, did a great job carrying on the legacy of Ed Saugestad. His roots run deep with Augsburg.

> *"I have learned that to be with those I like is enough."*
> —Walt Whitman (1819–1892)

THE THINGS WE DO WHEN WE ARE
YOUNG, OR MAYBE JUST DESPERATE

When the Minnesota Gophers football team beat West Virginia in a bowl game, it stirred a memory of a trip I took back in the spring of 1997 to the state of West Virginia.

After my one season with the men's hockey team at Augsburg, I was once again looking for a coaching position. I headed to Naples, Florida for the American Hockey Coaches Association convention. During the first day I was at the convention, I saw an ad for a head coaching job at West Virginia University. I emailed them my resume while I continued looking for job openings.

I had been down to the convention for a couple of years, and I usually would take a couple of days at the end to travel somewhere in Florida. One year it was Cocoa Beach, and another time it was Daytona Beach. This year I decided to drive across Alligator Alley and head to the Florida Keys. I got as far as Key Largo where I thought would be a great place to stay for the night before I eventually made my way to Key West the next day. I used the hotel phone and called home to my sister Margaret. She told me that there was a message from West Virginia asking me to call them right away. I called and spoke with the athletic director. He asked if I could come for an interview. The only catch was the interviews were being held that weekend on the West Virginia campus. What to do? Sure, jump in the rental car and drive 17 1/2 hours and 1,165 miles to Morgantown, WV. The university paid for my gas, as well as a hotel room. I got a quick three hours of sleep, gave the best interview I could at that point and after the interview I jumped back in the rental and drove back to Fort Meyers, Fla (16 1/2 hours and 1,078 miles) for my flight home. Crazy! Crazy! Crazy! Oh, and I didn't get the job. Turns out that it was a club team, and they would have had to find me a full-time job along with the coaching job. They had a local guy who already had a job and gave him the coaching position. It was a hard lesson to learn that Division 1 AHCA is not the same thing as Division 1 NCAA. Hey…I am a recovering goaltender. All lessons seem to be hard in my life. It was a heck of an adventure though and I saw some beautiful country on that long, long drive!

"We don't receive wisdom; we must discover it for ourselves after a journey that no one can take for us or spare us."
—Marcel Proust (1871–1922)

BUFFALO BISON/WAYZATA TROJANS

After my adventures on the east coast, I came back to Minnesota still needing a coaching job for the 1996-97 season. Two of my great friends, Carl Davis, head coach at Wayzata and Mike MacMillan (Mac) head coach at Buffalo, helped me out by hiring me to work with their goaltenders. I was going to work half-time at both schools. These two hockey schools were completely different. Wayzata, in Plymouth, Minnesota was a rich, suburban community. Buffalo, on the other hand, was a rural community with many working class, down to earth people. As the season progressed, I found myself more attracted to Buffalo, and thus, spending more time out there.

Now Mac may not admit this, but I was the best parent/coach liaison he ever had. Half the time that year he would see me talking to parents while practice was starting, usually with a cup of coffee in hand. He would just shake his head, wondering when I was going to get on the ice with the team. I felt that it was very important to smooth his edges some and let the parents know that the coaching staff cared about them. Mac didn't always agree with that philosophy though. To be honest, it was a tough year for me because working half time at each school didn't make me feel at home at either place. For me, coaching has always meant a sense of family. It was hard to attain that year.

During Christmas vacation, we often had early practice times at Buffalo. I was living in Minneapolis, and it was about a 50-minute, snowy drive to the Buffalo arena. One day, I was a little late getting on the ice for practice due to a snowstorm. I arrived, coffee cup in hand of course, and as I am getting on the ice Jackie, Mac's daughter, and our starting goalie on the boy's team (girls' hockey didn't start in Buffalo until the next season} storms off the ice swearing and throwing her stick. I skated up to Mac and asked what happened. He said Jackie told him to F off, so he kicked her off the ice. He then said that we would be having a meeting after practice, and I was going to be there. He then noticed the coffee cup and fixed me with the *"Mac Death Stare!"* Those of you who know him well, know that look.

"You had time to stop for coffee I see." He shook his head and skated away, probably swearing to himself.

Practice ended on an upbeat manner. Mac, Jackie, and I met in the coach's room. Dave Prokop, another assistant, was sitting in the corner waiting for the fireworks to go off. Mac and Jackie started yelling back and forth. Mac finally says,

"Listen, bottom line is that when you are on the ice you are one of my players and not my daughter!"

Jackie stands up and says, "Fine, maybe I'll quit then!" She then storms out!

Mac looks at me and says,

"TP, do you have an extra room at your place?"

I reply, "Yes Mac, but I don't think the school will approve of a 17-year-old living in my house."

And Mac says, "Oh, not for her. If she quits, I'll get kicked out of my house!" Thankfully Jackie didn't quit, and it all got smoothed over, as these things usually do in time with the cooling down of emotions. I did my best to make practice on time from then on and without coffee cup in hand.

"It is one of the blessings of old friends
that you can afford to be stupid with them."
—Ralph Waldo Emerson (1803–1882)

JANE RING, THE STRAUSS FLYERS AND
THE WRIGHT COUNTY BLADES

I coached mostly boys and men's hockey for 15 years before girl's hockey took off in the mid-1990's. I had a couple of years with the Armstrong softball team and a year at Roosevelt with the girls' soccer team, but the rest was all boys and men. I started coaching girls' hockey for the Wright County Blades in 1997-98. The Blades were a Co-op team made up of seven schools. Buffalo, Delano, Rockford, Watertown-Mayer, St. Michael-Albertville, Monticello, and Maple Lake.

I was head coach of the Blades for two years and at the same time, was an assistant hockey coach at the College of St. Benedict's, before ultimately getting the head coaching position at Saint Ben's. Bill Kelly, who was the first head hockey coach in St. Ben's history, and I switched positions after the second season, and I had to resign my position at Wright County. NCAA rules allow a person to be a high school head coach and an assistant at a college, but not a head coach at a college and any position at a high school of the same sport. While head coaching at Wright County and assistant coaching at St. Ben's, I decided I needed an additional challenge, so I coached the Strauss Flyers, a senior women's team in the WHAM League (Women's Hockey Association of Minnesota.)

For two years I would run practice in Buffalo or Delano from 3-5 PM, grab a bite to eat and then drive up to Richmond, Minnesota, an hour away where I would run the St. Ben's practice from 9-11 PM. On the weekends and some nights during the week, depending on schedules, I would coach the Flyers at various arenas in the Minneapolis-St. Paul metro area. I am not quite sure how I found the energy to coach all three teams. It was kind of an intense schedule. It was fun and quite the learning experience though. Coaching girls and young women after 15 years of coaching boys and men was a major adjustment. Girls like to know why you are doing a drill, they need some time to connect with one another, and they rally around each other when they feel a coach is being unfair. However, these are generalities and there are always exceptions. Once you get girls to understand why you are doing something, they will go through three walls for you. You must be able to connect with them through listening and communicating though. That is key whether you are a male coach or a female coach.

Now, all these teams of mine were completely different. The Blades were junior high and high school players in the grades 7th to 12th. St. Ben's, of course, was all college age players eighteen to twenty-two and on the Flyers, we had players from twenty-two years old to seventy-one-year-old Jane Ring. It was quite the experience working with all three different groups during the same time period. I was pretty used to a certain routine on game days. Usually, a little chat pre-game and adjustments in between periods and then a little wrap up at the end. I found out that I needed to adjust a bit with the Flyers. Players worked, had families, some were always running late, so the pre-game chat went away. Our games lasted an hour, so the time in between periods was brief. After one of my first games with the Flyers, I told the players to keep their stuff on and I would chat quick and then they could get changed. I walked in and one of my players is almost buck naked. She was 30 at the time and I was averting my eyes and I said,

"K, I told you guys to keep your stuff on!"

She just kept right on changing, and said,

"Tom, I don't have anything you haven't seen before!"

My reply? "I haven't seen yours...well now I have!"

Needless to say, the post-game talks went completely away with the Flyers.

Yep, coaching girls and women was different than coaching boys and men. It was, however, a positive change to my career. It came at a time when I needed change and a challenge to learn and grow. Generally speaking, women like to know why we are doing something and not just be told to do something. I learned to not say *"Because I said so,"* and explain things in better detail. In doing so, practices and games went a great deal better. I learned to have a female on the staff. This helped with communication and made the players feel more comfortable. We also instilled a *t-shirt rule* for all my women's teams, well except for the Flyers. They wouldn't have listened anyway; they kind of did their own thing. The t-shirt rule started at St. Ben's because our favorite fan Sister Lois Wedl and the other nuns could come knocking on the locker room at any given time. Bill Kelly and I felt it would be better if the players had a t-shirt on versus sitting around in sports bras. The rule helped everywhere I coached girls or women. My first couple of years I had to learn how far to push female players. It really isn't that you can't push them because you can. You just have to adjust how you push them. Yelling at them rarely works, explaining and communicating what you want to see happen is a better way to get your point across. You need to pick your spots a bit more carefully by getting to know your players more in depth. In retrospect, this is probably a better way to communicate with males as well as females.

As I said, with the Flyers we had a very large range in ages. Our oldest player was Jane Ring at a young seventy-one years of age. Jane was completely in love with the game of hockey and would give anything to play. Once, Jane had a heart attack and a week later she was back on the ice. I couldn't believe her drive and determination. Jane, her husband John, and their daughter Sue have sponsored a scholarship program to help young women hockey players graduating from Minnesota high schools to attend accredited colleges or universities. However, the winners of the scholarship don't have to play hockey in college, it's to help them attend and get an education. It's called The Jane Ring/Sue Ring-Jarvi Girls'/Women's Hockey Fund. Jane was an incredible woman and one I miss seeing around arenas. She died in 2015 at the age of eighty-nine, two days before her ninetieth birthday. RIP Jane. You can rest easy knowing that there are many young women that owe at least part of their education to your generosity, your passion, and your love for the game of hockey.

"Nothing in the world has ever been accomplished without passion."
—Georg Wilhelm Friedrich Hegel (1770–1831)

TOM BROPHY

As I have stated earlier, my first-year coaching girls' hockey was at Buffalo as coach of the Wright County Blades. The Blades were made up of seven different schools from all over Wright County, with Buffalo being the host school. The other schools included St. Michael/Albertville, Monticello, Delano, Rockford, Watertown-Mayer, and Maple Lake. During the preseason, myself and my coaching staff had a big group of Mites on the ice, and we were working with them on skating and other skills. I noticed that a couple of little guys were getting into a shoving match. I went over and I asked who started it. Well, you know how it is with kids they both said, "Not me, he did it!"

As soon as I start to skate away, one boy knocks the other one down. I skate back and tell the offender to come with me. I figured this would be a great teaching moment and I put the boy in the penalty box. The little guy was yelling at me that he didn't do anything, and I was a jerk. I told him he had two minutes in the penalty box and at the end of the two minutes, I would come get him out. As soon as I skated away, he stomped out of the back of the penalty box and walked around the rink on the cement in his skates to his mother. I told Tom Brophy, one of my assistants, about what just happened and to look at that boy ruining the edges of his skates while walking on the cement. Tom looked at me, shook his head and said, "Yeah, that's my kid."

Nice way to impress my assistant on the first day of practice. Tom was an excellent teacher who could coach any sport. He was an extremely valuable member of my staff and a great friend over the years. Tom had a way of connecting with our players. He was excellent at pushing them to be better, but he also made them feel valued. He was an ideal assistant coach. He understood his role and did a phenomenal job developing players. Thank you, Tom, for all your hard work and dedication. I learned a great deal from Coach Brophy in the two years I worked with him. I love you, big guy!

"The teacher who is indeed wise does not bid you to enter the house of his wisdom, but rather leads you to the threshold of your mind."
—Kahlil Gibran (1883–1931)

COLLEGE OF SAINT BENEDICT

I coached at St. Ben's for six years, two years as an assistant hockey coach and four as a head hockey coach. I loved being a head coach for a college hockey program. One of my greatest pleasures was coaching my niece Elizabeth Hancock, now Herman. I was tough on her but looking back on our four years together I loved seeing her at the rink every day and was proud to watch her confidence grow and see her develop into the awesome woman she has become. I truly valued her input on the team and her insight on the goings on in the locker room and within the team. She still plays senior women's hockey and is now the mother of a beautiful little girl, Valkyrie Noel Herman. One funny thing that happened was when Uncle Tommy was a bit tough on her and once or twice, even had to bench her. Inevitably I would receive a call from my sister Margaret, "So, I hear you benched my daughter."

I would just reply, "No, I benched one of my players." It's difficult when your sister is a tough hockey mom who loves her kids.

Our first year at St. Ben's was an awesome experience. We only had 3 or 4 players with any hockey background. Our best player was Anne Joswiak of South St. Paul. Anne was a great player in high school, was captain of her team during her senior year and helped lead South St. Paul to the first ever Minnesota Girls' State Hockey Tournament. She scored twelve goals and added sixteen assists for twenty-eight points in her only year of high school hockey. Anne was like another assistant coach for us, helping teach some of her teammates how to handle the puck, how to shoot and some of the finer points of being a hockey player. She loved that St. Ben's finally had a hockey team. She came to the rink with a huge smile on her face every day, put up with endless rudimentary skating drills, and helped all the other players develop throughout that year. I always admired her. I wish she could have been younger and played for us for a full four years.

Our goaltender, Mary Welle, was an awesome athlete whose first sport was softball. She had never played hockey or even skated before. Bill Kelly convinced her to try hockey. She worked so hard and hung with us for two years. She was awesome on shots she could stay on her feet to stop, but once she went down, well we needed to clear the puck to give her time to get back up. In our second year, Bill and I brought in sixteen first years and an incredible transfer from the University of Minnesota Gophers, Paula Vogt. Paula ended up being one of the best players to play at St. Ben's and was elected to the school's Hall of Fame in 2018. We were measurably better in that second year, but I'll always remember that first year and hold those players dear to my heart. It was an incredible first year.

"The beginning is the most important part of the work."
—Plato (427 BC – 347 BC)

CSB BONEHEAD AWARDS

When you coach a Division III college program you do some other things to go with your coaching position. At St. Ben's I taught some Physical Education and Health classes. One of them was *"Skills for Healthy Living."* I taught this class to a group of about thirty Saint John's students at 8:00 AM on the St. Ben's campus each semester for a few years. The boys hated having such an early class and on the St. Ben's campus to boot. I decided I needed to wake them up somehow, so I blasted Led Zeppelin on my boom box the minute they walked in. Of course, the boys loved *"Whole Lotta Love"* the best. I can't tell you how many guys I ran into in airports, parks, or at games and they always brought up the Led Zeppelin songs. Nothing else about the class, mind you, just the music.

I also was an assistant softball coach. The person who played the music at our games would always play *"Jump Around"* by House of Pain. Inevitably the players would convince me to jump up and down like a fool. We won our share of games and since a lot of softball is repetition, I tried to add some fun to practices and games.

One of the things that our staff at St. Ben's had created was called the "Bonehead Award." This was given to the full-time staff member who did something extra dumb during the year. I pride myself on winning this prestigious award twice in my four years as a full-time staff member. One of my two Bonehead Awards was for walking down the hall looking for our trainer Julie Deyak and singing at the top of my voice,

"Julie, Julie, Julie, do you love me?" This was a Top Ten hit in the early seventies by Bobby Sherman. Unbeknownst to me, Julie was teaching a class at the time. The whole class broke up in laughter when I walked in. Yeah, pretty dumb, embarrassing and worthy of the bonehead award!

The second one was even better. Bill Kelly's soccer team had a trip planned to Texas. Bill asked me to come with and drive one of the rental vans. We flew into San Antonio on a Saturday. At the airport we picked up two vans to transport the team. We first played against Southern University in San Antonio and lost 1-0 in double overtime. We then had a great day on the River Walk and seeing all the sites in San Antonio.

The next day, we drove to Austin, checked into our hotel and spent the day seeing the sites in Austin, including the Alamo, which was a great deal smaller than I thought it would be. On Monday, we played and lost to Trinity University in Austin 2-0. Not the results that Bill wanted, but a great trip all the same. The players flew out of Austin back to Minnesota after the game. Bill and I drove back to San Antonio to return the vans and then planned to fly out on Tuesday. We dropped one van off at the rental return and then met an alum for dinner and a couple of beers. It rained while we were in the restaurant and when we came out to the van, I noticed a huge scratch down the passenger side of the van. I showed the scratch to Bill. We decided to go to Walmart to get white touch up paint so we could fix the scratch. It was really dark out, but we were so proud of our solution. We then went to bed as we had an early flight the next morning. We came out in the morning and to our dismay, the van looked like a toddler had got into the finger paints and smeared paint all over the van. Oh my gosh, it looked bad. There was nothing we could do so we drove to the rental return at the airport. As we were driving, I got the paperwork out of the glovebox and noticed a long scratch drawn in on the side of the van on the paperwork. I said,

"Oh my gosh Bill, the scratch was already there!" We both laughed, hard.

So, we pulled into the return lot. Bill approached the man handling returns and handed him the van keys. The poor guy started to scratch his head.

He then said, "Hey, someone tried to fix the scratch."

Bill shows him the paperwork and asked,

"Why would someone try to fix the scratch, it's right here on the paperwork."

The guy says, "I know, I know, I work with this van. I know this scratch."

Bill just shrugged his shoulders, walked away, and joined me on the shuttle bus. The bus was leaving the lot and the poor guy was still both scratching and shaking his head, trying to make sense of why some bonehead would try to fix the scratch that was already on the van.

Yep, that was a well-earned bonehead award by Bill and me. Just for blabbing and telling the story when we got back. We probably deserved an extra award just for not keeping our mouths shut!

I have never worked with a closer staff than the group of coaches and administrators at CSB. It was a blast my whole six years there. Well, okay maybe the first five. My last year, Bill was leaving. His wife was hired to teach at Sienna College in New York, and they were moving east. Without my good friend to watch my back, it ended up being a stressful year. The college decided to go in a different direction for the 2003-2004 season. I was out, but it was a great run and Bill, and I were the first coaches in the history of St. Ben's hockey. I will always remember that time fondly.

> *"A true friend accepts who you are,*
> *but also helps you become who you should be."*
> —Unknown (From Pure Love Quotes)

HOCKEY TRAVELS

Hockey has been very, very good to me. It has brought me to tons of great places. I mean who else can say they have been to incredible places like Indus, Hallock, Crookston, Bottineau, ND, Mankato, and St. Peter? But in addition to those awesome places, I have been to Europe three times. When I coached in England, hockey brought me all over England, Scotland, Wales and Ireland. Then at St. Ben's we took both the hockey and soccer teams to Italy during the 2000-2001 season in January. We spent the first part of the trip in Northern Italy and had four hockey games. We then spent the second part of the trip in the central and southern parts of Italy and played four soccer games, plus a very interesting training session with the Italian women's national team coaches. The coaches were extremely impressed with Lisa Grefe, who was a first team All-American goaltender for the St. Ben's soccer team.

All in all, Venice was my favorite city, though I have to say that the outdoor hockey game we had in Merano in thirty-two-degree weather, with the backdrop of the Alps, was an incredible experience and one I will always cherish. I felt like we were in the movie *Mystery, Alaska*. We loaned a different line each period to the team we were playing as they were short players. I remember our players coming back saying,
"Tom. They are smoking and drinking in the locker room!"
I was like, "Yep, welcome to Europe you guys."
Both teams ended up on the ice together dancing and singing *"YMCA"* after the game. It was an incredible night. We even had a group of men supporters from Italy who followed our team to the next two games. I am sure it was just for the hockey though. Yeah right!

Our first game in Italy was against their Italian women's National Team, which was a good game and ended up in a 3-3 tie. We had a huge party after the game and the Italian players were extremely friendly. They gave me a team hat and even gave me a copy of their team calendar. The major difference of their calendar from a regular calendar, was that all the players were posing in a combination of hockey equipment and lingerie. The calendar was tastefully done, but somehow the athletic director at St. Ben's, Carol Howe-Veenstra didn't think us doing a similar calendar would fly with the Nuns, even though the Italian team made $25,000 selling the calendars.

Later coaching as an assistant at Augsburg we took the women's hockey team to Germany, Austria, and Italy in January of 2008. That was another incredible trip. It's funny, but the games were always fun, but the cultural experiences far outweighed the hockey aspects, even though hockey was the vehicle to make the trips happen. I have also had the pleasure of traveling to Colorado, New York, Boston, Ohio, Oregon, California, Utah, Wisconsin, Illinois, Michigan, Indiana, Alabama, Alaska, and Wyoming, as well as Sweden and the Czech Republic. Yes...hockey has been very, very good to me.

> *"The world is a book, and those who do not travel read only a page."*
> —Saint Augustine (354–430)

BILL KELLY AND MANY COACHING FRIENDS

I have worked with a lot of great coaches in my life. There are a few that really stand out. Bill Kelly is a dear friend that was a soccer guy his whole life. He and I worked at Luther Park Camp together when we were in our twenties. We always dreamed of coaching together and finally got our chance at St. Ben's. Bill was already the soccer coach there when CSB started its hockey program. He called me up and said,

"You owe me. I need you at St. Ben's."

For two years, Bill was the head hockey coach, and I was his assistant. Then we switched roles and for three of the next four years, I was the head coach, and Bill assisted me. Bill had helped me at Roosevelt when I was tabbed to be the interim head girls' soccer coach for a year. I had no clue how to run a real soccer practice. Bill ran the practices, and I did all the other duties. We reversed those roles at St. Ben's. Bill was great at recruiting, and he definitely has the Irish gift of gab. We had a good system. I would go out and watch the players, send Bill an email indicating which players to put on our recruiting list. Bill then made phone calls and set up campus visits.

It was also Bill's idea to plan a European trip. That trip was a great recruiting tool for us. It helped bring in some quality hockey and soccer players for St. Ben's. As an NCAA member, you can travel overseas once every four years. It does take a great deal of planning and fundraising. For our Italy trip, we worked in the concession stands at the Metrodome during Minnesota Vikings and Twins games. This helped the players come up with the cost of the trip. We had sixty-five hockey and soccer players make the trip and around forty-five parents. It was an incredible experience.

At St. Ben's, we also had a couple of young student-assistant coaches that were St. John's students. Ben Shanahan and Ian Anderson were great additions to the program in our first few years. Ian went on to work as the Minnesota Wild's video coach after graduating. He did an awesome job with the Wild. Ben was with us the longest and I think of him as the little brother I never had (well, younger He is bigger than I am.) and loved having him around. He was like a sponge, soaking up hockey and coaching knowledge. I seemed to be surrounded by Irish lads at St. Ben's. Shanahan and Kelly…you can't get more Irish than that.

And Bill Kelly? Well, it was simply an honor to work with him. As I said earlier, it was always our dream to coach together and we finally were able to accomplish that. Some of my fondest memories were my years of coaching with him at St. Ben's. It was just like we dreamt about it all those years ago. Working with Bill enriched my life in so many ways. We also had a lot of laughs coaching together. There was the time that one of the referees came out for warm-ups with one skate guard off and one on. We were laughing watching him figure out why his foot kept slipping. Also, Bill was a whiz on the soccer field, but that didn't necessarily translate to great skating skills on the ice. There was one day in practice when Bill caught an edge and fell in the corner of the rink. I looked over and Bill was spinning on his back like a turtle on its shell. It was very funny. On another day, when I was Bill's assistant, I had a high school hockey game in Buffalo. Bill had seen some videos of Russian skating and stickhandling drills. Bill designed practice and had the players skate through cones and then jump up on the boards, come down and regain the puck, just like the Russian players. This really wasn't normal for our style of hockey. I think the players thought his drills were a little crazy.

I loved working with him and to this day he is one of my best friends. I love you, Bill!

At Roosevelt I was fortunate to have one of the best assistant coaches. Bill Taleen was my trainer at Northwest Swim and Racquet Club. I found out that he loved coaching and had played hockey at St. Paul Harding, back when they regularly had good teams. He was a top player on their 1979 state tournament team. Bill had a way with the guys and was a key reason why we had the success we had with the Teddies. He knew his role, accepted it and excelled as a defensive coach, even though he was a forward in high school and youth hockey. Bill also had a smile on his face every day and the only time I saw him really nervous was when I got tossed out of a game against Washburn during our first year together. I had accidentally thrown my pen at the referee during a discussion on a penalty. I trusted Bill with the players and with running practice. He could have been a head coach anywhere he wanted to. And he had a hell of a shot. He even busted the glass behind the net once at Parade Ice Gardens. It was an incredible shot. I really enjoyed coaching with him. He was my trusted compadre and a great influence on the Roosevelt players and me. I love you, brother!

I had many incredible assistants along the way. There was Jim McGlade, Jim Rokala, Mark Bergum, Max San Roman and the incomparable Mike Mulvey, a man who bled Maroon and Gold with every heartbeat. Mulvey was a little crazy at times and he sometimes would let his passion override his thinking, but as I said, he was a Roosevelt Teddie through and through. Another friend who enriched my life and helped make me a better coach and person. Love ya Mulv!

> *"Even while they teach, men learn."*
> —Seneca the Younger (4 BC–65 AD)

PASSIONS BOIL OVER

Hockey is a very passionate game and sometimes those passions boil over, becoming both real and imagined slights. My first story I will now tell you happened because of real slights. The second was absolutely an imagined slight. I have changed the names to protect the innocent and for sure the guilty! Be forewarned, there is some blue language involved. Credit goes to Anne Sawyer Beach for reminding me of the first story.

I was coaching at St. Ben's, and I had a young player who I will call Annabelle. Annabelle was not our most talented player, but she had more heart than almost any player that I ever coached at St. Ben's. We were playing Concordia College and Annabelle was playing with her usual vim and vigor. She always played hard, and she was always hard to play against. Like I said, she always played with an immense amount of heart. In fact, that is how she lives her whole life with all her heart. All her friends loved her, and it was only the teams that played against her that didn't like her. Annabelle went into the corner, battling hard for the puck. The puck slid up the side boards and Annabelle and the Concordia player kept battling. Annabelle wins the battle and I see the Cobber yell something at her. She came to the bench and looked at me with this extremely confused look on her face. I asked her what was wrong, and she said, "That Concordia player called her a "c_ _ _t."

She then looked at the ice, looked back at me and in total confusion says, "Tom, what's a c _ _ _t?"

I kid you not! I took a deep breath, thought for a moment how to best answer that bombshell and said,

"Well Annabelle, that is a very nasty, derogatory word for a woman's vagina."

Annabelle got this completely horrified look on her face and she then played with even more drive and determination for the rest of that game. We beat Concordia that day in a game we probably shouldn't have. I like to think that we all had a little more heart, along with more spirit and more purpose that day.

The other story is definitely one of an imagined slight. In our first year together at St. Ben's, Bill Kelly had recruited a great softball player to try hockey. Her name was Mary Welle and she had never played hockey before. As a matter of fact, she had never skated before. She agreed to play goaltender, as we didn't have a goalie. The woman was an all-conference and all-region softball player, with great eye-hand coordination and she was as tough and as brave as they come. Of course, if you have never skated, well it's difficult turning, stopping and even staying upright. Which leads us to the second passionate event. Bill would do the heavy lifting on recruiting those first two years. My job was to find the players. His job was to get them to St. Ben's. I found a great goaltender at a private school in St. Paul. We will call her Karen. Kind of fits now 20 some years later during this crazy pandemic, but I digress. Karen was an exceptional goaltender. The night I watched her, she had almost 50 saves in a 3-2 loss. She was outstanding. However, she had a tough home life and was a bit quick with her temper. Let's just say she wasn't shy to speak her mind at the best of times and when she lost her temper? Look out! I copied a drill from John "Bah" Harrington, who was the St. John's head coach and a former player on the 1980 Gold Medal Olympic hockey team. All coaches steal lots of drills, don't you know? Anyway, in this drill, all your players have a puck at the blue line, including the goaltenders and one at a time each player shoots at the open net. If the player scores, no one skates. But, if a player misses, the whole team has to skate hard to the goal line, all the way to the opposite goal line and back to the blue line. You continue until everyone has shot their puck once. It seems easy, but you would be amazed how many players miss that wide open net! Anyway, Karen's turn came, and she missed the net. Mary was right on her heals and since Mary didn't skate so well, she tripped Karen. She tripped her physically and mentally. Both Karen and Mary went down in a heap. I skated over just in time to hear the end of Karen screaming at Mary that she did that on purpose. Mary's way of handling stressful situations was to laugh. Of course, this sent Karen well into the red zone and she looks at Mary and screams,

"You f@&king c_ _ _t!"

I was like the guy standing on the railroad tracks looking East when the train runs me over coming from the west. Totally shocked to say the least. Karen and I had a long talk about her temper and teammates after that practice. Not sure it made much of a difference. She transferred after that year. She could have been one of the best if she could have learned to get her emotions under wraps. Mary finished out the year, but then decided she was just going to concentrate on softball.

Mary was a great person, a great athlete, and a great friend. And she now has her kids playing the great game of hockey.

I will also be forever grateful to Mary for being brave enough to try the toughest, best sport in the entire world and to St. Ben's for providing hockey to many, many young women for the past 24 years.

"If passion drives you, let reason hold the reins."
—Benjamin Franklin (1706–1790)

A SCOTTISH COACH AND A REVELATION

Here's another couple of St. Ben's stories for you. Again, some of the names have been changed. My fellow coach and buddy Bill Kelly, soccer coach extraordinaire, was working a summer soccer camp out East and met a couple of Dartmouth College soccer players that were working at the camp. Dartmouth had hired a new soccer coach the previous year. He was a salty old coach from Scotland. He hadn't coached women before. He didn't quite understand the sensitivities of the young, well off, college women of the Ivy Leagues. Let's just say, it didn't work out so well for him. The first day, he wanted to see how fast the players could run, so he had them running some sprints. After watching for a while, he became more and more agitated. He didn't think that they were running fast enough. He then lost it and ran up to some of the players screaming at them in his Scottish Brogue,

"Oh, for Chris' sake, run ya fat f@&king pigs, run!"

Things digressed from there and needless to say, good old Dartmouth was once again in the market for a new women's soccer coach. Bill and I pretty much figured that if we ever treated our players that way, we probably wouldn't have any skin left on us after our AD, Carol Howe-Veenstra finished tanning our hides.

It is true that sometimes firm words would be necessary and appropriate with our St. Ben's hockey teams. We had a player I will call Alexi. Alexi was a decent player who sometimes let her frustration control her actions and get the better of her emotions. Occasionally she would have an emotional melt down on the ice and I would be forced to take her off the ice or bench her. During one home game, Alexi blew a gasket and came off the ice screaming and swearing. She then threw her stick or slammed it, I forget. Anyway, I said in a loud and firm, but calm voice,

"Alexi, sit down until I tell you different."

That is when Alexi started crying. Bill Kelly looked at her and in an extremely loud voice he yelled,

"Why do you do this to yourself? Woman?!"

I don't believe Alexi had ever been spoken to in this manner. She immediately stopped crying and looked at Bill and I with the biggest shocked look on her face. Alexi didn't have any more meltdowns the rest of that year.

It really turned out to be a great message for the whole team. Your emotions are yours and it's up to you to control them. Alexi today is a great mother to her kids and she and her sister are leading their best lives with their kids loving to play hockey. They were a great addition to our team, and both were extremely intelligent and great students.

"We might be the masters of our own thoughts,
but we sometimes are still slaves to our own emotions."
—Unknown (From Quotes Lover)

GILMOUR ACADEMY

I coached at St. Ben's for 6 years. Loved the players and loved the staff and the comradery that we all had. However, the athletic director felt we weren't winning enough and let me go after the 2003 season. Well in all fairness, she gave me a choice, continue coaching at less than half my current salary or resign. I walked. Life happens. I was upset at first but recovered and got a job at Gilmour Academy in Cleveland, Ohio as head coach of the girls Prep hockey team. It is a Catholic prep school that was started by the same order that started the University of Notre Dame. John Malloy is the Director of Hockey for both the boys and girls programs and does a phenomenal job running things. They have two rinks and one of the most beautiful campuses I have ever seen. Plus, it didn't hurt that I was making more as the head girls prep coach at Gilmour than I did as a head coach for Saint Ben's. I coached hockey and eighth grade softball, taught lower school skating, and supervised lunches. It was a sweet gig. I stayed one year, should have stayed longer, but I was getting married the next summer and we were going to move back to Minnesota where my fiancé was working on her master's degree.

The first thing I discovered was that we had a pretty good team, but they didn't exactly have much of a system of play. We had a couple of future Division I players, along with a group of better than average players, interspersed with some average players who worked hard. If I had stayed at Gilmour longer, we would have had a very good hockey team the next year. One thing I found out early was that my best player, Katy Beach, was a distant cousin. Small world, right? Katy ended up playing at Providence College and had a good career there. She is now a nurse and from what I hear, an exceptional one. We had several players go on and play college hockey. Rebecca Allen at Princeton, Missy Hall at RIT to name just a couple.

I coached a lot of tough players over the years, but one of the toughest players that I have ever had on any team was a female player named Niki Calvillo. She had no fear when playing the game and would rather go through someone than around them. Niki was part Italian and part Mexican, a little quick on the temper and fiercely loyal to anything and anyone she cared about. I had to stop her from beating up one of her teammates, K.K., one day because K. K. said Mexicans were dirty. K.K, was a little rich girl with a nice house and had all the toys. She didn't quite get the fact that Niki was a tough working-class girl from the west side of Cleveland. Big mistake on K.K.'s part.

One of my favorite players was Kate Budaji. She had great parents, worked hard, and had a great attitude. She did have a penchant for pulling pranks and for getting caught. Sorry Kate, you know it's true. Her dad Joe would say that her elevator doesn't go all the way to the top, but hey I won't go there! The two stories I can tell occurred on a trip to Boston, both on the same night.

First, Kate, a couple other players, and a boys assistant coach ventured out in a major snowstorm to get pizza. The pizza place said it was too snowy out to deliver. So of course, they all pile into the boys' assistant coach's car to pick the pizza up. Of course, they get lost. They stop at a police station to get directions and Kate has to carry in her teammate Debbie because Debbie didn't have socks and shoes on. Why would she? Who would wear shoes and socks in a major snowstorm? Eventually they find the pizza joint and get back to the hotel. I see them walk in, inquire as to where they were, lecture them a bit (I'm sure for a slice or two of that pizza) and send them to bed. They did fail to mention that it was the boy's assistant coach who also wanted pizza but needed someone to drive his car as he was drunk. Probably a smart decision at the time.

Like I said, I sent them to bed, but K.K. got the great idea to prank coach Peart. She left me a nice present on a paper towel outside my door, knocked and ran down the hall. I open the door and there was what appeared to be dog poop on the paper towel. Except it wasn't from a dog. I could hear giggling and followed the sound. I found K.K. and a couple of others thinking that they were oh so clever. I asked who left the present and K.K. finally fessed up to the transgression. I made her clean it up. The next day, I considered what her consequences would be all the way home. A nice long bus ride, contemplating how to handle this situation. I suspect the suspense was killing K.K. After all, it was a 14-hour bus ride. When we arrived back at Gilmour, I asked the arena guys what their nastiest job was. They said cleaning off gum from under the bleachers. K.K. got to spend a week under there on her hands and knees chipping away at nasty old gum. She wasn't too keen on pulling pranks on me from then on.

It was, and still is the nastiest prank ever pulled on me in my over 50 years in the game of hockey!

"Fool me once, shame on you!
Fool me twice, shame on me!"
—Unknown (Also, one of Herb Brooks favorite sayings.)

IN DEFENSE OF WOMEN'S AND GIRL'S HOCKEY

When I was coaching at Gilmour Academy in 2003-2004, one of my players, Debbie came steaming into my office, and I mean STEAMING! She had just come from a speech communication class. Their assignment was to write a speech about something that affected them personally.

One classmate of hers, a male hockey player got up and gave the following speech. Debbie went to her teacher and asked for a copy, which she gave to me. Here is the speech.

> *Have you ever looked at something and been completely grossed out? Well, I do every day when I go to the rink and see the girl's hockey team practicing. I am here to tell you why girls should not play hockey. Personally, I think that they should cancel girls' hockey everywhere as soon as possible. One reason why a girl should not play hockey is that her body will resemble one of a male. If you looked around the Gilmour campus lately you can clearly separate the girls that play hockey from the girls that don't. For example, when you walk through the halls glance down at the student center and you will see all of the hockey girls gathered around one area hitting each other. Other than the fact that they may look like guys is that they are not as strong as guys. It is scientifically proven that women do not have the muscle structure that men have. If you ever have watched the guy's prep team play a game and then watched the girls prep team play it is like night and day. The girls are not even contenders with the boys' varsity B team. It is also impractical for a girl to play a man's sport. At the beginning of the year during prep team tryouts we went to Detroit to play a few games and after our games there was a college girls team playing. We were watching the warm-ups and one of the coaches said, "Come on boys, we can watch Bantam hockey at home." I personally have played against girls on boys' teams, and it is very uncomfortable playing against a girl. I feel that I have to bring down my level of play so that I do not hurt a girl if I hit her, or I*

don't want to make her look like a complete fool. I have a quote from a sophomore teammate Mark N., "I would feel bad if I totally railed a chick unless it is a chick that looks like a dude." It is also immoral for a girl to play a contact sport like hockey because when they get hurt, they bitch and moan about their injury for weeks. I live with Sean C., and before the break he experienced a season ending injury. He dislocated his wrist and fractured it. This is the worst wrist injury a person can have, and it is usually seen in car accidents. He also had a stage 2 concussion that he is recently getting over. Sean took his injury and is making the best of the situation. Although earlier this year a girl broke her collar bone and cried about it forever and still does. After her injury she went home for a month so she could recuperate. She took her injury and let it get the best of her but still we never see Sear with a tear in his eye. In conclusion, if you can't take the consequences of the sport than you shouldn't play the game.

I needed a day or two to ruminate on the best way to approach this situation. At first, I was as mad as Debbie and consequently the rest of the team was also mad at this boy as well. If any of the boys on the prep team wanted a date for the winter dance, they were better off avoiding my girls' prep team. I talked to my assistant coach, Mike Mortellaro, about the situation. What we came up with was that I would give a rebuttal speech. I wanted my players to know that I believed in them and that I supported them completely.

I approached Debbie's teacher and asked for the chance to give a speech to contradict this male player's absurd assertions. After getting assurances from me that I wouldn't embarrass this boy completely, I set up a time to go to the class and give my rebuttal.

As the day approached, my players all wanted to be there, but most had other classes at that time. There was only a couple of them on hand, but I knew that the word would spread to the rest of the team.

I spoke extemporaneously about my background to set up some credibility and let the male players in the class know that I played the game, coached boys and men, and that I now coached the girls because they don't have attitudes about the game of hockey. They don't think that hockey owes them something and they work just as hard, if not harder than the boys' teams. And yes, I had watched many of their practices.

I pointed out the contradiction made during the speech that a girl shouldn't play hockey because her body will resemble one of a male. Yet later, it was pointed out that girls are scientifically proven to have less muscle than boys. So, which is it? Will the girls look like boys simply by playing hockey or is that an impossibility? I also asked why was hockey merely a man's sport? Where do the rules state that fact?

I further pointed out that a few of my players would hold their own in a physical matchup with some of the boys. Not all, but quite a few of them. In fact, the boys would be hard pressed to spot which of my players were girls if they didn't have a ponytail. I then went on to refute the argument that it was immoral for a girl to play a contact sport. I indicated that many of my players handle pain better than even I could handle pain. And the girl that went home to recuperate? Her parents brought her home against her will. It was not her decision. I challenged the boys to come skate with us and see if they could keep up with our conditioning drills. I was not surprised when none of the boys in the class took me up on the challenge. To be truthful, it would have been a no-win situation for the boys. If they won, they were supposed to and if they lost, they would not live it down.

I concluded my speech by saying that hockey is a game for everyone and instead of tearing down the girls for playing, we should all be supporting one another. As it turns out the boy that wrote the speech had asked out one of my players and she shot him down. It appears that this was a personal vendetta against her, versus the whole team. Teenage angst can be so tough to handle.

"A boy told me that I skate like a girl. I told him,
if he skated a little faster, he could too!"
—Unknown~

JILL POHTILLA AND AUGSBURG AUGGIES-WOMEN

When I started coaching girls and women, there were some minor adjustments that I needed to be aware of. I mentioned earlier that women and girls generally liked to connect when they got on the ice. They would be stretching and warming up and chatting about their day or classes. My niece Elizabeth was my touchstone on the St. Ben's team. I would come on the ice at St. Ben's and ask my niece,

"How you guys doing today?"

On the days she would give me a sharp, "Fine!" as an answer, I would just say, "Okay, the coaches will be down on that end, you guys warm up. And we'll start when you are ready."

Just a bit of awareness of their moods was needed. Once they adjusted and were warmed up, we would jump into the practice plan.

After my one year at Gilmour Academy, I got married over the summer and also lined up an assistant coaching job with the Augsburg women's hockey program. It was at Augsburg that I had the distinct honor coaching with one of the best coaches I have ever worked with, Jill Pohtilla. Jill is in the Minnesota Girls Hockey Coaches Association Hall of Fame. She started the Augsburg program in 1995 and was one of the leading coaches in the MIAC until her retirement from coaching in 2010. Jill also has been inducted into The WHAM (Women's Hockey Association of Minnesota.) and was inducted into the Augsburg College Athletic Hall of Fame in 2021. I learned a great deal from Jill. She is one of the most morally upstanding coaches I have ever known. It was a true privilege to work with Jill for the four years that I was at Augsburg with the women's program. She is one of my most treasured friends. Love you, Jilly.

As I stated earlier, I was fortunate to travel on a fantastic trip to Germany, Austria and Italy when I worked with Jill. It was an incredible experience. One of my favorite nights was playing in the city of Augsburg. We had a party afterwards and the home-town players were amazed that a college in the United States had the same name as their town. It was so incredible to be playing hockey in other countries. There is a sense of community that is sometimes missing when the teams in college hockey are competing. The pressure to win obscures the enjoyment of playing. Don't get me wrong, I am very competitive and want to win, but there is something about playing for the pure joy of the sport. It brings you back to your youth and playing pick-up hockey on the pond it's a very special experience.

One final example of some of the differences between coaching females versus males. There was one practice that Jill and I were coaching, and she noticed a first-year player not giving her all in practice. Jill skated up to her and challenged her by saying,

"Why aren't you working hard to make your teammates better?!"
The player looked at Jill and responded, "I have my period!"
Jill just looked at her and said, "Well, I have mine too, so suck it up!"
That is something male coaches can't say.

I learned a great deal from Jill. She is one of the most moral, upstanding individuals I have ever met. She is a true friend. I love you Jill!

"Women, like men, should try to do the impossible.
And when they fail, their failure should be a challenge to others."
—Amelia Earhart (1897–1937)

Thomas H Peart

BILL HALBREHDER

My friend Bill Halbrehder died from pancreatic cancer on April 2, 2023. He fought hard to beat the cancer, but ultimately lost his battle. Bill was a very passionate person. His first passion was his wife, Barb. He met Barb on a soccer field and they both quickly realized that they were soulmates. They were together for forty-one years and had a love for each other that many people can only dream about. I always admired the love that they have had for one another. Bill also loved his grandkids. They brought great joy to him, especially as he fought the insidious disease that took his life.

Bill also had a passion for Willy Cars, especially the Willy Street Rods made from 1933-1942. When he and Barb built their new house, Bill made sure that his garage had a high enough ceiling that he could work underneath a car when it was on the car lift. Over the years, he rebuilt quite a few cars and showed them off with great pride. He leaves behind many friends who shared this "hot rod" passion with him.

One of Bill's greatest passions was coaching and teaching. His love of the game of hockey was evident anytime you spoke with him. He absolutely loved the game and devoted his life to making kids better people and better hockey players. He worked and coached at North St. Paul for thirty-one years where he won over 300 games as a head coach, but his biggest contribution to North St. Paul, as well as any other program he worked with, was his genuine love of kids and desire to make them the best people they could be. Everyone he coached and worked with he considered to be part of his family.

I had every intention of getting over to see Bill before he passed. I didn't make it in time. I was in Belize when Bill went to join Herbie Brooks and Keith "Huffer" Christiansen and other hockey players that he played with that had left this world before him. It is one of the biggest tragedies of life that we sometimes put things off for too long, and then it is too late. I wanted to tell him thank you for all the years of his friendship. All the moments of support. All the great times that we talked about hockey and coaching. All the things that he taught me over the years. I would have had my Bacardi Limon and Diet Coke and Bill would have had his beer with the two or three olives in it. There was no limit to how long Bill could talk about hockey. Barb would sometimes roll her eyes and shake her head, but she also knew that talking hockey with people who loved the game as much as he did was when he was happiest. And I would have told him that I loved him. Men seem to struggle with this concept. It's considered by some as unmanly or inappropriate. To that I say bull. It isn't said enough between men. It needs to be said and heard. Bill, I love you!

We will meet again "partner" and it will be glorious to talk hockey and skate with you once again.

> *"A teacher affects eternity; you can never tell where his influence stops."*
> —Henry Brooks Adams (1770–1831)

THE TRAINERS

There are a great many things that go into running a successful hockey program, especially on the college level. You need a supportive athletic director who shares in the vision of your program and will provide you with the tools and money needed to run that program effectively. You need a great admissions department that will work hard to get qualified student-athletes admitted to your school. You also need great assistant coaches who understand their roles and work hard to fulfill them, trust amongst coaches is paramount. And you need a recruiting vision. Some coaches just try and get the most talented players they can, while other coaches try and fill specific spots or positions. It all depends on your goals and objectives. Along with this, you need a game plan for the season because every team has a little different flavor. Great goaltending, some steady defense and some consistent goal scorers always help. Lastly, you need some luck. Making the right decisions at the right time, your best players stepping up when you need them too, and your role players playing above themselves. The one thing people always seem to forget in this equation is that you need great athletic trainers. I have been fortunate in my career to have known and worked with some fantastic athletic trainers. Early on, Nancy O'Connor at St. Cloud State. Kelly Flynn when I was coaching at Roosevelt and Dave Matzoll at Totino-Grace were three of the best trainers out there. Then there were two that were extraordinary and made a great impact on the programs I worked with. These two, Julie Deyak at St. Ben's and Missy Strauch at Augsburg were key to our success as college hockey programs. You could trust them both to put the student-athletes' health as priority one and they were extremely honest with the coaches they worked with. Their job was to protect kids, but also to get them back on the ice, the court or the field of play. They worked extremely long hours and put their heart and souls into their jobs. Without them our programs would not have had the successes that they did, To all you athletic trainers out there, thank you. We love you! You never get the credit that you deserve.

Oh, and one last shout out to Ben Jangula. Ben ran the Blue Line Medical Group and did a phenomenal job providing EMT's for the MGHCA programs and did the same for many years for the Minnesota Hockey High Performance programs. He is now retired and living in Savannah, Georgia. He is a great person!

"To keep the body in good health is a duty...otherwise we shall not be able to keep our mind strong and clear."
—Buddha (564 BC–483 BC)

UNIVERSITY OF ST. MARY'S

I worked with Jill Pohtilla for four years as a part time assistant at Augsburg, so when the opportunity to go full time with St. Mary's men's hockey program opened up, I jumped at the chance. My good friend, Bill Moore was taking over the head coaching position at St. Mary's in 2008. He hired me and I was excited about the new position as assistant hockey coach. However, it required me moving to Winona. Winona is a beautiful little town in the bluff country of the Mississippi River. I moved down there and found an apartment by Winona State.

My two years coaching men's college hockey were both tough years. First off, with Augsburg in 1995-1996, Ed Saugestad had all his health problems. Then my mom died in January of 1996. In my only year with the men's team at St. Mary's, 2008-2009, I was in the process of getting divorced. Things didn't work out between my ex-wife and me. As I told my players at St. Mary's,

"Things happen to you in life. To all of us. What is important is how you deal with those things after they occur."

St. Mary's was a tough year, both on the ice and off for me. I personally worked through the aftermath of getting divorced and the team improved throughout the season, but it certainly was a roller-coaster ride for the boys, as they had to adjust to new coaches, new systems and become more disciplined.

Our team had a good deal of talent, but we didn't know how to win consistently. As I said, we had a very up and down season. We finished up with a record of 9-14-2. We won a couple that we maybe shouldn't have won and a lost bunch that we should have won. It wasn't all bad, however. Everything that happens in life is a learning experience and I certainly learned a great deal working there. I believe that the players did as well.

One of my fondest memories of my time there happened early in the season. There is a tradition at St. Mary's where the two assistant coaches draft their teams for a red/white intersquad game that takes place after the first two weeks of practice and before the beginning of games in the regular season. It's a big thing on campus and certainly competitive between the assistant coaches. J, the other assistant played at St. Mary's and had been coaching there for a year or two prior to my arrival. We scouted players for two weeks and then picked the teams. J picked mostly upper-class returners and I went with the younger, hungrier guys. We were given a two-hour time slot to practice alone with our team. A closed practice mind you. Like there are really any secrets other than a few minor plays in the game of hockey. How you run your power play, penalty kills, or face offs are three examples, but once you watch the first power play or penalty kill, you adjust as you go. Just to rib J a bit, I snuck up to the Alumni Room that overlooks the ice and faked like I had a video camera set up. J freaked out and accused me of cheating. I just laughed and said it was a prank. I really could care less what they were doing in practice. Heck, he, and the boys on his team could have watched our practice. I really could have cared less. We ended up beating them 4-1, but I think some of them really thought it was because I watched some of their *closed practice.*

All in all, it was a tough year. I felt pretty much alone. Bill and I hung out some and I occasionally would have the goaltenders over for dinner, but the rest of the time I felt lonely. My buddy Bobby Olson came down one weekend when his son was playing for Concordia. We had a great weekend together, but other than a few times here and there, I was happiest when I was on the road recruiting. At the end of the year, Bill and I met, and he let me know that St. Mary's wasn't renewing my contract. That was okay, I had already decided that I was leaving and was going to hand in my resignation. It all worked out for the best really. I became the girls head hockey coach at Totino-Grace high school. I really enjoyed the players that I worked with though, there were a lot of great kids on the team. Winona and SMU just weren't the right fit for me.

"What would life be if we had no courage to attempt anything?"
—Vincent Van Gogh (1853–1890)

TOTINO-GRACE

My last six years of coaching were spent at Totino-Grace high school as head coach with the girl's hockey program. This was 2009-2015. We made the section finals four of those six years, but never could get over the hump and make it to the state tournaments. We practiced and played our home games at Parade Ice Gardens. Every day before practice, we coaches would put on our skates right by the rink and players would come out of the locker room. As they each came out, I would ask how their day was or tease them about something, just anything to each of them prior to practice just to connect in a small way. One of my assistants asked one day if I thought the players even cared that I interacted with them. Maybe they were just humoring me. So, the next day I told my assistant coach Maria Swanson that I was trying an experiment. The players streamed out to the ice, and I didn't say a word to any of them, not a one. We started practicing and about halfway through practice Maria skated up to me. She told me almost every player had asked if I was mad at them. I guess they did listen and felt connected because of my little comments to each of them.

Later that same year we were in the quarterfinals of the section playoffs against Simley. We were down by three goals after a bad second period. I came into the locker room and the whole team was subdued, probably thinking I was ticked off and would yell at them because this was a team that we should have been beating by three goals. I looked at them, sighed and just said, "Ladies, I really don't know what to say. Really, unless we want the season to be over, we need to go balls out in the third period."

Then I stopped talking as I realized what I had said. I am sure that the look on my face was one of shock, because I always tried to be respectful around my players. I didn't cuss around them and surely didn't allow them to cuss either. I started to apologize and one of my toughest players and captain of the team, looked at me and replied, "Don't worry coach we have bigger balls than boys do!"

The locker room cracked up. And by gosh, we came out like a team possessed and beat Simley to move on to the semi-finals.

In the semi-finals we faced St. Paul United. A very good team. We again were down going into the third period. United's locker room was right next to ours and you could hear them laughing and talking about how they were going to beat South St. Paul in the finals. I propped the door open and told the team to listen,

"Listen to them, they think they have already won this game. I think we have a bit more left in the tank. Let's let them know you have to play until the end whistle when you play Totino-Grace."

We played South St. Paul in the finals later that week and lost in double overtime, but that is a story for another day.

"Don't let a win get to your head or a loss to your heart!"
—Anonymous (From Picture Quotes.com)

TOTINO-GRACE GOALTENDERS AND
THE CHAMPIONSHIP GAME

I have been very lucky to have worked with some great goaltenders in my career. John Zimmer, Derek Hanson, Joe Girod, Jim Koltes and Greg Nelson at Armstrong. Andy Kruppa, Brett Olson, Mike Grover and Shawn Haroldson at Roosevelt. John Noctor and Dean Russell-Samways in England. Jackie MacMillan, Amy Hockett and Rachel Young at Buffalo. Kate Hall, Amanda Reed and Kristin Blumberg at St. Ben's. Rebecca Allen and Lauren Mellen at Gilmour Academy. Toni Menth and Amanda Bockman at Augsburg. And last but not least, Greg Moore at St. Mary's. I have been very fortunate, because you aren't going to have consistent success without steady goaltending. I worked with two of the best at Totino-Grace. Brittany Fussy and Logan Knip.

Brittany came to Totino-Grace from Blaine and was one of the better high school goaltenders during her three years with us. When Brittany was done playing, she held, or was in the top five, of every goalie record for Totino-Grace. She had the most saves in a game with fifty-four, most saves in a season with 703, 2nd in career saves with 1,781, Second in shutouts for a season with seven. Brittany was also a great mentor for the younger goaltenders, and she took Logan Knip under her wing, teaching her how to handle different situations that she would face as a starter.

When I retired Logan had attained three school goaltending records. She set the record for most saves in a game with fifty-five. Most saves in a season with 812. And most starts in a season with twenty-eight. She also was all conference for the two years she played for us and was All State in 2013-2014.

I believe Logan's best game came in the Section 4A Championship game against South St. Paul. We lost 2-1 in double overtime, but Logan played the game of her life. She ended up with a school record fifty-five saves on fifty-seven shots. She did everything in her power to help us try and win.

We were down 1-0 with about fifty-seven seconds left. We were pressing hard when South St. Paul's goaltender covered the puck. I called timeout. I had noticed that their goalie would kick the puck out towards the bottom of the opposite circle from where the shot came from. The faceoff was on the left of the goaltender. So, I put out my best face off center in Abby Huber to take the draw. I told her to draw the puck back to Laura Minkoff at the top of the circle and I told Allison Parnell to start at the far circle, face off dot, read the puck and put the puck in the goal when it rebounded to her. I had a feeling that the puck would come right to her. And it worked, although not exactly how I drew it up. We didn't win the draw, but their defender tried to clear the puck and passed it right to Laura. She put a perfect shot on net. The South St. Paul goalie kicked it right to Allison who scored to tie the game up. We played our butts off the whole game and sadly lost on a lucky bounce with fifty-two seconds left in the second overtime. I just felt if we could have gotten a rest with the time in between overtimes, we may have won the game in the third overtime. What was undeniable was how good Logan and Brittany played in their careers, and how fortunate I was to have not one, but two exceptional, intelligent, and outstanding young goaltenders like Brittany and Logan on my teams at Totino-Grace.

"Never confuse a single defeat with a final defeat."
—F. Scott Fitzgerald (1896–1940)

A DARK SIDE OF COACHING

At the beginning of each season, I would have a player/parent meeting with all of the players and parents. My message was pretty much the same every year to the parents. Their son or daughter is the most important thing to them. To the coaches, all the players on the team are equally important. I would say 90% got it and understood and supported the staff. 5% didn't understand and 5% didn't care or didn't listen.

I have written in previous stories about some of the great parents of players that I have coached. Now, I will tell you about one of the crazy experiences I have had with a parent. Overall, I have run into great parents over the years and generally have gotten along with most. There have been a few over the years that haven't seen eye to eye with me though. Here is a story about one parent at Totino-Grace. For obvious reasons, I have changed the name of the parent involved.

We had an incident on a road trip early in the season. One of my players snuck booze into the hotel room in a Gatorade bottle. When I found out, I called my athletic director, and he told me to sit the four roommates down and ask them who was involved. In retrospect, it was counterproductive, as no one wanted to tell on their teammate. Probably should have anticipated that, but I was following his directions.

Later that season, we, as coaches, called a mandatory community service project for the players with the group called "Feed My Starving Children." Each of the Totino-Grace sports programs were required to do at least one community service project per season. In my letter to the parents and players, I stated that *"T-G gives us lots of gifts and this is our way to give back to the community. Any players with a conflict need to check with me if you have a conflict."* I kid you not, this is the email I received from the parents of one of my freshman players. Now keep in mind, this dad's daughter was one of the roommates in the hotel room drinking situation, though she was not the offending player. Please note, I have changed the name of the girl and her family.

"Excuse me, but you're the hockey coach. I don't need to clear anything with you. You, nor TG, have been appointed the director of charitable giving of time and money for the (Sanderson) family. You should be plenty busy just trying to coach the girl's hockey team, as it appears you are already in over your head just trying to accomplish that task. This is evident with your overstepping your authority into trying to be the social conscience for TG families. While I am on the topic of how great you are not, let's visit the alcohol incident involving your team. You must be the world's biggest moron to think the best way to get to the facts as to 'what happened', in any conflict, is to get all the players involved to sit in one room and discuss the incident. Did you learn the Catholic way of handling abuse and conflict from the pedophile priests? I have zero intention of letting someone like you, with such poor communication skills and morals to spend any 'mandatory' extra time with my daughter. I send my kids to TG for the education. Hockey is extracurricular and you have your hands full just teaching the basics. Save your energy for that and leave saving the world, having a social conscience and giving back to the community to the parents! (Mandy) will not be at your 'mandatory' event, nor will she make it up in some way.' I strongly suggest you clear ANY and ALL 'mandatory' additions to the hockey schedule with me before you decide to approve them. We the parents and students of TG, afford you the privilege of teaching and coaching our sons and daughters. It is your privilege, not a right. Let me make this very clear, YOU HAVE NOT EARNED THE OPPORTUNITY, MUCH LESS THE RIGHT, TO TELL ME WHAT MY DAUGHTER IS GOING TO DO WITH THEIR TIME OUTSIDE OF THEIR NORMAL CLASS TIME OR EXTRA CURRICULAR TIME. GOT IT?"

Now obviously the "mandatory" aspect pushed a few buttons for the dad. Well, he pushed a few buttons with me as well. I talked to my friend Mike MacMillan, and he had some good advice. He advised me to contact my athletic director and don't go to the guy's house. See, I could care less if the guy thought I knew what I was doing on the ice. This is the one area that I have always been confident in what I was doing, coaching. But when the parent compared me to the pedophile priests and called into question my morals, well that crossed the line in my mind. I forwarded the message to my athletic director and told him that he needed to handle this situation, or I would, and it would be in the parking lot and then he would have to resolve the bigger problem of an altercation between myself and this parent. The school brought in both parents and had a meeting. The situation was resolved to a certain degree, though the father's personal insult to me did not get resolved. As it turns out, what this parent was upset about was that they were going to Duluth for their son's tournament and didn't feel comfortable leaving their ninth-grade daughter home alone. It turns out that he had sent a similar letter to the Admissions department laying the groundwork with the high school league to leave Totino-Grace and still maintain his two kids' eligibility. They transferred the next year. The funny thing is that all these parents would have had to do was call me and tell me that the reason she was going to miss was because her brother had an out-of-town hockey trip, and they didn't want to leave her home alone. Easy peasey. Go on the trip. See you when you get back. Some parents!

"Life is really simple, but we insist on making it complicated."
—Confucius (551 BC – 471 BC)

THE OFFICIALS

I thought I would delve into a few stories of some of my encounters with referees during my coaching career. First off, I have known a lot of great referees over the years. Some of my favorites include Mark Whipple, Denny and Matt Roach, Jim Larson. Terry Abram, Bill Newhouse, Scott Parker, Greg Hughes, Rob Shattuck, Jim Bergstrom, Rick Tibesar, Bill Kronschnabel, and the crazy Bill Rhody. They all worked hard and were firm, but fair.

We start with a JV game when I was at Armstrong. We were getting hammered by Edina, and I was really frustrated, although in all fairness Edina was a better team. We were trying our hardest, but it just wasn't in the cards that day. So, I am stewing on the bench and the kids are taking a few penalties which just leads to more goals against us. Now the benches at Braemar at the time had a slide bolt to close the gate. I had tried to summon the referee over to our bench a few times. He wouldn't come over, which just frustrated me more. Finally, I slid the bolt so the gate would not close and called the ref over. One of my players is trying to show me how to close it and I am telling him to be quiet and batting his hand away. Finally, the referee comes over and we look at the door. He slides the bolt back so the gate would close. I then looked at him and asked him if he had a green Edina jersey on under those stripes. He didn't appreciate that very much and dinged me for a bench penalty. Bob O'Connor, the Edina JV coach, and one of the legends of Edina hockey asked me after the game what I said to the referee. I told Bob what I said. He looks at me and in a very serious tone and says, "Oh, you can't do that. But that was pretty good!" And then he started laughing.

During my first year at Roosevelt, we were playing Edison in a game. I was on Jim Larson pretty hard. Jim usually was quick tempered, but he was in a good mood that day and let me harp and question almost every call. Edison was really good that year. I made a rookie mistake and got my third line out there against their first line. Boom, Edison scored right away. Jim skated over, called me down to the end of the bench. He looked at me and says, "Nice F'ing line change dummy!"

Then he skated away laughing. I understood his point. When coaching, you need to worry about your team and let the officials worry about the game. From

Thomas H Peart

then on, I tried to pick my spots and not complain to the referees as much. Though it sure was hard some days. In 2018, I ran into Jim at the Veteran's Hospital. He had cancer and died later that year. Semper Fi my friend, rest in peace.

Another time when I was coaching in Buffalo with the Wright County Blades, one of my assistants was just hammering the referee on an offsides call. The referee had heard enough. He threw the puck down on the face-off dot. He turned and started pointing and yelling at my assistant. None of us were sure if he meant for the play to begin. Or if he was just pausing the play to yell at my assistant. I took it that the play started, and I yelled at my players to take the puck. My center grabbed the puck, and we caught the other team flatfooted. We almost scored on that play. It was a pretty funny moment as the other referee was as confused as we all were.

I was only tossed out of one game in my career. It was during my first year at Roosevelt. We had a referee named Jerry Bergstrom. Nice guy, except for this day. I always chewed gum on the bench and always had a pen and notepad to jot down notes and who was on the ice for goals for and against. During one pause in play, I was ripping on Jerry about some call. I am empathetically making my point by slamming my notepad with my pen. Suddenly two things happened. One, my pen flew out of my hand and two, my gum flew out my mouth. Both right at Jerry. I caught the gum, but the pen hit him. Jerry thought I threw my pen on purpose and kicked me out of the game. He didn't buy my explanation that it was a mistake.

I really appreciated referees like Mark Whipple and Denny Roach. If they made a mistake, they would look you in the eye and say,

"Hey Tommy, I missed that one."

I made sure to shake the refs' hands after the game. I always believe that they tried hard and tried to be fair. They just didn't always see things the way I saw them!

"Whatever you do in life, surround yourself with smart people
who'll argue with you."
—Unknown~

THE REFS ARE OFTEN...CORRECT!

Now, I was a pretty passionate coach and would defend my players. However, sometimes I would speak before I thought out the consequences. I was coaching a junior varsity game at Armstrong, and we were playing Jefferson at New Hope Ice Arena. Jefferson scored a couple of PP goals with a player behind my goalie in the crease. I complained vehemently to the officials, that the goals should be disallowed because the opposing player couldn't be in the crease. I might have even mentioned that if I was wrong, I would eat the darn rule book. I stopped in the ref's room after the game. Yep, they had changed the rule. The trainer stopped me after I ate the first three pages of the rule book. Thankfully. I probably would have been tossing my cookies or spending a lot of time in the bathroom, if I ate the whole thing. There are a lot of pages in those rule books. I need to note that generally, I got along with all the officials. They were trying their best to run a fair game and make it fun for the kids to compete. Doesn't mean I didn't say something at times. Or stick my foot in my mouth on occasion!

I only went out on the ice after one official in my entire career. My Roosevelt team was playing Southwest and up to this point we had never beaten them. One time against them at Parade Ice Gardens, we tied up the game late and we were in overtime when our goaltender Andy Kruppa made a save and had the puck trapped in his upper body. A Southwest player then collided with him knocking the puck into the net. For some reason the referee allowed the goal to stand. It was an emotional loss. Yours truly felt that the referee should have called a penalty for contact with my goaltender and waved the goal off. He didn't and I pretty much lost it. My players were trying to keep me away from the referee, they knew the look on my face. Unfortunately for me, the athletic director for the entire city, Ed Prohofsky, was in attendance. I received quite the dressing down from Ed.

"How do you expect your players to be respectful when you are acting like a fool and losing your temper?"

Ed was a man that I deeply respected and admired. It was a tough night.

*"I've spent pretty much my whole life realizing that
I should have shut up ten minutes ago!"*
—Unknown (From AZ Quotes)

ATHLETIC DIRECTORS

A key aspect of every high school and college program is the relationship between a coach and his or her athletic director (AD). I have had good ones and a few great ones. At Armstrong, since I was an assistant coach, my time with the athletic director was very limited. Same thing at Augsburg with both the men and women, as well as Buffalo and Wayzata. In England, the Director of Hockey Operations was Ron Charbonneau. His position was similar to an athletic director. He was in charge of the overall program. Ron and I got along pretty well, but he and three of our imports were having lunch with the owner every week and planning changes for the club, namely my position. As the season was wrapping up, I came up with a list of items that needed to be put into effect to improve the professionalism of the team. Almost all my suggestions were implemented the next season, even though I was let go and Ron had on hand in it. I don't blame him however, as I know that at least two imports pushed to have me removed. Ron stayed on as GM for a couple more years and the team had some success. All I can say is thanks Ron for giving me a chance. It didn't work out for more than a year, but you are a great guy, for a Canuck!

At St. Mary's I was a full-time assistant, so I had a bit more contact with the AD, Nikki Fennern. Part of my duties was fall and spring sports supervisor. A supervisor sets up for the games and makes sure that the officials are taken care of, that there are student workers at the games to assist with anything needed and make sure that the tickets and money gets turned in after the games. Nikki was fair, but firm with the people that worked for her, but she wasn't overly warm towards us. It comes with the position of being the boss. Like a head coach, you need to have a separation from the people working for you.

As a head coach, the relationship I had with the best AD's was a little different at each program. At Roosevelt, my AD Eric Magdanz, was phenomenal to work with. He was a very hands-off supervisor and trusted me to run my program. As I had written about earlier, the team had a lot of issues that first year. I was in Eric's office at least once a week. He was always fair and straight with me. Eric was a great basketball player at the University of Minnesota in the early 1960's and was the team MVP during his senior year, so he understood sports and athletes, as well as coaches. I had always intended to get over to Eric's house and tell him this in person. Unfortunately, he passed away in 2021, before I could make the trip to his house. One of my regrets in life.

At Gilmour Academy the Hockey Director was John Malloy. Another great man to work for. John made sure I had the money and budget to run the program and recruit quality student-athletes. He was another hands-off boss who was there if you needed him but allowed me the latitude to run the program the way I saw fit. John was also a great hockey player at Miami University-Ohio.

Two of the other AD's I had were more hands-on type AD's. The first was Carol Howe-Veenstra at St. Ben's. She was the most organized AD I have worked with in my career. Carol paid attention to all the little details and challenged her coaches to do their best. I learned a great deal about organizing my program and paying attention to details from Carol. She was also a very accomplished volleyball coach at St. Ben's and cared greatly about all the women who wore the red and white.

The second hands-on and last AD of my career was Mike Smith at Totino-Grace. Mike and I have a unique connection as I coached his wife Michelle in softball at Cooper High School back in the 1991 and 1992 seasons. Michelle was an incredible athlete and is an even better person. Mike is probably more of a mixture of a hands-on AD and a hands-off AD. He is not totally hands off, as the school is a little closer knit as a whole than other schools I have worked at, but he doesn't hover over you and every decision you make. He expects you to always keep the school's morals and values in mind. He has always been there when I needed him though He is an excellent AD and also an excellent baseball coach at Totino-Grace. I have really been fortunate with the Athletic Directors that I have worked with.

"Find your course & remain steadfast to its outcome."
—Toussaint Louverture (1783–1803)

"THE MIRACLE ON ICE" 1980 GOLD MEDAL TEAM

I would be remiss if I didn't write a story about the single greatest sporting event in my life! 2020 marked the 40th Anniversary of the "Miracle on Ice" 1980 Gold Medal winning Olympic Hockey Team's improbable win against the Russians. I was a Resident Advisor in my dorm (Hill-Case Hall) at St. Cloud State University. I was on duty the weekend the games were played against Russia on Friday and the Gold Medal game against Finland on Sunday. My sister had taped both the Russia and Finland games for me. The USA/Russia game played during the afternoon in Lake Placid and was on a tape delay. I purposely stayed away from any televisions as some of the guys in the dorm who were huge hockey fans, and I were going to watch the game later that evening. I went out to a college bar called the Trader and Trapper for happy hour prior to my weekend on duty. I drank a Coca-Cola, socialized a bit and then left for campus. I turned on my car. Just as I was reaching to turn off the radio I heard, "The USA wins! They beat Russia today 4-3 in an incredible game!" Ugh.

Of course, it did not diminish the awesomeness of the game, but it would have been fun and nerve racking to watch it without knowing the result. Heck, I still watch it today and it is just as exciting 40 years later. The dorms were just crazy that whole weekend and there was a huge party on my floor. SCSU is a dry campus and unfortunately if you saw booze, you had to throw it out. I was one of those RA's that didn't go looking for guys or gals to bust but would follow the rules if I caught someone. I told my guys to be smart. Stay in their rooms, keep the music down etc. Well, you know what happens as people get intoxicated, they get louder and louder. I received a complaint, and I went up, knocked on the door of the room where the music was coming from, and a young man opens the door. There in his hand is a whole fifth of booze unopened. I had to confiscate it and pour the whole thing down the drain. I thought the kid was going to cry. The party pretty much broke up after that.

On Sunday, a whole group of the guys on my floor met in the community room and watched the USA win the Gold Medal. You could hear the cheers all throughout the dorms,

Thomas H Peart

"U-S-A! U-S-A! U-S-A!"

On Monday I was called into the Dorm Director's office. He looked at me and said,

"I hear that there was a knee hockey game going on up on your floor at 11:30 last night."

I replied, "Yeah, I heard some guys out there playing. Just as I stepped out of my room the overnight supervisor came off the elevator. Just a coincidence."

(My room was right across the hall from the elevator, and it was a great place to play knee hockey if you were so inclined.)

He looked at me with a smirk and said,

"Oh Yeah? Why does my note from the night supervisor say that you were winning 3-2?"

Whoops, busted! He was a pretty cool guy and just made me work an extra weekend as punishment.

The cool thing about being involved with USA Hockey and the Coaching Education Program is that I have had the chance to meet some of that 1980 team. Most probably would never recognize me, but I had met many of them at different USA Hockey clinics including Buzzy Schneider, Phil Verchota, Neal Broten, Rob McClanahan, Mike Eruzione, Bill Baker and Jim Craig. I have a minor connection with Mike Ramsey since he is a Roosevelt Teddie and married to a St. Mane from the famous St. Mane family that owns St. Mane's Sporting Goods right by Roosevelt High School. I also know Mark Johnson because one of my Totino-Grace players (Laurel Miller) played for him at Wisconsin. And I had the awesome experience of working with John "Bah" Harrington at CSB/SJU. John and I became good friends and had some fantastic discussions about his Olympic experience. I also was fortunate to meet Herb Brooks, the coach of the 1980 team, in person, down in Naples, Florida. Herb was incredibly fascinating to speak with and it was amazing to me that he would take the time to speak with a me, a D III women's coach, who he had just met. It was an incredible morning. Rest In Peace Herb!

Lastly, I have one other connection with the 1980 team. The third goaltender for most of their pre-Olympics season was Bruce Horsch. He was cut just before the Olympics. Bruce played at Michigan Tech and is the winningest goaltender in Michigan Tech history. He won a National Title in 1975. He was coaching at Tech when I worked the summer hockey camps. I haven't seen him in a number of years, but he was always fun to hang out with and interesting to talk with.

"Great moments are born from great opportunities."
—Herb Brooks (1937–2003) (By Permission)

JOHN "BAH" HARRINGTON

As I have already written, I worked with Bah at St. Ben's and St. John's. We were the head coaches for our respective programs. We got along really well even though we had different personalities. There was a movie in the late 1990's called "Planes, Trains and Automobiles." It starred Steve Martin, as a very fastidious, organized, reserved person and John Candy, who was very positive and basically a very happy person. This is my real-life movie equivalent. Bah would be Steve Martin and yours truly would be John Candy.

Bah and I were asked to speak at a combined St. Ben's/St. John's alumnus gathering at Jax Cafe in Minneapolis. Bah called me and asked if I could drive. I had just gotten my car out of the shop the day before, so we were good to go. I picked him up at his house and we headed to the Twin Cities. It was a great drive down, talking hockey and his experiences on the Olympic team. I was in Heaven. We were a little confused as to where the restaurant was located, and we first stopped at the place where I thought it was. It turns out not to be the right place. While Bah ran in to get directions, I noticed that my check engine light was on. I ignored it, I figured I could bring it back to the shop the next day. Besides, we needed to get to the Alumni event. We got to Jax in Nordeast Minneapolis, had a great dinner, both gave talks about our programs, had a couple of drinks with the alums and went out to my car at about 10:00 PM. It wouldn't start. One of the alums gave us a jump and Bah and I took off for home. We got about six blocks, and my car died. We coasted into the Super America gas station on the corner of Broadway and University. I had AAA, so I called for a tow. We waited and waited and waited. I even asked a policeman that stopped for a cup of coffee if he could help. He couldn't or wouldn't. I called AAA again. It was going to be another hour.

By now it's around 11:30 PM, so I called my sister Margaret who lived in Minnetonka, a good thirty-five miles away. She and my nephew Jeff came together in her car to help. Margaret thought we could jump my car and I explained to her that a jump was not going to help. I had hoped that Jeff would have followed her with his Chevy Blazer rather than ride with her. This way Bah and I could take his Blazer and follow the tow truck. Jeff didn't bring his car, so we all talked about it and decided the best bet was to go get Jeff's Blazer back in Minnetonka. We piled in Margaret's car, a Chevy Suburban and I noticed that Bah is getting quieter and quieter.

We drove to Minnetonka and then back to Minneapolis in Jeff's vehicle arriving back at the SA around 12:45. I checked with the clerk. Sure enough, the tow truck had come and gone. When I told Bah this, he didn't say a word, he just gave me that steely glare of his. He was pissed. I was trying really hard to look on the positive side and laughed a bit. Bah was not having any of it and didn't see the humor in the situation. He was just pacing back and forth like a tiger in a cage.

By 1:15 AM, the tow truck finally showed up again, and we got my car towed to a repair shop in St. Anthony. It's 1:35 AM and we were finally on our way back to St. Cloud in Jeff's vehicle. Bah is still quiet, but the tension has eased now that we were on our way. We would get home by 2:45 AM. Just a few hours late.

We got a mile and a half past the St. Michael exit on I-94. when Jeff's Blazer sputtered and conked out. Bah glared at me again and yelled,

"Geezus Cripes! This is a f'ing nightmare! Don't you guys have any cars that run?"

So here we are, at about 1:45 AM walking on I-94 for at least a mile to the nearest exit hoping to find a phone. We see a well-lit gas station at the Albertville exit ramp. We hoofed it up there. The station was all lit up, but it was closed for the night. I spotted an outside pay phone, but it was not working. I think if Bah would have had a gun, he might have shot me at this point. We see another gas station two blocks away and start walking to it. It's also closed and doesn't have a pay phone outside. Suddenly a spotlight from a sheriff's car lit us up. Thankfully the deputy gave us a ride back to the St. Michael exit, where we found a phone and called sister Margaret, again.

Margaret and Jeff picked us up at 3:30 AM and we finally got Bah home at about 4:30 that morning. He had fallen asleep in the car; I woke him up when we arrived at his house. He got out of the car without a word, he slammed the door, stopped, opened the door, looked at me and said,

"TP, I am NEVER, EVER going anywhere with you again!"

And then he slammed the door a final time. Thankfully Bah forgave me and we are still good friends to this day.

"If you could kick the person responsible for most of your troubles, you wouldn't sit for a month."
—Theodore Roosevelt (1858–1919)

RANDOM THOUGHTS ON COACHING

I was talking with Tim Morris, and he told me that the entire girls hockey staff at Hutchinson has resigned due to parental pressure. And every year lately, on both the boys' and girls' side of the game, coaches are hanging up their whistles. There are lots of reasons, but many are due to parents coming after them and administrators not backing them up. One of my best friends, Bill Kelly, lost his college soccer job because two disgruntled players, who both had marginal ability, went after him and the college administration refused to back him up. They claimed that he had violated their Title IX rights. Title IX doesn't mean that every player has to play equally, it states that the opportunities to play sports between men and women have to equal. Is this how we want to treat people who spend their lives dedicated to trying to make young people into better adults?

So, what does make a good coach? What goes into it? Is it winning? I was fortunate enough to have the players to win over 400 games as a head coach. Does this make me a great coach? I also lost a little over 300 games. Does this make me a bad coach? What really goes into it? I worked with some incredible coaches. Coaches who cared about their players, worked hard to give them the best opportunities to succeed and more importantly, worked hard to make them better people. Some of these include Bruce Johnson, Don Moore, Bill Taleen, Mike Mulvey, Mike Macmillan, David Prokop, Larry Hendrickson, Dick Emahiser, Jill Pohtilla, Bill Halbrehder, Amy Cardarelle, Tom Brophy, Ed Saugestad, Steve Houge, Steve Carroll, Bill Kelly, Ben Shanahan, Denny Malarkey, Maria Swanson and Bill Moore. I could go on forever. And my apologies to anyone I missed. Plus, this is not counting the coaches that my teams played against. My point is that there are some bad coaches out there, but in my opinion, there are many more good coaches who put a great deal of time and effort into kids and the game of hockey, as well as all the other sports in our society.

Thomas H Peart

I believe that these are some of the things that make up a great coach.

- They are dedicated to the sport and their craft. Going to clinics. Learning new ways to coach. Learning new ways to communicate with their players.
- They treat kids with respect, and with a firm, steady hand. You need to teach kids to be accountable for their decisions.
- They make practices and games fun. Kids play because they love the sport, want to be with their friends, want to become better, and want to have fun. Winning factors in, but it's not the end all or be all.
- They help players grow and mature into solid, upstanding adults.
- They make an impact on their players lives.

There certainly are many more things that I haven't listed. What I can tell you is that I am proud of the kids I coached. I am proud of how many of them have gone on to become successful coaches, policemen, teachers, firemen, lawyers, airline pilots, chefs and parents. I love seeing and hearing about their kids' playing hockey or any other sport. and watching them grow up. It is awesome. I have never had kids of my own, but I like to think that a part of me lives on in the over one thousand kids I have had the pleasure of coaching over the years. Was I perfect? No. I made a lot of mistakes, but as I tried to teach all my players, making mistakes is how we learn and grow. What we should try and avoid is making the same mistakes over and over again! To all the coaches out there… keep fighting to help kids. You are valued by the people that care. The people that understand. You have a position in these kids' lives that can't be measured in wins and losses but is measured in the pleasure of seeing them succeed in life.

"You have to be able to go home, look at yourself in the mirror and say, 'I gave my best today!' Then you can be proud of yourself and your efforts."
—Thomas L. Peart (1915–1991)

MORE RANDOM THOUGHTS ON HOCKEY AND LIFE

It was a busy day with picking up hockey jerseys for the Minnesota Girls Hockey Coaches Association fall league tryouts. Then I had to pick up hockey bags and table covers. Next, I met a couple former teaching buddies for happy hour, then I went home and answered another bunch of hockey related emails to go with the two hundred and fifty or so I had already answered throughout the week. I would be rich if I was paid per email.

Have you ever wondered why some kids struggle with making decisions? In my opinion it's because their parents never make them decide for themselves. Almost half of the emails I deal with are from parents,

"Bertha has (the Icup/ rodeo nationals/water skiing tryouts/a lacrosse tourney/a golf outing etc.) can she switch her tryout times?"

Now this is after they put down their first and second choice of tryout days. I love the ones that put down First Choice: Saturday. Second Choice: Saturday. If they would just teach their little darlings that they need to decide what is important to them, it would go a great way in helping the little cherubs later in life. Is trying out for and making this fall league important enough to miss whatever else you have going? If not, then don't tryout. We have 197 players signed up. We'll put you on a waiting list. Seriously, it will help the kids far more in the long run. I once even had a dad try to get his daughter a free pass to play in the league.

"Well Bob (another staff member) knows how good she is. She will be one of your best players."

Sheesh, why hold tryouts? Let's just name people to the spots. But that is one of the problems with hockey in other states and even in Junior Hockey. Teams have tryouts and charge big bucks for those tryouts, when in actuality the coaching staff has already decided who will make the team. It's not fair to the players, and in my opinion it's wrong to do it just to raise money for your team. Oh, and by the way, the scene in "Miracle" where Herbie says that he has the list of his players picked before the end of the tryouts didn't happen. Herb watched them all the way through the week-long tryouts. That scene was changed to make the movie more dramatic.

Okay, I apologize. I just reread this, and it sounds pretty whiny. I am in a down mood. Just found out that a former players hubby died today. Life is fleeting and I am going to quit whining right now. My issues are trivial compared to losing the love of your life. Rest In Peace Forrest Renick. And to leave you with a more positive mood...a quote on friendship. To all my friends...thank you for being in my life!

"The language of friendship is not words but meanings."
—Henry David Thoreau (1817–1862)

AND EVEN MORE RANDOM THOUGHTS

I originally started this writing project on Facebook under the title "Stories from the Coronavirus Quarantine" and numbered the days. After eighty-five days or so, I decided to drop the days concept. Originally it was to keep track and I thought maybe I had twenty or so stories in me, which soon became twenty-five, then thirty-five, then fifty and now over eighty. It's kind of like jokes at a party. People tell one joke, which triggers a joke from me and then that joke triggers another person and so on and so forth. People will contact me and another story pops into my brain.

One of the experiences that was incredible for me personally was working with my fantastic friends Mike (Mac) MacMillan, Dave Prokop, and Larry Hendrickson. Mac started a hockey company called *The Hockey Development Company*. We would run various skills clinics, fall pre-season warm-ups for hockey associations and summer hockey camps. Two towns that turned out to be the most fun were Manitowoc, Wisconsin and Morristown, New Jersey.

At Manitowoc we ran a summer camp for their youth association. The kids were great to coach and really wanted to learn. We had a great time in that beautiful city on Lake Michigan. And in the evenings, we did our best to help the local economy. I believe that Bonkers Saloon was one of our nightly stops. When you work hockey schools, clinics, and camps, you work hard, but you also play hard. I am glad I was younger then. I don't think I could keep up anymore.

Morristown was another incredible experience. We spent at least three years running their pre-season warm-ups. Larry would do the dry-land portion, David would run the skating portion, I would be on the ice running some practices and Mac would skate and oversee the entire operation.

It was really something to see. All of the Morristown players had the best equipment that money could buy. Some of the Mite players had $700 skates and $400 sticks. That is crazy. Anyone who has been involved in hockey knows how fast young kids grow out of skates and equipment. However, Morristown is a bedroom community for the Financial District in New York City. There is no lack of money in that area. As a matter of fact, eleven people from Morristown lost their lives in the 9-11 attacks on New York City and the World Trade Center. Once again, all of our coaches did their best to give back to the economy of Morristown and New York. There were plenty of nights of sitting around the hotel and talking hockey with Larry, Mac and David. Let me tell you, Larry could tell some stories. Rest in Peace my friend.

One other thought, my friend Marilyn gave me a great book. "The Boy, The Mole, The Fox and The Horse" by Charlie Mackesy. It is outstanding. I can't quote the book as it would be a copywrite infringement, but I can assure you that the book is well worth your time to buy it and read it. It is one of my favorite books. It is a children's book, but certainly pertains to adults as well.

Essentially it is about life, friendship and growing up. The book is also about asking for help. Something that many of us struggle with. Somehow, we are taught, especially men, that we have to figure out life on our own and that asking for help is weak. When in essence, asking for help shows strength. It has taken me a long time to figure that one out and to do so in my life.

Have a brave and magnificent life everyone!

"It's not what we have in life, but who we have in our life that is important."
—Unknown (From Quotespedia.com)

ANOTHER SAD PART OF COACHING

I mentioned earlier that I thought cutting kids from your team was one of the hardest parts of coaching, and that is true. However, I am certain the hardest part about being a parent is losing a child, and in turn the hardest part of coaching is losing to an early death a player that you have worked with and praised and disciplined and fought for and developed into a young man or woman. That is truly the hardest part of coaching young people. I have lost way too many of the kids I coached over the years. I suppose it's true for all coaches, but it doesn't make it any easier. Here are the players, coaches, and friends that I would like to remember and pray that they are resting in peace. These are the ones that I know of, there may be more that I am not aware of.

Teammates, Players, and Coaches

Alexandria Cardinals: Raymond Devine, Gordy Vipond, Bill Theiss, Frank Verdugt, Brian Lynch, Scott Thompson, Tim Fitzgerald. Ron Domschot Football coach, Ross Larson Football coach, Ed Christopherson Football Coach.

Mesabi Community College Norsemen: Dan Rogers. Pat Finnegan Hockey coach and Jim Matchefts Hockey coach.

St. Cloud State Huskies: Doug "Boots" Randolph. Charlie Basch Hockey coach.

Armstrong Falcons: Allison Musech, Brian Boeder, Tom Reiswig, Derek Hanson. Don Moore Hockey coach and Lois Johnson Wife of Bruce Johnson Hockey coach.

Roosevelt Teddies: Shawn Haroldson, Elias Papalidis. Eric Magdanz Athletic Director.

Augsburg Auggies: Ed Saugestad Hockey coach

Thank you all for the impact that you had on my life.

"Ubuntu" A Zulu saying that means "Humanity." Its translation is: "I am because we are."

THE PANDEMIC

We have just gone through a major worldwide pandemic. Well, I guess we are still going through it. We were quarantined for a few months, and I started getting very agitated and too political, that is why I started writing these stories. I always thought that I should write down some of the stories from coaching and it has now happened. It was a very cathartic process. Another one of my projects during this quarantine was to go through all the plastic bins which I had filled with a lifetime of coaching memories and mementoes. I collected a lot of stuff, er, treasures, yeah that's it, treasures over the course of a lifetime. I did pare these treasures down from fifteen bins to ten bins. So that's good, right? Anyways, I coached hockey for thirty-seven years, but also coached softball, soccer and football. During a few years, I coached three different teams during the hockey season. Among the items I collected were the home and away jerseys from almost every team I coached and for sure, from all the teams that I served as a head coach. I also discovered that during this career of mine, I coached over one thousand players. That just seems amazing to me! And that is just my players during the regular season, it doesn't include the many hundreds of players that I coached in the spring, summer and fall. Or the kids I had in class. But you know what? I can't say that I liked every player that I coached or taught. I don't think anyone could, but I loved being their coach and teacher. I loved trying to help them grow into awesome women and men. Every one of them touched my heart in some way. And as happy as I was of the success stories, I was sad for the ones that I couldn't help more. There was a quote or a statement that I saw, and it touched me deeply. I am not sure who wrote it initially, but it is awesome!

Thomas H Peart

*"Coaching is a calling. Your players will break your heart, your colleagues don't consider you a real teacher, your critics roast you on social media, and you work countless hours for low pay. What keeps you going is changing lives.
That is a calling!"*
—Unknown

"You can't reach them all, but the hope is to reach enough."
—Bill Heslin (By Permission)

FRIENDS, OLD AND NEW

One of the greatest rewards which comes from being involved in the game of hockey for over fifty years is that I met and incredible number of people who became my friends. Some ended up being life-long friends and some were in my life for just a short period of time. What I have learned now that I am older (and hopefully wiser.) is that you always remember your friends. Little snippets of time come back to you in moments of reflection, and you remember fondly something that happened ten, twenty, thirty years ago. Just as if it happened yesterday.

You also never know what impact you may have on someone or the impact someone has on you. I remember attending the Bemidji Summer Hockey Camp in Bemidji. Gary Gambucci, who was playing professionally for the Minnesota North Stars, was one of the instructors. Somehow, we decided to bet on who would win in a shootout, him or me. The grand sum of a Dairy Queen malt was on the line for the winner. Gary let me stop a couple and then put my jock up in the stands with some incredible moves to win the shootout. It wasn't the outcome that impressed me. What I remember is that a professional athlete took the time to interact with me when he didn't have to. He made that hockey camp fun and I tried to emulate him with every player that I worked with over the thirty-seven years of coaching.

"We have three types of friends in life: friends for a reason, friends for a season, and friends for a lifetime."
—Anonymous (From Search Quotes)

Thomas H Peart

SOME FINAL THOUGHTS

There is a saying attributed to Confucius, often repeated throughout history, that states, "If you do what you love, you will never work a day in your life." I can attest to the truth of this statement. I loved being a hockey coach and a teacher. I believe that it was what I was truly and genuinely destined to do with my life. I am very fortunate that I could do what I loved for the past fifty plus years, including playing, coaching and administrating the great game of hockey. It wasn't always rosy or easy. I have made mistakes, but I have also learned from those mistakes. I have had fifteen surgeries in my life, ten of them directly resulting from my life in hockey. I have had two ankle surgeries from a broken bone in my lower leg. Three hip replacements (two on the left hip due to a fall on the ice after a hockey game, shaking hands no less.) Two surgeries on my left shoulder, two on my right shoulder and one on my left thumb. I have also had a broken tail bone, broken thumbs, lost four teeth, sustained numerous bruises and contusions as well as too many concussions to count. (Maybe why I was a goaltender in the first place.) I have had over one hundred stitches from cuts. And I now have arthritis in many of my joints. Even though I have had all of these injuries, I would do it all over again. There is nothing like the feel of skating, experiencing being free and fast and oh so cold! It was truly worth all of the later pain and agony, just to feel the wind on your face and hear the sound of your skates cutting into the ice. My sisters never were able to experience the feeling. Some of them skated, but none of them fell in love with hockey like I did. Hockey has given me a lifetime of joy. I have been very fortunate as well.

I have won over four hundred games as a head coach. I led Minneapolis Roosevelt to the Minnesota High School Hockey Tournament where we won the Consolation title. I was named Section Coach of the year four times, which goes to a coach in each high school section who has been deemed by his/her peers as the top coach in that section. I have been presented with the Ted Brill Award, which is given to an individual who is dedicated to the player development programs of Minnesota Hockey. It is presented annually and requires at least ten years of service to one of the various Minnesota Hockey programs. I have been presented with the Brano Stankovsky award, which is presented in honor of Brano Stankovsky, long time coach of the Blake School. The award is presented to an individual who has been involved in the Minnesota Girls Hockey Coaches Association and the many programs it offers for the advancement of girls' high school hockey in Minnesota. I have been presented with the Breaking Barriers Award, which is given annually to an individual who successfully tore down barriers to provide opportunities in sports for girls and women of all races, ages and levels of ability.

I have been awarded the Minnesota Wild/3M Coach of the Year Award, given to a girls and boys high school coach for excellence in coaching. To honor these coaches and leaders, the Minnesota Wild partnered with 3M to give this award to two coaches each year. Candidates for this award must embody the following qualities. They must display good sportsmanship towards teams, parents, fans and officials. They must display a positive sports experience and teaching methods through the game of hockey. They must display respect for players, parents, fans and officials in all situations. They must teach positive life skills allowing athletes to benefit from the team experience and they must dedicate time both on and off the ice to support community initiatives.

And lastly, I have been inducted into the Minnesota Girls Hockey Coaches Hall of Fame. I tell you all of this, not to brag, though I am certainly proud of my accomplishments, but to emphasize that hockey has been so, so good to me. It has been my calling, my life and my true destiny. I would still feel this way, even if none of the accolades had come my way. For me, it was the smile on the players' faces, day in and day out, the joy of seeing them grow as athletes, as teammates, as human beings. Most of what happens on a team is never shown to others, not to fans, not to parents, not even to boyfriends or girlfriends. It is the comradery in the locker room, on the bench and on the ice. It is striving for a common goal, sometimes reaching that goal, and sometimes missing that goal. It is all about the sport and the joy of competing and the friends that you make along the way. It's about the journey. It all has been a rich and rewarding ride all the way!

Thank you for reading my stories. They are all true, with some names changed so as not to embarrass the particular player or person. I never believed in being negative when I coached my players, and I certainly don't believe it would be right to be negative now. If you have watched the "Bosch" series on Amazon

Thomas H Peart

Prime or read the Michael Connelly books, I truly tried to live this quote my entire career and with all my teams…

"Everybody counts or nobody counts!"
—Harry Bosch (By Permission. Courtesy of Michael Connelly)

ABOUT THE AUTHOR

Thomas H. Peart is a born-and-bred Midwesterner, an ex-US Marine, and a veteran coach of hockey, softball, football, and soccer with a career spanning thirty-seven years. In his native Minnesota, he spent twenty-one years coaching girls' and boys' hockey, twelve years coaching college hockey for men and women, and three coaching senior women, before moving to England to coach professional men's hockey for a year. His time coaching has always served as inspiration for him, in his life and his writing. He began sharing stories of his coaching on Facebook during the COVID-19 pandemic, sparking his inspiration for this project. As a member of several hockey coaching associations from the local to the national level and with over fifty years of playing and coaching hockey under his belt, he hopes these stories will serve to inspire others interested in coaching.

Thomas lives in Little Canada, Minnesota. Interested in getting in touch? You can reach him at @tompeart27 on Twitter, @thpeart on Instagram, or on Facebook under the name Tom Peart.

Milton Keynes UK
Ingram Content Group UK Ltd.
UKHW010225230124
436511UK00002B/22